Scientific Workflows

Jun Qin • Thomas Fahringer

Scientific Workflows

Programming, Optimization, and Synthesis with ASKALON and AWDL

 Springer

Jun Qin
Amadeus Data Processing GmbH
Erding
Germany

Thomas Fahringer
Universität Innsbruck
Innsbruck
Austria

ISBN 978-3-642-43679-6   ISBN 978-3-642-30715-7 (eBook)
DOI 10.1007/978-3-642-30715-7
Springer Heidelberg New York Dordrecht London

ACM Computing Classification (1998): H.4, C.2, C.3, J.3, I.2

dedicated to our families

Preface

Distributed systems enable the sharing, selection, and aggregation of a wide variety of distributed resources for solving large-scale, resource (computation and/or data)-intensive problems in science. Workflows represent a main programming model for the development of scientific applications. Creating scientific workflow applications, however, is still a very challenging task for scientists due to the complexity of distributed computing environments, the complex control and data flow requirements of scientific applications, and the lack of high-level languages and tool support. Particularly, sophisticated expertise in distributed computing is often required to determine the software entities to perform computations of workflow tasks, the computers on which workflow tasks are executed, the execution order of workflow tasks, and the data communications among them. The composition of an optimized scientific workflow can be even more difficult. Existing work suffers from being limited to specific implementation technologies, modeling low-level tasks, limited mechanisms to express iterative, conditional, and parallel execution, naive dataset distribution, no semantic support, no automatic workflow composition, or automatic workflow composition limited for special cases, etc.

This book presents a novel workflow language called Abstract Workflow Description Language (AWDL) and the corresponding standards-based, knowledge-enabled tool support with the aim to simplify the development of scientific workflow applications, as well as to optimize and to synthesize them. AWDL is an XML-based language for describing scientific workflow applications at a high level of abstraction. AWDL is designed such that users can concentrate on specifying scientific workflow applications without dealing with either the complexity of distributed computing environments or any specific implementation technology. A rich set of control flow constructs is provided in AWDL to simplify the specification of scientific workflow applications which includes directed acyclic graphs, conditional branches, parallel and sequential iterative constructs, alternative executions, etc. Properties and constraints can be specified in AWDL to provide additional information for workflow runtime environments to optimize and steer the execution of workflow applications. The AWDL modularization mechanism, including sub-workflows and workflow libraries, enables easy reuse and sharing of scientific workflow applications among research groups. To streamline scientific workflow composition, a standards-based approach for modeling scientific workflow applications using the Unified Modeling Language (UML) Activity Diagram is presented, along with the corresponding graphical scientific workflow composition tool, which can automatically generate AWDL code based on graph representations of scientific workflows.

To meet the complex dataset-oriented data flow requirements of scientific workflow applications, AWDL introduces a data collection concept and the corresponding collection distribution constructs, which are inspired by High Performance Fortran (HPF). With these constructs, more fine-grained data flow can be specified at an abstract workflow language level, such as mapping a portion of a dataset to an activity, and independently distributing multiple collections onto parallel loop iterations. The use of these constructs improves the performance of scientific workflows by reducing data duplications and simplifies the effort to port scientific workflow applications onto distributed systems.

With the help of Semantic Web technologies, AWDL introduces a novel semantic based approach for scientific workflow composition. This approach features separation of concerns between data semantics and data representations and between Activity Functions (AFs) and Activity Types (ATs). It simplifies scientific workflow composition by enabling knowledge support and automatic data conversion. On the basis of this semantic approach, an Artificial Intelligence planning based algorithm for automatic control flow composition of scientific workflows using an Activity Function Data Dependence (ADD) is presented. The algorithm employs progression to create an ADD graph and regression to extract workflows, including alternative ones if available. The extracted workflows are then optimized based on data dependence analysis. Following automatic control flow composition, data flow composition is automated by semantically matching each data sink in scientific workflows against the corresponding data sources obtained through backward control flow traversing.

The newly introduced techniques and algorithms are implemented in the framework of the ASKALON development and runtime environment for workflows on distributed systems. The effectiveness of our techniques is demonstrated through a variety of experiments on a distributed computing infrastructure.

The topic covered in this book is of interest to a broad range of computer science researchers, domain scientists who are interested in applying workflow technologies in their work, and engineers who want to develop workflow systems, languages, and tools.

Munich, Germany   Jun Qin
Innsbruck, Austria   Thomas Fahringer
April 2012

Contents

List of Figures

List of Tables

List of Tables

List of Algorithms

Part I
Overview

Chapter 1
Introduction

The continuous demand for computing power has led to the development of parallel and distributed computing technologies since the beginning of computer technology in the mid-twentieth century. *Parallel computing* is a form of computation where multiple concurrent processes cooperate to fulfill a common task. It operates on the principle that large problems can often be divided into smaller ones, which are then solved concurrently, i.e., *in parallel*. Early parallel computers were developed based on various models such as vector processors, Symmetric Multiprocessing (SMP), and Massively Parallel Processing (MPP). *Distributed computing* is a form of parallel computing where concurrent processes run on different computers interconnected by networks. Distributed computing often deals with heterogeneous environments, network links of varying latencies, and unpredictable failures in the network or the computers. *Cluster computing* is a form of distributed computing operating in local networks. A computer cluster is a group of loosely coupled computers that work together closely, so that in many respects they form a single computer. Cluster computing is motivated by the need of high performance and/or availability and low cost, especially compared with traditional SMP and MPP parallel computers.

In the early 1990s, driven by large-scale, resource (computational and data)-intensive scientific applications that require more resources than a single computer (PC, workstation, supercomputer, or cluster) could provide in a single administrative domain, computer scientists began to explore the design and development of an infrastructure for distributed computing in wide area networks. As a consequence, middleware, libraries, and tools were developed to allow the cooperative use of geographically distributed resources unified to act as a single powerful platform for the execution of a range of parallel and distributed applications. This approach to computing has been known by several names, such as *metacomputing, scalable computing, global computing, Internet computing*, and lately as *Grid computing* [152]. The term *Grid computing* originated as a metaphor for introducing computing as a utility and making it as pervasive, reliable, and easy to access as an electric power grid in Ian Foster and Carl Kesselman's book *The Grid: Blueprint for a New Computing Infrastructure* [56]. The vision of the Grid is to provide

J. Qin and T. Fahringer, *Scientific Workflows*, DOI 10.1007/978-3-642-30715-7__1,
© Springer-Verlag Berlin Heidelberg 2012

a transparent and pervasive computing infrastructure in which computing power can be used as a utility that is delivered over the Internet. The key to fulfilling this vision is to enable the sharing, selection, and aggregation of a wide variety of geographically distributed resources including supercomputers, storage systems, data sources, and specialized devices owned by different organizations for solving large-scale resource intensive problems in science, engineering, and commerce.

Ian Foster, Carl Kesselman, and Steve Tuecke led the efforts to create the Globus Toolkit [57, 58] which includes computation management, storage management, security provisioning, data movement, monitoring, agreement negotiation, notification mechanisms, information aggregation, etc. While the Globus Toolkit remains the de facto standard for building Grid solutions, a number of other tools have been built, such as UNICORE [192] and gLite [68]. The global standardization efforts are taking place under the umbrella of the Global Grid Forum (GGF) that transformed into the Open Grid Forum (OGF) [131] in 2006.

Cloud computing is a large-scale distributed computing paradigm that is driven by economies of scale, in which a pool of abstracted, virtualized, dynamically scalable, managed computing power, storage, platforms, and services are delivered on demand to external customers over the Internet [61]. The term *Cloud* was originally a metaphor used to describe the telephone network and the network infrastructure powering the Internet. Cloud computing extends this metaphor to computing services which can be delivered on demand.

Clouds generally provide services at three different levels: Infrastructure as a Service (IaaS), Platform as a Service (PaaS), and Software as a Service (SaaS). IaaS provisions hardware, software, and equipment to deliver computing environments; PaaS offers a high-level integrated environment for building, testing, and deploying custom applications; and SaaS delivers special-purpose software that is remotely accessible through Internet [61].

Clusters, Grids, and Clouds are all distributed systems with the objective to allow access to large amounts of computing power and delivering computing as a utility. On one hand, these distributed systems enable solving complex scientific applications in a powerful computing environment that consists of diverse resources interconnected by networks. On the other hand, the scientific applications often consist of a collection of computation and/or data intensive tasks which are executed in a certain order such as sequence, parallel, loops, and conditional branches. One challenge here is to provide powerful and easy to use programming environments for scientists to develop their applications and execute them on distributed systems.

Workflows represent a main programming model for the development of scientific applications on the distributed systems. While existing techniques for workflows in Business Process Management (BPM) (i.e., Business workflows) can be used for scientific workflows, the latter have their own unique characteristics: (a) scientific workflows are executed on distributed systems where resources may join and leave at any time. Scientific workflows must be able to adapt to the dynamic nature of distributed systems. (b) scientific workflows are normally composed by scientists who are not necessarily computer scientists. The low-level complexity of the distributed systems must be shielded from scientists; and (c) scientific applications may have complex control flow and data flow requirements which must be supported by scientific workflows. Therefore, a high-level scientific workflow language and an easy to use scientific workflow composition tool are required.

Apart from the composition of scientific workflows, the execution of scientific workflows also requires high performance because one of the main reasons to execute scientific applications on distributed systems is to finish the execution and to obtain the results in the shortest possible time. This emphasizes the need for optimization of scientific workflows. Dataset-oriented data flow optimization plays a key role in this aspect since dataset processing is very common in scientific applications.

Recently, researchers have begun to take a step further from information to knowledge [152] by involving domain knowledge support in the process of the workflow composition and execution on distributed systems. To strengthen this vision, we introduce semantics in the development of scientific workflow applications by using state-of-the-art Semantic Web technologies. It further simplifies the process of scientific workflow composition by enabling domain knowledge support, thereby automating scientific workflow composition in terms of control flow composition and data flow composition.

1.1 Motivation

In recent years, the interest in scientific workflows has increasingly grown in the scientific community as a means of describing, composing, and executing scientific workflow applications on distributed systems such as Grids or Clouds. Programming scientific workflow applications that can effectively utilize distributed systems, however, still remains very difficult due to the lack of high-level languages and tools support. The challenges and motivations that have been driving the research in this book are summarized as follows.

1.1.1 Adaptability

A distributed system is a dynamic and heterogeneous computing environment without central ownership or control typically. Computers can join or leave at any time. The computational and networking capabilities can vary significantly over time. Software components, executables, and services can be deployed or undeployed during the execution of scientific workflows. Therefore, scientific workflows must be able to adapt to the dynamic nature of distributed systems in order to benefit from them.

1.1.2 Abstraction

The software resources in distributed systems provide diverse functionalities that can be used in scientific workflow applications. These functionalities are implemented with different technologies and are represented in different forms such as executables (binaries or scripts), Web services, Java classes, or software components. Understanding all of these implementation technologies is difficult for scientists who are in general only interested in their own domain knowledge. Scientific workflows need to be abstract and independent of any specific implementation technology. The advantages are twofold: scientists can concentrate on specifying scientific workflow applications without dealing with the complexity of different implementation technologies; and abstract descriptions of workflow tasks can be dynamically mapped to concrete software resources which are available at runtime and implement the required functionality.

1.1.3 Single System Image

Programming for distributed systems is more difficult than programming for a single computer. It is important for a scientific workflow programming environment to provide a Single System Image (SSI) for scientists, such that they do not have to care about whether their workflow will be executed on a distributed systems or a local computer, nor where, when, and how to start/stop workflow tasks and how to queue/transfer data. Scientific workflow programming environments should shield as many low-level complexities as possible from scientists in order to simplify the scientific workflow composition process.

1.1.4 Complexity of Scientific Applications

Scientific applications usually consist of a collection of tasks that are executed in a certain order like sequence, parallel, sequential or parallel loops, conditional branches, and Directed Acyclic Graphs (DAGs). The data used in scientific applications can be a single value (with type of *string*, *integer*, *boolean*, etc.), a file in a file system, or a collection of such data (i.e., dataset). All of these complex control flow and data flow requirements of scientific applications must be supported by scientific workflow programming environments.

1.1.5 Workflow Modularization

With the increase in the number, size, and complexity of scientific workflows, workflow modularization mechanisms become essential. For example, a scientist wants to invoke part of his/her workflow multiple times (e.g., based on a `for` loop) within the workflow, a scientist in one research group wants to invoke a scientific workflow from another research group in his/her own workflow, without knowing the details of the invoked workflow. Scientific workflow programming environments should effectively enable sharing and reuse of parts of or entire scientific workflows.

1.1.6 Standard Based Graphical Tools

Graphical tools provide scientists a simple way to compose scientific workflow applications by dragging and dropping workflow tasks and connecting them with control flow and/or data flow. However, the exploitation of user-defined workflow notations hinders the collaboration among different workflow projects because scientists have to learn different graphical notation systems. There is a need for a standards-based approach to streamline the task of scientific workflow modeling.

1.1.7 Data Flow Optimization

Besides the complex control flow requirements of scientific workflow applications, data flow in scientific workflow applications can also be very complex, especially when datasets are involved. For instance, a scientific application consumes a portion of a dataset produced by another application, a parallel iterative construct consumes multiple datasets, and each of its loop iterations processes a variable number of elements in different datasets. The dataset-oriented data flow need to be supported by scientific workflow languages in order to reduce data duplication during scientific workflow execution. Thus the communication overhead can be reduced and the performance of scientific workflows can be improved.

1.1.8 Semantics Based Scientific Workflow Composition

The selection of workflow components is an essential step of scientific workflow composition. The components providing user-required functionality may have different input and output data structures, e.g., different number of input and output data, different input and output data types. Scientists have to understand the complex data type systems supported by scientific workflow languages in order to select suitable workflow components and establish correct data flow. Ontology technologies provide vocabularies with explicitly defined, unambiguously understandable and automatically machine-interpretable meanings that can simplify scientific workflow composition by enabling the workflow components selection and data flow composition at the semantic level. In other words, scientists can compose scientific workflows with their own domain knowledge without dealing with complex data type systems. The conversion between different data types, if necessary, should be automated by scientific workflow programming and execution environments.

1.1.9 Automatic Scientific Workflow Composition

The simplest way to compose scientific workflow applications is to compose them automatically based on the input data provided by scientists and their required output data. This is more effective if semantics is enabled, because matching workflow components and data can be done at the semantic level, i.e., based on component functionalities and data semantics. The advantages of automatic scientific workflow composition are (a) the selection of workflow components is done semantically and automatically. This is especially useful in the case where hundreds or thousands of them are available for selection; (b) alternative workflows can be built automatically. In case a workflow component is not available or fails at runtime due to the dynamic nature of distributed systems, an alternative workflow can be adopted; (c) automatically composed workflows can be optimized such that workflow components can be executed as soon as their required input data are available.

1.2 Research Goals

Motivated by the problems outlined in the previous section, this book presents the Abstract Workflow Description Language (AWDL) and the corresponding workflow composition tool that are developed as part of the ASKALON development and runtime environment for workflows on distributed systems. The main goals are (a) to develop an abstract workflow language that meets the complex control flow and data flow requirements of scientific workflow applications while shielding the low-level complexity of distributed systems, implementation technologies, and data type systems from scientists, (b) to implement a knowledge-enabled scientific workflow composition tool based on standards that simplifies and automates the process of scientific workflow programming, and (c) to optimize the control and data flow of scientific workflows.

1.2.1 Abstract Workflow Description Language

This book proposes an Abstract Workflow Description Language (AWDL) for describing scientific workflow applications at a high level of abstraction. AWDL is an XML-based language which is designed such that users can concentrate on specifying scientific workflow applications without dealing with the complexity of distributed systems or any specific implementation technology (e.g., Web service). AWDL allows programmers to define a graph of workflow activities that refer mostly to computational tasks in an intuitive way. A rich set of essential constructs is provided in AWDL to simplify the specification of scientific workflow applications which includes conditional branches, parallel and sequential iterative constructs, parallel sections, directed acyclic graphs, alternative branches, etc. In addition, users can specify high-level constraints and properties for activities and data flow links which provide additional information for scientific workflow programming and execution environments to steer and optimize workflow composition and execution. AWDL is the main interface to ASKALON and has been applied to numerous real-world applications.

AWDL is the successor language of our prior work Abstract Grid Workflow Language (AGWL) [53, 149]. We have been making AWDL simpler and more compact by merging the original 11 compound activities into 4 compound activities without losing simplicity and expressive power. We also introduced a new compound activity `alt` to support alternative executions in scientific workflows. The `alt` activity also facilitates the automatic composition, scheduling, and execution of scientific workflows.

1.2.2 Workflow Modularization

The workflow modularization mechanism of AWDL includes the definition and invocation of sub-workflows, as well as workflow libraries. The workflow modularization mechanism provides a simple and consistent way for reusing workflow components, sub-workflows, and workflows and enables efficient workflow sharing and reuse in ASKALON. With the workflow modularization mechanism, scientists can build workflows based on already existing workflows. The workflow composition time can be reduced and the quality of workflows can also be improved by reusing established and validated workflows. The ASKALON Workflow Hosting Environment (AWHE) is developed as a workflow library which enables easy publishing and sharing of scientific workflows among research groups.

1.2.3 UML-Based Scientific Workflow Modeling

We compare the relationship between scientific workflows and UML Activity Diagrams and propose a novel approach for modeling scientific workflows based on the standard UML Activity Diagram notation system. We extend the UML Activity Diagram by defining some new *stereotypes* with associated *tagged values* based on existing elements, each corresponding to a specific AWDL construct.

The corresponding graphical user interface is developed for scientists to compose scientific workflows through dragging and dropping workflow components and connecting them with control and data flow.

1.2.4 Data Flow Optimization

To provide a flexible dataset-oriented data flow support for scientific workflow applications, this book introduces a data collection concept together with sophisticated collection distribution constructs, which are inspired by High Performance Fortran (HPF), but applied to scientific workflow applications. A data collection is used to model a static or dynamic dataset at a high level of abstraction. The collection distribution constructs are used to map data collections to workflow tasks and to distribute data collections onto loop iterations. With these collection distribution constructs, more fine-grained data flow can be specified at an abstract workflow language level, such as mapping a portion of a dataset to an activity, independently distributing multiple collections onto parallel loop iterations. Our approach reduces data duplication, optimizes data transfers, and simplifies the effort to port workflow applications onto distributed systems.

1.2.5 Semantics-Based Scientific Workflow Composition

This book presents a novel semantic approach for scientific workflow composition which features separation of concerns between data semantics and data representation (i.e., the storage-related information) and between Activity Functions (semantic representation of workflow components) and Activity Types (syntactic representation of workflow components). The key to this approach are Abstract Scientific Workflow Ontologies (ASWO). ASWO include an upper ontology which consists of three main concepts: *Data*, *DataRepresentation*, and *Function*, as well as domain-specific ontologies which are defined by extending the concepts in the upper ontology. This approach allows users to compose scientific workflows at the semantic level, i.e., the level of data semantics and Activity Functions, and leave the task of dealing with data representations and Activity Types, including data conversions between different data representations, to scientific workflow programming and execution environments.

1.2.6 Automatic Scientific Workflow Composition

In order to further automate the process of scientific workflow composition, this book presents a formal Stanford Research Institute Problem Solver (STRIPS) based definition of the scientific workflow composition problem, followed by an Artificial Intelligence (AI) planning based algorithm for automatic control flow composition using an Activity Function Data Dependence (ADD) graph. The algorithm employs progression to create an ADD graph, and regression to extract workflows, including alternative ones. The alternative workflows are useful; when the execution of one workflow fails, an alternative one can be taken. The algorithm also optimizes workflows by analyzing data flow dependences among Activity Functions. In contrast to existing approaches, our algorithm is not limited to any workflow modeling notation such as Petri Nets, and can efficiently and automatically compose high quality (portable, fault tolerant, and optimized) scientific workflows. The complexity of our algorithm is a quadratic in the number of Activity Functions defined in ASWO. Following this algorithm, this book also presents an algorithm for automatic data flow composition.

1.3 Organization

This book is organized into six parts: overview, programming, optimization, synthesis, and conclusion, followed by appendices.

1.3.1 Part I: Overview

This part provides an overview of this book which includes *Introduction* (this chapter) and *Prerequisites* (Chap. 2). Chapter 2 presents an overview of distributed systems, its architecture and characteristics with special focus on programming for distributed systems. Then we briefly survey the existing programming models, followed by the introduction of scientific workflows and some Semantic Web techniques that are helpful for scientific workflow composition. An overview of the ASKALON development and runtime environment for workflows on distributed systems, part of which has been developed for this book, is also presented in Chap. 2.

1.3.2 Part II: Programming

This part focuses on scientific workflow programming. Chapter 3 presents the Abstract Workflow Description Language (AWDL) for describing scientific workflow applications at a high level of abstraction. We present the specification of AWDL which includes atomic activity, control flow constructs (compound activities) such as conditional branches, parallel and sequential iterative constructs, parallel sections, directed acyclic graphs, and alternative branches, data flow, as well as properties and constraints. We describe a real-world material science workflow application that has been successfully ported to a distributed system based on an AWDL specification. Chapter 4 introduces the workflow modularization mechanism of AWDL which enables efficient workflow sharing and reuse in ASKALON. The workflow modularization mechanism includes the definition and invocation of sub-workflows, as well as workflow libraries. An algorithm for detecting incorrect recursive sub-workflow invocations is presented and two case studies are discussed. Chapter 5 discusses the UML Activity Diagram and its relationship with scientific workflows, followed by a UML Activity Diagram based approach for scientific workflow modeling which includes modeling AWDL control and data flow constructs by directly using or *stereotyping* existing UML Activity Diagram modeling elements. A case study of modeling a real-world scientific workflow application is illustrated to demonstrate our approach. Chapter 5 also presents our graphical scientific workflow composition tool and our workflow library ASKALON Workflow Hosting Environment (AWHE), through screenshots.

1.3.3   Part III: Optimization

This part focuses on scientific workflow optimization. Chapter 6 presents an approach to meet the flexible dataset-oriented data flow requirements of scientific workflow applications. We introduce a data collection concept and the corresponding collection distribution constructs, which are inspired by High Performance Fortran (HPF), but applied to scientific workflow applications. Five collection distribution constructs are presented and case studies are shown. The experimental results of applying these constructs to real-world scientific workflow applications are demonstrated to illustrate the effectiveness of our approach.

1.3.4   Part IV: Synthesis

This part takes a step further to simplify and automate the process of scientific workflow composition by applying semantic technologies. Chapter 7 presents a novel semantic approach for scientific workflow composition which features separation of concerns between data semantics and data representation and between Activity Function (semantic description of workflow activities) and Activity Type (syntactic description of workflow activities). We present how a scientific workflow can be described by Activity Functions, followed by an algorithm for mapping semantic scientific workflow representations to syntactic ones. The corresponding implementation and experimental results are demonstrated to show the effectiveness of this approach. Chapter 8 gives a formal definition of the scientific workflow composition problem based on STRIPS, followed by an automatic scientific workflow composition algorithm. The algorithm consists of two sub-algorithms dealing with control and data flow composition, respectively. The control flow composition algorithm is an Artificial Intelligence planning based algorithm. It composes control flow of scientific workflows at the semantic level using an Activity Function Data Dependence (ADD) graph. The three phases of the algorithm, i.e., ADD graph creation, workflow extraction and workflow optimization, are presented and the time complexity is analyzed. Once control flow among AFs is determined, data flow links of scientific workflows can be established automatically by the data flow composition algorithm in two steps: (a) locating possible source data ports of each sink data port through backwards control flow traversing, and (b) matching source data ports against sink data ports based on data semantics. The experimental results on the execution time of applying the control flow composition algorithm to compose scientific workflow applications are presented. The performance improvements of scientific workflow applications resulting from the adoption of the workflow optimization phase are illustrated. The experimental results of the data flow composition algorithm are also discussed by applying it to a real-world scientific workflow application.

1.3.5   Part V: Related Work

This part outlines the most relevant related work in the three scientific workflow research areas presented in this book: programming, optimization, and synthesis. Chapter 9 starts with an overview of a few main workflow languages and systems which is followed by a systematic comparison between the related work and our approach in each of the three areas.

1.3.6   Part VI: Conclusions

This part concludes the book by highlighting contributions and future research directions.

1.3.7   Appendices

Appendix A and B list main acronyms and mathematical symbols we have used in this book.

Chapter 2
Prerequisites

2.1 Distributed Systems

A distributed system can be visioned as a *metacomputer* formed by connecting computers, storage systems, etc. through networks. Formally, we have the following definitions.

Definition 2.1. A *distributed system* is a computing system that consists of a set of resources $\mathcal{R}$ (Definition 2.2) and enables the sharing, selection, and aggregation of those resources. The resources in the distributed system may be graphically distributed across multiple administrative domains. A distributed system may consist of multiple nodes (Definition 2.3).

Definition 2.2. A *resource r* in a distributed system is an entity that contributes or facilitates to contribute some capability to the distributed system. Such resources include not only physical resources such as computer clusters, computers, storage systems, network devices, and scientific instruments, but also logical resources deployed in the system such as Web services, executables, and Java Classes.

Definition 2.3. A *node g* is a set of resources that share the same local security, interconnects, and resource management policies and are managed under a single administrative domain.

2.1.1 Programming Architecture

Figure 2.1 illustrates the distributed system programming architecture. Each layer is compared with the corresponding layers in the conventional programming architecture.

- *Fabric:* The *fabric* layer consists of the resources that users want to share and access. These resources can be physical resources or logical resources by nature.

J. Qin and T. Fahringer, *Scientific Workflows*, DOI 10.1007/978-3-642-30715-7_2,
© Springer-Verlag Berlin Heidelberg 2012

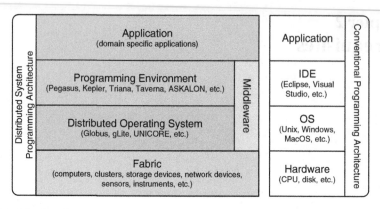

Fig. 2.1 Distributed system programming architecture compared with conventional programming architecture

Physical resources include, but are not limited to, computers, clusters, storage devices, network devices, sensors, and scientific instruments. Logical resources include Web services, executables, Java classes, etc.

- *Middleware:* The *middleware* layer consists of software tools that manage and facilitate access to the resources available at the fabric layer. The middleware can be categorized into two groups: *distributed operating system* and *programming environment.*

   - *Distributed Operating System:* The *distributed operating system* layer provides a fundamental framework for interaction with resources in the fabric layer. It includes job management, data transferring facility, information services, security infrastructure, etc. Examples of distributed operating systems are Globus [69], gLite [68], UNICORE [192], etc.
   - *Programming Environment:* Based on the functionality provided by the distributed operating system layer, the *programming environment* layer provides an integrated environment for users to develop, schedule, execute, and monitor their domain-specific applications. Examples of such a programming environment include Pegasus [41], Karajan [196], Kepler [105], Triana [174], Taverna [133], ASKALON [51], P-GRADE [136], etc. The focus of this book is scientific workflow programming as part of the ASKALON development and runtime environment.

   The layered middleware is mainly used to shield low-level complexities from users.
- *Application:* The *application* layer corresponds to the domain-specific applications which are constructed with the help of the programming environment layer. For example, a meteorology workflow application [159] that needs to execute thousands of tasks each taking as input some parameters and/or files and producing some results.

2.1.2 Characteristics

Computers in a distributed system are usually heterogeneous with different operating systems, distinct hardware architectures, and various programming languages. A generalized distributed system has the following characterizing aspects: heterogeneity, adaptability, and scalability [152]:

- *Heterogeneity:* The computational and network resources in distributed systems are heterogeneous, e.g., different processors, various operating systems, different memory size and network bandwidth, distinct communication protocols, etc.
- *Adaptability:* The distributed system may be dynamic. Resources join and leave the distributed system at any time without prior notification. In such an environment, the probability of resource failures is high, which has to be dealt with by the middleware layer.
- *Scalability:* A distributed system might grow from a few resources to millions. This raises the problem of potential performance degradation as the size of the distributed system increases due to the heterogeneous bandwidth and latency of resources. This emphasizes the requirement of highly scalable middleware.

2.2 Programming for Distributed Systems

Programming for distributed systems is the development of distributed applications which are defined as follows.

Definition 2.4. A *distributed application* is a software that is distributed. An application is said to be distributed when it can be executed on distributed systems and exploit their potential.

Distributed applications tend to be heterogeneous and dynamic, that is, they are executed on different types of resources whose configuration may change at runtime. Distributed applications often require high performance because a main reason for executing applications on distributed systems is to finish their executions in shortest possible time. The goal of *distributed system programming* is the study of programming approaches (or programming models) that support effective development of portable, high-performance distributed applications [99]. Programming models for distributed systems (or *distributed programming models*) can be presented in many different forms, e.g., languages, library APIs, tools, frameworks, portals, or problem-solving environments.

2.2.1 Programming Issues

Because of the characteristics of distributed systems (see Sect. 2.1.2), programming for distributed systems requires capabilities and properties beyond that of simple sequential programming. Distributed application programmers have to manage computations and data in an environment that is typically open-ended, heterogeneous, and dynamic in composition with a deepening memory and bandwidth latency hierarchy.

- *Discovery:* Distributed applications need to discover suitable resources on which to run. Distributed system programming models must be aware of available discovery services, and either offer distributed application developers explicit mechanisms to exploit those services for the development of distributed applications or postpone and automate resource discovery for distributed applications at runtime.
- *Adaptability:* Distributed programming models must support distributed applications to adapt themselves to the dynamic nature of distributed systems, that is, resources may join and leave at any time.
- *Fault tolerance:* As the number of resources involved in distributed systems increases, so does the probability that some resources fail. The dynamic nature of distributed systems means that some level of fault tolerance is necessary. Distributed programming models must be able to check for faults of communication and/or computing resources during the execution of distributed applications and provide actions to recover from or react to faults.
- *Performance:* Due to the heterogeneous bandwidth and latency of distributed systems, it is difficult for distributed applications to achieve high performance and good utilization of distributed resources. The communication-to-computation ratio that can be supported in the typical distributed environment will make it especially difficult for tightly coupled applications [99].

2.2.2 Programming Models

In principle, programming addresses three basic problems: data (how data is represented), computation (how data is processed), and control (in which order data is processed). In order to simplify programming and facilitate code reuse and maintenance, data, computation, and control are often encapsulated in subroutines (also called procedures, functions, or methods), or objects in Object Oriented Programming (OOP). In the context of distributed systems, computations are distributed and typically executed on different computers. This implies three aspects to be addressed by distributed programming models: (a) data exchange between different computations; (b) encapsulation of distributed computations; and (c) coordination of distributed computations. This section provides a brief survey of existing distributed programming models categorized according to the aforementioned aspects. Readers may refer to [63, 98, 99, 167] for more detailed information.

- *Data Exchange*
  Data exchange refers to the way how data are passed among computations. This is an important aspect of distributed system programming because distributed applications are typically executed across computers.

- *Shared State Models:* Shared state programming models are typically intended for shared memory computers or distributed memory computers with a dedicated interconnect network that provides high bandwidth and low latency. In the context of distributed systems, shared state programming models imply that the data exchange among different computations is based on shared state and the producers and consumers of data are decoupled. An example of shared state programming models is JavaSpaces [62]. It is a Java-based implementation of the Linda tuple space concept [64] and considers an application as a collection of processes communicating through putting and getting objects into one or more *spaces* which are shared and persistent object repositories that are accessible via a network.
- *Message Passing Models:* In message passing programming models, processes run in disjoint address spaces, and data are exchanged using message passing of one form or another. An example of message passing models is MPICH-G2 [89], which is a Grid-enabled implementation of the Message Passing Interface (MPI) [115, 116] that automatically converts data in messages sent among machines of different architectures.
- *RPC and RMI Models:* Remote Procedure Call (RPC) and Remote Method Invocation (RMI) provide the same capabilities as message passing models, but they structure the interaction between sender and receiver more as a language construct, rather than as a library function call that simply transfers an uninterpreted buffer of data between two processes. Examples of RPC and RMI programming models are GridRPC [162] and Java RMI. GridRPC is a RPC model and API for the Grid. Java RMI inherits basic RPC design and is truly object oriented.
- *Hybrid Models:* In hybrid models, applications may run multithreaded within a shared address space, and also by passing data and control between computers with disjoint address spaces. Examples of hybrid programming models are the combination of OpenMP [32] and MPI [115,116], OmniRPC [157] and Message Passing Java (MPJ) [16]. OmniRPC uses OpenMP to manage thread-parallel execution while using RPC to manage cross machine interactions. MPJ provides multithreading, RMI, and message passing all in one package.

• *Encapsulation*
  In the context of distributed system programming, encapsulation of data and computations is often used to shield the low-level complexity of distributed systems from programmers by providing simple Application Programming Interface (APIs) at a high level of abstraction, in order to simplify distributed system programming.

  - *Distributed Object Models:* Distributed objects are objects that are distributed on multiple computers, communicating via messages across networks. Examples of distributed object programming models include ProActive [14], CORBA [194], and JavaSymphony [87]. CORBA is an Object Management Group (OMG) defined standard that enables software components written in multiple computer languages and running on multiple computers to work together through Object Request Brokers (ORBs). ProActive extends Java with a Grid API library for the creation, execution, and management of *active* distributed objects. It provides simple methods to transform standard objects into *active* objects which possess synchronization capabilities and location transparency. JavaSymphony is a Java library that allows programmers to distribute any type of Java objects by encapsulating them in JavaSymphony remote objects.

– *Distributed Thread Models:* In distributed thread models, computations are encapsulated into distributed threads that span multiple address spaces. Examples of distributed thread programming models are Alchemi [107] and Grid Thread Programming Environment (GTPE) [168]. Alchemi is a Microsoft .NET Grid computing framework that views a Grid application as a collection of Grid threads capable of running on remote computers. GTPE is a thread library in which the *GridThread* object forms the atomic unit of remote and independent computation, and the *GridApplication* is responsible for thread management and provide near transparent access to Grid resources.

– *Component Models:* In component models, components extend the object-oriented programming paradigm by enabling objects to manage the interfaces they present and discover those presented by others [169]. Examples of component models include Common Component Architecture (CCA) [10] that allows individual components to export interfaces that can be remotely invoked by other components and provides some features to support high performance computing, and XCAT [74,94] that is an implementation of CCA with focus on leveraging the advantages of both component models and web services technologies.

– *Service Oriented Models:* In service-oriented models, computation is encapsulated in services which are network-enabled entities providing some capability through message exchange. A *Grid service* is a Web service that provides a set of well-defined interfaces and that follows specific conventions [59]. The Open Grid Services Architecture (OGSA), developed within the Open Grid Forum (OGF) [131], is a set of standards for creating, naming, discovering, and communicating with Grid services. OGSA is based on several Web service technologies, notably Web Services Description Language (WSDL) [189] and Simple Object Access Protocol (SOAP) [185]. Grid technologies are evolving toward an OGSA which views the Grid as an extensible set of services that can be aggregated in various ways. The Globus [69] Toolkit 4 is an implementation of OGSA.

• *Coordination*
  Coordination models aim to provide means to integrate a number of possibly heterogeneous tasks by interfacing with each task in such a way that the collective set forms a single application that can execute on distributed systems [9].

– *Bag of Tasks Models:* Bag of Tasks (BoT) models treat applications as a set of independent tasks that can be executed in parallel. An example of BoT models is parameters sweep, which distributes the same program across multiple computers to work on different parameters. ZEN [144] is a directive-based language for the specification of arbitrary application parameters through annotations of arbitrary application files, without any source code modification or adaptation.

- *Peer-to-Peer Models:* In Peer-to-Peer (P2P) models, computers that have traditionally been used solely as clients communicate directly among themselves and can act as both clients and servers. JXTA [73] is a set of open, generalized P2P protocols, defined as XML messages that allow any connected device (i.e., peer) to communicate and collaborate in a P2P manner.

- *Workflow Models:* A workflow is a collection of tasks that are processed in a well-defined order to accomplish a specific goal. Different workflow models have been developed in various distributed systems, including the data flow based workflow models adopted in Kepler [105], Triana [174], and Taverna [133], the Directed Acyclic Graph (DAG) based workflow models adopted in Pegasus [41] and P-GRADE [136], the Petri Nets based workflow models adopted in GWorkflowDL [1] and Grid-Flow [76], and the UML Activity Diagram based workflow model adopted in ASKALON [51], [143] and [79], etc.

2.3 Scientific Workflow

The concept of *workflow* has been used in the business world for more than a decade. The Workflow Management Coalition (WfMC) defined a workflow in 1996 as:

> The automation of a business process, in whole or part, during which documents, information or tasks are passed from one participant to another for action, according to a set of procedural rules [178].

It defines a workflow as a business process based on Business Process Management (BPM). That is, a business workflow is an instance of any well-defined task that is often repeated as part of a standard enterprise task, for example, the steps required to complete a purchase order.

In the context of science, *workflows* are used to describe scientific experiments. A scientific workflow is a flow of tasks, mostly computational tasks, that are part of a scientific experiment. Scientific workflows are usually executed on distributed systems because of their huge demand of computation power.

2.3.1 Comparison of Scientific Workflows with Business Workflows

While many techniques and standards that are developed for business workflows can be used for scientific workflows, there are some characteristics that are unique to scientific workflows [17]. Business workflows are typically less dynamic and evolving in nature and they are usually predefined and executed in a routine fashion in the business domain. Scientific research is exploratory in nature. Scientists carry out experiments often in a trial and error manner, wherein they modify the steps of the task to be performed as the experiment proceeds. Therefore, scientific workflows tend to change more frequently. While business workflows tend to be constructed by professional software and business flow engineers, scientific workflows are often constructed by scientists themselves—experts in their domains, but not necessarily experts in information technology, the software or networking domains in which the tools and workflows operate. Finally, scientific workflows typically involve long lasting tasks and/or a large number of data flow connections. The control flow found in business workflows may not be expressive enough for highly concurrent scientific workflows and data pipelines found in leading-edge simulation studies. For example, while most business workflow languages require the programmer to enumerate all concurrent flows, scientific workflows require a new control flow operator to succinctly capture concurrent execution and data flow [17]. Therefore, compared with business workflows, scientific workflows require considerably different interfaces and end-user robustness during both the construction stage of the workflows and their execution.

Business Process Execution Language (BPEL), abbreviation for Web Services Business Process Execution Language (WS-BPEL), is an executable language for specifying interactions with Web Services. BPEL was first conceived in July 2002 with the release of the Business Process Execution Language for Web Services (BPEL4WS) 1.0 specification [39], a combination of IBM's Web Services Flow Language (WSFL) and Microsoft's XLANG specification. After more contributors joined, BPEL4WS 1.1 [6] was released less than a year later and received more attention and vendor support. In April 2007, the OASIS standard WS-BPEL 2.0 [129] was released as a revision of BPEL4WS 1.0 and BPEL4WS 1.1, with significant enhancements. The change in name was done in order to align BPEL with other Web Service standard naming conventions which start with *WS-*. However, BPEL is not a good fit for scientific workflows because (a) BPEL focuses only on Web Services, while scientific workflows may consists of not only Web Services, but also executables, shell scripts, and Java classes; (b) Early versions of BPEL have limited mechanisms to express parallelism. For example, when the research described in this book was conducted, BPEL 1.0 and 1.1 did not support parallel loops. The addition of parallel loops into WS-BPEL 2.0 illustrated the importance of parallel loops; (c) BPEL does not support *file* data type which are frequently used in scientific workflows; (d) BPEL contains numerous constructs that are of no use in scientific workflow applications such as *pick* activity and *wait* activity; and (e) As a combination of WSFL and XLANG, BPEL contains both graph-based and block-based [138] programming which makes BPEL more complex and harder to use for domain scientists.

XML Process Definition Language (XPDL) [179, 180] is an intermediate language defined by the Workflow Management Coalition (WfMC) [178]. It is a format to interchange Business Process definitions between different workflow products such as modeling tools. XPDL is not suitable for scientific workflows because: (a) it does not guarantee precise execution semantics. Generally, it is not possible to take a workflow representation from one vendor's design tool, and process it in another vendor's engine, because of vendor-specific information; (b) although services or tools invoked by XPDL processes can be declared without specific implementation, e.g., just by being named, XPDL does not provide how the named services or tools can be mapped to concrete computational entities. This is probably enough for XPDL as a language only dealing with the store of process definitions, but not sufficient for scientific workflow languages where workflow executions must be considered; and (c) furthermore, XPDL does not have data types such as *file* or *collection* which are very common in scientific workflow applications.

2.3.2   Scientific Workflow Basics

In this section we introduce some basic concepts and definitions of scientific workflows, focusing on scientific workflow composition.

Definition 2.5. A *scientific workflow application w*, is a distributed application (Definition 2.4) that consists of a set of activities A (Definition 2.6) that are processed in a well-defined order to accomplish a specific goal. A scientific workflow w is formulated as a pair:

$$w = \langle A, \vec{D} \rangle \tag{2.1}$$

where A is a set of activities, and $\vec{D}$ is a set of dependences. Each dependence $\vec{d} \in \vec{D}$ is either a control flow dependence (denoted by $\overrightarrow{d^{CF}}$) or a data flow dependence (denoted by $\overrightarrow{d^{DF}}$) associated with an ordered pair of activities (a_m, a_n), where $a_m, a_n \in A$.

Definition 2.6. An *activity* $a \in A$ in a scientific workflow is a computational task of the scientific workflow. It may refer to a computational entity (Definition 2.7) which will be invoked or executed when the scientific workflow is executed.

Definition 2.7. A *computational entity* is a logical resource (Definition 2.2) such as a Web service, an executable, a shell script, a software component, a Java class, etc. that can be assembled in a scientific workflow as an activity (Definition 2.6).

Definition 2.8. The *composition* of a scientific workflow refers to the process of the identification of the activities of a workflow, and the establishment of necessary control flow and data flow dependences among identified activities, such that a specific goal, e.g., to obtain simulation results of a meteorological simulation, can be fulfilled when the scientific workflow is correctly executed.

In a distributed system, the computational entities may have different function-alities, various interfaces, different performance behaviors, distinct requirements on CPU architectures, network bandwidths, storage spaces, and Operating Systems (OS). They may be executed on geographically distributed heterogeneous resources where the computational and networking capabilities can vary significantly over time. These distributed, heterogeneous, and dynamic characteristics of distributed systems impose many challenges for scientific workflow application developers to compose a scientific workflow. Undoubtedly, scientific workflow programming models should alleviate or, if possible, eliminate these challenges by facilitating the tasks such as the identification of suitable computational entities which can be assembled in a workflow, and the establishment of the corresponding control flow and data flow dependences among the identified activities.

2.4 Semantics

One of the key challenges to use distributed systems is the need to deal with resources such as computers, data, and services that are distributed and heterogeneous. An approach to overcome this challenge is to add semantics to distributed resources. In a semantic enabled distributed system, computing resources, data, and services are given well-defined meaning by using Semantic Web technologies, e.g., Ontology [75], Resource Description Framework (RDF) [183], and Web Ontology Language (OWL) [20, 137], such that they are both understandable for human beings and processable for computers. It is believed that this approach is essential to achieve the full richness of the vision of distributed systems (see Chap. 1), with a high degree of easy-to-use and seamless automation enabling flexible collaborations and computations on a global scale [161].

2.4.1 Ontology

An *ontology* is an explicit specification of a conceptualization [75]. In other words, an ontology is a formal representation of a set of concepts within a domain and the relationships between those concepts. An ontology provides a shared vocabulary, which can be used to model a domain, that is, the type of objects and/or concepts that exist, and their properties and relations. Two basic components of ontologies are *Classes* and *Individuals*. *Classes* in an ontology are those concepts that are abstract groups, sets or collections of objects, in contrast to *Individuals* which are instances or objects (the basic or *ground level* objects). For example, *ProgrammingLanguage* is a class and a specific language is an individual of this class. Importantly, a class can subsume or be subsumed by other classes; a class subsumed by another is called a *subclass* of the subsuming class. For example, *ProgrammingLanguage* subsumes *ObjectOrientedProgrammingLanguage*, since (necessarily) anything that is a member of the latter class is a member of the former.

A domain ontology (or domain-specific ontology) models a specific domain, or part of the world. It represents the particular meanings of terms as they apply to that domain. For example, a meteorology ontology models the concepts and relations used in the meteorology domain. An upper ontology (top-level ontology, or foundation ontology) is a model of the common concepts that are generally applicable across a wide range of domain ontologies. It contains a core glossary in whose terms concepts in a set of domains can be described. For example, an ontology consisting of two classes: *Function* and *Data*, and two relations: *hasInput* and *hasOutput* can be considered as an upper ontology. The upper ontology can be used to model data processing in a wide range of domains including Meteorology.

Ontologies are commonly encoded using ontology languages such as Resource Description Framework (RDF) [183], RDF Schema (RDFS) [182], Web Ontology Language (OWL) [20, 137].

2.4.2 Web Ontology Language

The Web Ontology Language (OWL) is an extension of the Resource Description Framework (RDF) and RDF Schema (RDFS), two early Semantic Web standards endorsed by the World Wide Web Consortium (W3C). RDF is a graph-based data model with labeled nodes and directed, labeled edges. The fundamental unit of RDF is the statement, which corresponds to an edge in the graph. An RDF statement has three components: a subject, a predicate, and an object. By itself, RDF is just a data model; it does not have any significant semantics. RDFS is used to define a vocabulary for use in RDF models. In particular, RDFS defines classes used to type resources and properties that resources can have. One problem with RDF Schema is that it has very weak semantic primitives, e.g., lack of disjointness of classes, boolean combinations of classes, and cardinality restrictions [8]. In order to provide a powerful expressiveness and fact stating ability, OWL extends RDF and RDFS by adding more vocabulary for describing properties and classes: among others, relations between classes (e.g., disjointness), cardinality (e.g., exactly one), equality, richer typing of properties, characteristics of properties (e.g., symmetry), and enumerated classes [112]. In our work, OWL is used to capture a hierarchy of concepts and their relations which is then used for semantic workflow composition, with the aim to simplify the scientific workflow composition process by automating it.

2.5 ASKALON

ASKALON [51] is a development and runtime environment for distributed applications developed by the Distributed and Parallel Systems group, led by Prof. Fahringer at the University of Innsbruck. Figure 2.2 illustrates the architecture of ASKALON.

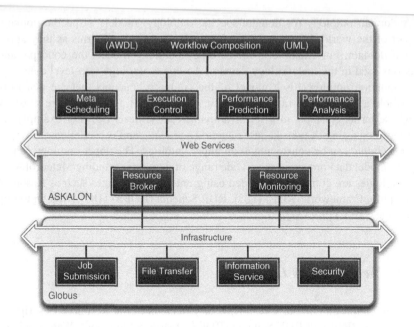

Fig. 2.2 The architecture of ASKALON

2.5.1 Workflow Composition

Workflow composition, the topic of this book, includes the AWDL and the corresponding graphical workflow composition tool. AWDL is an XML-based language for describing scientific workflow applications at a high level of abstraction. It is the main interface to ASKALON and has been applied to numerous real-world scientific workflow applications. AWDL has been designed such that users can concentrate on specifying scientific workflow applications without dealing with either the complexity of distributed systems or any specific implementation technology (e.g., Web Service, software components or Java classes, etc.). The workflow composition tool enables users to composes scientific workflow applications graphically using the standard UML Activity Diagram [176]. The UML-based workflow composition tool can also generate AWDL representations of scientific workflow applications, which can then be given to the ASKALON middleware services for scheduling and reliable execution on distributed systems.

2.5.2 Resource Management

The Resource Manager is a service that provides resource discovery, advanced reservation, and authorization [164]. Besides physical resources such as processors, storage devices, and network interconnections, the Resource Manager also covers logical resources comprising Web services and executables in its integral part GLARE [165]. GLARE provides a distributed framework for dynamic registration, automatic deployment of services required to execute distributed applications, and an effective mapping between high-level abstract activity descriptions and concrete computational entities [165]. In combination with AWDL, the Resource Manager shields the user from low-level complexities of distributed systems.

2.5.3 Workflow Scheduling

The Meta-Scheduler [54, 200, 201] is a service that determines effective mappings of single or multiple workflows onto distributed systems using graph-based heuristics and optimization algorithms that benefit from Performance Prediction and Resource Manager services. Additionally, the Meta-Scheduler provides Quality of Service (QoS) by dynamically adjusting the optimized static schedules to meet the dynamic nature of distributed systems through execution contract monitoring.

2.5.4 Workflow Execution

The Enactment Engine service [44, 45] is responsible for executing scientific workflow applications on distributed systems based on the mapping decided by the Meta-Scheduler. It coordinates workflow execution according to the control flow dependences and the data flow dependences specified in AWDL. The Execution Engine service also targets fault tolerant execution of workflows through techniques such as checkpointing, migration, restart, retry, and replication.

2.5.5 Performance Analysis and Prediction

Performance Analysis [128, 145] supports automatic instrumentation and bottleneck detection (e.g., excessive synchronization, communication, load imbalance, in-efficiency, non-scalability, etc.) within scientific workflow executions. A Performance Prediction service [126, 127] estimates execution time of scientific workflows and activities through a training phase and statistical methods using the Performance Analysis service.

2.6 Summary

This chapter presents some prerequisites of this book. It starts with a general description of distributed systems, its architecture, and characteristics. Then it discusses distributed system programming issues and surveys existing programming models for distributed systems. As the topic of this book, scientific workflows and the problem of scientific workflow composition are then defined. The Semantic Web technologies such as ontology, OWL which are helpful to scientific workflow composition are also discussed. Finally, the ASKALON development and runtime environment for workflows on distributed systems, part of which is the topic of this book, is presented by its architecture and the introduction of each component.

The next chapter starts with the description of the Abstract Workflow Description Language (AWDL) and its application in real-world scientific workflow applications.

Part II
Programming

Chapter 3
Abstract Workflow Description Language

3.1   System Overview

Figure 3.1 shows an overview of the development process of scientific workflow applications from an abstract representation to an actual execution in the
ASKALON development and runtime environment for workflows on distributed
systems [51]. The development process consists of three fundamental procedures:
Composition, *Reification*, and *Execution*.

Composition: The user composes a scientific workflow by writing an AWDL
program. At composition time, activities correspond mostly to computational tasks
and the specification of their input and their output data. There is no notion of how
the input data are actually delivered to activities and how activities are implemented,
invoked, and terminated. Such a program is an abstract definition of the scientific
workflow application. The abstract workflow contains all the information specified
by the user during the workflow composition. An AWDL program at this level of
abstraction cannot be executed until it is reified.

Reification: The ASKALON runtime system compiles the abstract workflow to
a concrete workflow by extracting concrete information that is required for the
execution of workflow activities (e.g., the URL of the WSDL [35] document in
case of Web Services, the working directory and command line usage in case of
Unix executables, etc.) from an activity registry (i.e., the GLARE service [165],
see Sect. 2.5.2) and inserting them into the workflow. The concrete workflow can
be executed because it contains all necessary information which is required to
execute the workflow. In contrast to the abstract workflow, the concrete workflow is
implementation dependent, i.e., each activity in the concrete workflow is associated
with a specific computational entity (see Definition 2.7). Note that the concrete
workflow is not seen by the AWDL programmer. Instead, users compose scientific
workflows at the abstract level. The detailed reification process is presented in
Sect. 3.4.

Execution: The ASKALON Enactment Engine (see Sect. 2.5.4) interprets the
concrete workflow and executes it on the distributed infrastructure. Details about

J. Qin and T. Fahringer, *Scientific Workflows*, DOI 10.1007/978-3-642-30715-7_3,
© Springer-Verlag Berlin Heidelberg 2012

Fig. 3.1 The development
process of scientific
workflows in ASKALON

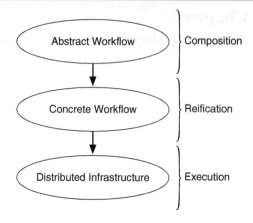

the execution of scientific workflow applications in ASKALON are presented in
Sect. 3.4 and more detailed information can be found in [44, 45, 51].

3.2   Specification

An AWDL workflow consists of activities, control flow constructs, data flow links,
properties, and constraints. An activity can be either an *atomic activity*, which refers
to a single computational task, or a *compound activity*, which encloses some atomic
activities or other compound activities that are connected by control and data flow.
A workflow is a compound activity. The composition of a workflow application
or a compound activity is done by specifying all its enclosed activities as well as
the control and data flow among them. Properties and constraints can be specified
for activities and data flow links to steer and optimize the execution of workflow
applications.

AWDL considers a scientific workflow as a set of activities to be executed in a
certain order. Each activity is described by a set of input *data ports* which represent
the input data to this activity, and a set of output data ports which represent the
output data of this activity. Activities are connected through control flow constructs
(such as branches, iterations, and directed acyclic graphs) which determine the
execution order of the activities. An activity can be executed as soon as all of its
input data are available and the control flow is at the entry of this activity.

When an activity is executed, the input data are processed and the output
data are produced. The produced data of an activity can be processed again
by subsequent activities. Thus, data flow dependences among activities can be
established. Processing data in an activity does not affect the availability of the
data. Data can be processed by any number of activities, and each activity processes
its own copy of the data without considering how the data are processed by other
activities. From this point of view, activities act as side effect-free functions or
methods in high-level programming languages.

```
1  <activity name="name" type="type">
2    <dataIns>
3      <dataIn name="name" type="type" source="source"? >
4        <value> constants </value>?
5      </dataIn>*
6    </dataIns>
7    <dataOuts>
8      <dataOut name="name" type="type" saveto="saveto"? />*
9    </dataOuts>
10 </activity>
```

Fig. 3.2 Atomic activity

In order to make the text easier to read, the AWDL specification is given in the following subsections using an informal syntax to describe the XML grammar of an AWDL workflow.

- The syntax appears as an XML instance, but the values indicate the data types instead of values.
- Wildcard characters are appended to elements and attributes as follows: "?" (0 or 1), "*" (0 or more), "+" (1 or more).
- Elements ending with "... " (e.g., `<element.../>` or `<element...>`) indicate that elements or attributes irrelevant to the context are being omitted.

3.2.1 Atomic Activity

The definition of an atomic activity is shown in Fig. 3.2.

Activity Name: The activity name serves as an identifier for the activity. Activities must be organized in an AWDL workflow or a sub-workflow. In a workflow or a sub-workflow, the name of each activity is unique.

Activity Type: In AWDL, atomic activities are described by *Activity Types (ATs)*. An AT is an abstract description of a group of *Activity Deployments (ADs)* (concrete implementations of computational entities deployed in distributed systems) which have the same functionality, but probably different performance behaviors, QoS characteristics, costs, etc. For instance, an AT *MatrixMultiplication* can be used to describe a group of two ADs which are deployed as an executable and a Web service respectively and implement matrix multiplication. ATs shield the implementation details of ADs from the AWDL programmer. In ASKALON, ADs and ATs are organized based on their domains (e.g., Mathematics, Meteorology, Material Science, etc.). The mapping between ADs and ATs are managed by the activity registry service GLARE [165]. For example, the AT *MatrixMultiplication* can be accessed by the URL *actt://mathematics/MatrixMultiplication*. Once ATs are specified in workflows, locating and executing the corresponding ADs are done

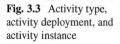

Fig. 3.3 Activity type,
activity deployment, and
activity instance

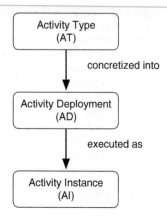

in combination of a Meta-Scheduler (retrieving AD–AT mappings and making scheduling decision based on performance prediction), a Performance Predictor (predicting performance of ADs), a Workflow Enactment Engine (executing ADs), and a Resource Manager (providing AD–AT mappings). See Sect. 2.5 for the details of each of these components. An invocation or execution of an AD is called an Activity Instance (AI). Figure 3.3 summarizes the relationship among AT, AD, and AI.

DataIn/DataOut Ports: The input or output data of activities are specified through `dataIn` or `dataOut` ports. The number and the `type` attributes of the dataIn/dataOut ports are determined by the chosen AT. The `dataIn` port DP can be specified by (a) setting its `source` attribute to either the name of a data port DP' of another activity in the same workflow in the form of *activity-name/data-port-name*, or the name of a `dataIn` port DP'' of the workflow in the form of *workflow-name/data-port-name*. In this case, the data port DP' or DP'' is called the *source data port*, and the data port DP is called the *sink data port*; (b) setting its `source` attribute to a specific URL referring to a file, or an ordered list of URLs referring to an ordered list of files; or (c) specifying a constant or an ordered list of constants in the `value` element such as an *integer*, a ordered list of *string*, an XML constant, etc. No `source` is specified in this case. The data associated with a `dataOut` port can be stored in the location specified through its `saveto` attribute. Linking the data ports of different activities through the `source` attributes defines data flow of AWDL workflows. The data in activities can be interchanged through the exchange of data along the specified data flow.

Data Type: The `type` attribute of a data port indicates the data type of the data port. The data type system used in AWDL is a subset of the XML Schema Datatypes [181], including *xsd:boolean, xsd:string, xsd:integer, xsd:float*, etc., plus two additional types, *awdl:file, awdl:collection*. Here *xsd* and *awdl* indicate the namespace of XML Schema Datatypes and AWDL, respectively. The data type *awdl:collection* will be explained in detail in Chap. 6.

```
 1  <activity name="CalcKPoint"
        type="actt://MaterialScience/CalcKPoint" >
 2    <dataIns>
 3      <dataIn name="num1" type="xsd:integer"
            source="WIEN2k/integerFraction"/>
 4      <dataIn name="num2" type="xsd:integer">
 5        <value>0</value>
 6      </dataIn>
 7    </dataIns>*
 8    <dataOuts>
 9      <dataOut name="kpoint" type="xsd:integer"/>
10    </dataOuts>*
11  </activity>
```

Fig. 3.4 The atomic activity *CalcKPoint*

Figure 3.4 shows an example of an atomic activity *CalcKPoint* specified in a material science workflow application named WIEN2k [25]. Its activity type is *actt://MaterialScience/CalcKPoint* which is defined in the activity type registry service GLARE [165]. Determined by the activity type, the activity *CalcKPoint* accepts two integers as its inputs, and produces an integer *kpoint* as its output. While the value of the dataIn port *num1* (Line 3) is derived from the dataIn port *integerFraction* of the workflow (note that *WIEN2k* is the name of the workflow), the value of the dataIn port *num2* (Lines 4–6) is a constant. Based on the specified activity type, the workflow runtime system can search the activity type registry to get the corresponding ADs for scheduling and execution.

3.2.2   AWDL Control Flow

After having defined activities as building blocks, we can now discuss the AWDL control flow constructs (compound activities), which specify the execution order of activities, the condition under which activities can be executed, etc.

In a compound activity, the specifications for its name attribute, its dataIn or dataOut ports, the source attribute of its dataIn ports, and the saveto attribute of its dataOut ports are similar to that in an atomic activity. To avoid redundancy, we will not explain them again in the following sections.

A compound activity contains some *inner activities* which are executed in the order defined by the compound activity. The inner activities are called *children activities* of the compound activity; the compound activity is called the *parent activity* of the inner activities. Note that if an inner (or child) activity is a compound activity, the term *inner activity* or *child activity* refers to this compound activity as a whole, i.e., without referring to any of the inner (children) activities of this compound activity. In the following explanation of compound activities, the XML segment <activity .../>+ indicates multiple activities, which include not only atomic activities but also compound activities. Unless explicitly stated, the *activity* in the remainder of this book means either an atomic activity or a compound activity.

AWDL provides a rich set of compound activities to simplify the specification of scientific workflow applications. In our prior work [53, 148, 151], we have introduced 11 compound activities, namely, sequence, parallel, if, switch, while, doWhile, for, forEach, dag, parallelFor, and parallelForEach. In order to make AWDL simpler and more compact without losing expressive power, we merge the 11 compound activities into 4 main compound activities in this book, namely, dag, for, while, and if. sequence and parallel are considered as special dag activities. In addition, we introduce a new compound activity alt to support alternative executions in scientific workflows. In the following, we explain the five new compound activities by showing their definitions and some illustrative examples from real world scientific workflows. We will also discuss how these compound activities can be used to express the original 11 ones.

3.2.2.1 dag Activity

Directed Acyclic Graph (DAG) is a commonly used construct to express control flow dependences among activities in scientific workflows. In AWDL, the dag activity is used to express control flow in DAGs, where each vertex is represented by a node. A node can be specified as the predecessors of another node. The activities contained in a node can be executed as soon as all of the predecessors of this node finished their execution. The dag activity has a potential for sequential or parallel execution of its inner activities. The definition of the dag activity is shown in Fig. 3.5.

Node: Each node (Line 8) contains some activities and has a unique name in the dag activity. The activities contained in a node can be atomic activities or compound activities such as if, for, and while. The predecessors attribute (Line 8) of a node is a comma separated list of names of some other nodes that must be executed before the execution of this node starts. Those nodes without predecessors or with the predecessors attribute referring to the dag activity itself are the *roots* of the dag activity. Multiple roots can exist in a dag activity. The roots, as well as those nodes whose predecessors have finished their execution, can be executed immediately in parallel with other nodes.

DataOut Ports: For the dag activity and all other compound activities, the source attribute (Line 13) for dataOut ports is introduced to specify internal data flow from dataOut ports of inner activities to dataOut ports of the compound activities themselves. In the dag activity, the value of the source attribute is similar to that of the source attribute of a dataIn port, except that it

```
 1  <dag name="name">
 2    <dataIns>
 3      <dataIn name="name" type="type" source="source"? >
 4        <value> constants </value>?
 5      </dataIn>*
 6    </dataIns>
 7    <body>
 8      <node name="name" predecessors="predecessors">
 9        <activity .../>+
10      </node>+
11    </body>
12    <dataOuts>
13      <dataOut name="name" type="type" source="source"
               saveto="saveto"? />+
14    </dataOuts>
15  </dag>
```

Fig. 3.5 dag activity

refers to dataOut ports of inner activities of the enclosing compound activity. The source attributes for dataOut ports is especially useful in case of the if, for, and while compound activity which will be explained later.

Figure 3.6 illustrates an example of a dag activity *dagRAMS* specified in a meteorology workflow *MeteoAG* [159]. The dag activity *dagRAMS* contains eight nodes, with their predecessors specified at Lines 4, 7, 10, 13, 16, 19, 22, and 25, respectively. The node *RAMSMakevfile* is a root because its predecessors attribute refers to the dag activity itself (Line 4). The node *RAMSAll* has two predecessors (Line 16): the node *SoilConv* and the node *LandCoverConv*. This is similar for the node *REVUAll*. Other nodes each has a single predecessor. The corresponding graphical representation of the dag activity is illustrated in Fig. 3.7.

For the reasons of convenience, AWDL provides two special dag activities: sequence and parallel , where no explicit predecessor information needs to be specified. The definition of the sequence activity is illustrated in Fig. 3.8. The sequence activity imposes a sequential control flow on all of its inner activities being either atomic activities or compound activities. The inner activities in a sequence activity are executed sequentially in lexical order. If an AWDL programmer specifies two activities lexically one after the other, it is assumed to be a sequence activity by default. The definition of the parallel activity (Fig. 3.9) is syntactically similar to that of the sequence activity except that the outermost XML element is parallel. The parallel activity indicates that all of its inner activities can be executed simultaneously.

```
 1  <dag name="dagRAMS">
 2    <dataIns ... />
 3    <body>
 4      <node name="RAMSMakevfile" predecessors="dagRAMS">
 5        <activity name="RAMSMakevfile" ... />
 6      </node>
 7      <node name="RAMSInit" predecessors="RAMSMakevfile">
 8        <activity name="RAMSInit" ... />
 9      </node>
10      <node name="SoilConv" predecessors="RAMSMakevfile">
11        <activity name="SoilConv" ... />
12      </node>
13      <node name="LandCoverConv" predecessors="RAMSMakevfile">
14        <activity name="LandCoverConv" ... />
15      </node>
16      <node name="RAMSAll" predecessors="SoilConv,LandCoverConv">
17        <activity name="RAMSAll" ... />
18      </node>
19      <node name="REVUCompare" predecessors="RAMSInit">
20        <activity name="REVUCompare" ... />
21      </node>
22      <node name="RAVER" predecessors="REVUCompare">
23        <activity name="RAVER" ... />
24      </node>
25      <node name="REVUAll" predecessors="RAMSAll,RAVER">
26        <activity name="REVUAll" ... />
27      </node>
28    </body>
29    <dataOuts ... />
30  </dag>
```

Fig. 3.6 The dag activity *dagRAMS*

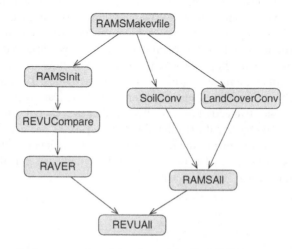

Fig. 3.7 The graphical representation of the dag activity *dagRAMS*

```
1  <sequence name="name">
2    <dataIns>
3      <dataIn name="name" type="type" source="source"? >
4        <value> constants </value>?
5      </dataIn>*
6    </dataIns>
7    <body> <activity .../>+ </body>
8    <dataOuts>
9      <dataOut name="name" type="type" source="source"
            saveto="saveto"? />+
10   </dataOuts>
11 </sequence>
```

Fig. 3.8 sequence activity

```
1  <parallel name="name">
2    <dataIns>
3      <dataIn name="name" type="type" source="source"? >
4        <value> constants </value>?
5      </dataIn>*
6    </dataIns>
7    <body> <activity .../>+ </body>
8    <dataOuts>
9      <dataOut name="name" type="type" source="source"
            saveto="saveto"? />+
10   </dataOuts>
11 </parallel>
```

Fig. 3.9 parallel activity

3.2.2.2 if Activity

The if activity enables the conditional execution of inner activities. Unlike the *if* construct in high-level programming languages, the if activity in AWDL directly supports more than two conditional branches without using *else-if*, thus the *switch* construct in high-level programming languages can be easily supported by the if activity. The definition of the if activity is illustrated in Fig. 3.10.

Branch: Each branch (Lines 7–12) consists of a condition (Lines 8–10) (explained later) and some activities to be executed in this branch. A branch can be executed only when its condition evaluates to *true*. Multiple branches can be included in the if activity and their conditions are evaluated in lexical order. Only the first branch holding a *true* condition is selected for execution when the if activity is invoked. The condition in a branch is optional. An absence of the condition indicates a *true* condition, that is, the branch without condition will be executed if no previous branches hold a *true* condition. This is similar to the *else* branch in the *if* construct, and the *default* branch in the *switch* construct in high-level

```
 1  <if name="name">
 2    <dataIns>
 3      <dataIn name="name" type="type" source="source"? >
 4        <value> constants </value>?
 5      </dataIn>*
 6    </dataIns>
 7    <branch>
 8      <condition combinedWith="and|or"? >
 9        <acondition not="0|1"? left="data"
                  operator="operator" right="data" />+
10      </condition>*
11      <body> <activity .../>* </body>
12    </branch>+
13    <dataOuts>
14      <dataOut name="name" type="type" source="source"
                saveto="saveto"? />+
15    </dataOuts>
16  </if>
```

Fig. 3.10 if activity

programming languages. The body of a branch can be empty. In particular, if all branches in the if activity have their condition specified, it is assumed that there is also an implicit empty branch without condition specified as the last branch in the if activity. This is to ensure that there is always one branch being executed and the output of the if activity is well defined.

Condition: In the if activity, the condition is a set of *atomic conditions* combined with either *and* (the default value) or *or*. Each atomic condition consists of left (left operand), right (right operand), operator, and not (negation operator). The operators supported in AWDL are equality operators $==$ and $\neq$, relational operators $>$, $\geq$, $<$, and $\leq$, as well as *string* operators *contains*, *startsWith*, and *endsWith*. The negation operator is either 0 (which is the default value, indicating no negation) or 1 (indicating negation). For the reasons of simplicity, we limited the operands to *boolean*, *integer*, *float*, and *string* constants or data ports with these types. The condition specification in the if activity also applies to the condition in the while activity (explained later).

DataOut Ports: The source attribute of the dataOut ports specifies the possible internal data flow from dataOut ports of inner activities to the dataOut ports. The value of the source attribute is a comma separated list of data ports. This list must contain one dataOut port of an inner activity in each branch, in the same order as the branches are specified in the if activity. If an implicit empty branch exists, there must also be a data port in the list corresponding to this branch. More details about the data flow in the if activity is discussed in Sect. 3.2.3.2.

Figure 3.11 illustrates an example if activity *runhist*. The if activity contains one branch which is executed when the dataOut port *decision* of the activity *raver* (a predecessor of the if activity, not shown in the figure) is *true* (Line 5). Because the only branch of the if activity has condition specified, an empty branch

```
1   <if name="runhist">
2     <dataIns ... />
3     <branch>
4       <condition>
5         <acondition left="raver/decision" operator="=="
                right="true">
6       </condition>
7       <body>
8         <activity name="ramshist" ... />
9         <activity name="revudump" ... >
10          <dataIns ... />
11          <dataOuts>
12            <dataOut name="dump" type="awdl:file"/>
13            <dataOut name="logfile" type="awdl:file"/>
14          </dataOuts>
15        </activity>
16      </body>
17    </branch>
18    <dataOuts>
19      <dataOut name="casedump" type="awdl:file"
              source="revudump/dump, revucompare/dump"/>
20    </dataOuts>
21  </if>
```

Fig. 3.11 The if activity *runhist*

without condition is added implicitly. The dataOut port *casedump* (Line 19) of
the if activity refers to the dataOut port *dump* (Line 12) of the inner activity
revudump as one possible output, and the dataOut port *dump* of the activity
revucompare (a predecessor of the if activity, not shown in the figure) as another
possible output.

3.2.2.3   for Activity

The for activity is one of the two iterative activities supported in AWDL. It is
used to execute its body multiple times. The for activity behaves as the *foreach*
construct in high-level programming languages such as Java (since version 1.5) and
Python, etc. Counter loops can be implemented by using the *range(start,stop,step)*
construct, in a similar way as Python does. Parallel loops can also be achieved by
setting the attribute parallel of the for activity to *yes*. The definition of the for
activity is illustrated in Fig. 3.12.

Parallel: The attribute parallel of the for activity indicates whether all
iterations can be executed in parallel. By default, parallel= *"no"*, that is, all
iterations must be executed sequentially.

DataLoop Ports: dataLoop ports (Lines 7–11) are inputs to the for activity
and used to express cyclic data flow when the parallel attribute is set to *no*.

```
 1  <for name="name" parallel="yes|no">
 2    <dataIns>
 3      <dataIn name="name" type="type" source="source" >
 4        <value> constants </value>?
 5      </dataIn>*
 6    </dataIns>
 7    <dataLoops>
 8      <dataLoop name="name" type="type" initSource="source"?
            loopSource="source" >
 9        <value> constants </value>?
10      </dataLoop>*
11    </dataLoops>
12    <loopElement name="name" type="type" collection="collection" />
13    <body> <activity .../>+ </body>
14    <dataOuts>
15      <dataOut name="name" type="type" source="source"
            saveto="saveto"? />+
16    </dataOuts>
17  </for>
```

Fig. 3.12 for activity

dataLoop ports get their initial values via the attribute initSource or the
value element before these loop activities are executed. The loopSource
commonly refers to a dataOut port of an inner activity, in the form of *activity-
name/data-port-name*. After the execution of each iteration, the dataLoop ports
receive the new values specified by the loopSource attributes. The dataLoop
ports receive the final results of the loop body after the for activity terminates.
When the attribute parallel for the for activity is set to *yes*, dataLoop ports
must not be used.

Loop Element: The loopElement specifies a data collection (through the
collection attribute) over which the for activity iterates. The collection can
be provided statically as a collection of constants or URLs referring to files, or
dynamically as an output of a parallel loop activity. If the data collection is empty,
then the loop body is never executed. The loopElement provides an implicit
dataIn port for the activities in the loop body. A counter loop can be achieved
by using a data collection expressed with the range(start,stop,step)
construct. The values of start, stop, and step in the range construct can
be *integer* or *float* constants, or refer to data ports with these types. The values of
start, stop and step are only evaluated once at the beginning of an invocation
of the for activity.

DataOut Ports: In case of parallel=*"no"*, the source attributes of the
dataOut ports refer to the dataLoop ports which are set to the final results
after the execution of the for activity. In case of parallel=*"yes"*, the source
attributes of the dataOut ports refer to dataOut ports of inner activities. In this
case, each dataOut port of the for activity is a data collection, each element of

```
1  <for name="pForAkmin" parallel="yes">
2    <dataIn ... />
3    <loopElement name="akmin" collection="range(0:80:10)"/>
4    <body>
5      <activity name="ramsmakevfile" ... />
6      <activity name="ramsinit" ... />
7      <activity name="revucompare" ... >
8        <dataIns ... />
9        <dataOuts>
10         <dataOut name="dump" type="awdl:file"/>
11         <!-- other dataOut ports -->
12       </dataOuts>
13     </activity>
14     <!-- other activities -->
15   </body>
16   <dataOuts>
17     <dataOut name="dumpcol" type="awdl:collection"
                source="revucompare/dump" />
18   </dataOuts>
19 </for>
```

Fig. 3.13 The for activity *pForAkmin*

which corresponds to the data produced by an inner activity in a different iteration. In both cases, subsequent activities of the for activity can only access the final results through the dataOut ports of the for activity after the for activity terminates.

Figure 3.13 illustrates an example for activity *pForAkmin*. It is a parallel counter loop. All iterations of the for activity are executed in parallel, each corresponding to a different *akmin* value determined by the range construct *range(0:80:10)* at Line 3. The dataOut port *dumpcol* (Line 17) of the for activity is a data collection, each element in which corresponds to the output data *dump* (Line 10) of the inner activity *revucompare*.

3.2.2.4 while Activity

The while activity is another iterative activity supported in AWDL. The while activity can be used to execute the loop body multiple times based on certain conditions. The while activity can behave as either the *while* construct or the *do-while* (or *repeat-until*) construct in high-level programming languages, depending on the lexical order of the loop body and the loop condition: if the loop condition comes first, the evaluation of the loop condition is done first (behaving as *while*); if the loop body comes first, the loop body is executed first (behaving as *do-while*). The definition of the while activity is illustrated in Fig. 3.14, where the dataLoop

```
1  <while name="name">
2    <dataIns>
3      <dataIn name="name" type="type" source="source" >
4        <value> constants </value>?
5      </dataIn>*
6    </dataIns>
7    <dataLoops>
8      <dataLoop name="name" type="type" initSource="source"?
               loopSource="source" >
9        <value> constants </value>?
10     </dataLoop>+
11   </dataLoops>
12   <condition> condition </condition>
13   <body> <activity .../>+ </body>
14   <dataOuts>
15     <dataOut name="name" type="type" source="source"
              saveto="saveto"? />+
16   </dataOuts>
17 </while>
```

Fig. 3.14 while activity

ports and the source attributes of dataOut ports are similar as they are in the for activity with parallel=*"no"*.

Condition: The condition in the while activity is similar to that in the if activity. It controls how often the loop body is executed. The while activity continues execution until the condition is evaluated to *false*.

DataOut Ports: Similar to the for activity with parallel=*"no"*, the source attributes of the dataOut ports refer to the dataLoop ports which are set to the final results when the while activity terminates. If the loop body of the while activity is not executed at all, the dataOut ports would hold the value specified by the initSource attribute of the dataLoop port. In this way, we guarantee that the dataOut ports of the while activity are well defined in any case.

Figure 3.15 shows an example while activity *whileConv* in the material science workflow WIEN2k [25]. The while activity has a dataLoop port *val* (Line 4) which is assigned its initial value from the workflow input *WIEN2k/val*. After each iteration, the dataLoop port *val* is assigned a new value (Line 4) from the dataOut port *outVal* (Line 15) of the inner activity *TestConverge*. The condition to exit the while activity is *whileConv/val==true* (Lines 6–8). The source attribute of the dataOut port *outVal* (Line 20) refers to the dataLoop port *val* of the while activity which represents the final result when the while activity terminates.

3.2.2.5 alt Activity

The alt activity consists of alternative branches and is used to specify alternative executions in scientific workflows. Different from the branch selection in the if

```
1  <while name="whileConv">
2    <dataIns> ... </dataIns>
3    <dataLoops>
4      <dataLoop name="val" initSource="WIEN2k/val"
               loopSource="TestConverge/outVal" ... />
5    </dataLoops>
6    <condition combinedWith="and">
7      <acondition left="whileConv/val" operator="=="
               right="true" />
8    </condition>
9    <body>
10     <activity name="LAPW0" ... />
11     <!-- other activities -->
12     <activity name="TestConverge" ... >
13       <dataIns> ... </dataIns>
14       <dataOuts>
15         <dataOut name="outVal" ... />
16       </dataOuts>
17     </activity>
18   </body>
19   <dataOuts>
20     <dataOut name="outVal" source="whileConv/val" ... />
21     <!-- other dataOut ports -->
22   </dataOuts>
23 </while>
```

Fig. 3.15 The while activity *whileConv*

activity, the selection of the alternative branches in the alt activity is not based on the conditions evaluated against workflow data (as represented by data ports), but based on user preferences, scheduling decisions, and runtime execution statuses of activities (e.g., failed). Only one branch is selected for execution when an alt activity is invoked. The alt activity can be used to provide fault tolerance support by the underlying workflow runtime system in the sense that if the execution of one branch fails, the alternative branch can be taken. Note that this is different from the fault tolerance supported by mapping an activity from an AT to ADs where, in the event of a failure, a different AD is used for another attempt, but the AT remains the same. With an alt activity, the alternative branch taken after a failure occurs may be totally different from the previously tried branch in terms of which and how many ATs are specified in these branches. The alt activity is also useful when multiple solutions (therefore multiple branches) are identified by an *automatic* workflow composition algorithm. In this case, the automatic workflow composition system can put multiple solutions into an alt activity, and the workflow runtime system can take whichever branch applicable for execution, depending on the availability of ADs, the performance, costs, and/or execution statuses of the included branches. The definition of the alt activity is illustrated in Fig. 3.16.

Branch: A branch indicates an alternative execution branch specified in the alt activity. Each branch element is associated with a weight and contains

```
 1 <alt name="name">
 2    <dataIns>
 3       <dataIn name="name" type="type" source="source"? >
 4          <value> constants </value>?
 5       </dataIn>*
 6    </dataIns>
 7    <branch weight="weight">
 8       <activity .../>+
 9    </branch>+
10    <dataOuts>
11       <dataOut name="name" type="type" source="source"
                  saveto="saveto"? />+
12    </dataOuts>
13 </alt>
```

Fig. 3.16 `alt` activity

activities each of which can be either atomic or compound activities. The value of the `weight` attribute is an *integer* indicating the weight of a `branch`. The weight values of branches indicate user preferences: the lower the weight of a branch, the more the branch is preferred. The weight values can also represent estimated execution or economic costs of branches. When the `alt` activity is executed, only the `branch` with lowest weight is selected for execution. In the case where multiple branches have the same weight, any of them can be selected. By default, all branches have a weight of zero. Users can also specify the weights of branches during the process of scientific workflow composition based on, for example, estimated costs of these branches that users might have, the number of activities in these branches, or the complexity of these branches. When a scientific workflow is scheduled, the scheduler can also calculate a weight for each `branch` based on scheduling factors such as predicted execution time or economic costs. Combining this with the user's weights, the scheduler can determine the final weight of each `branch`. How the combination can be done is not specified in AWDL and it is up to the implementation of the underlying workflow runtime system. If at runtime the execution of the branch with lowest weight fails, then the branch with the next lowest weight is taken. There must be more than one branch specified in an `alt` activity.

DataOut Ports: Same as in the `if` activity, `dataOut` ports are also defined for the `alt` activity. The `source` attributes of the `dataOut` ports is comma separated lists of data ports in the order as the branches are defined in the `alt` activity. Each data port in the list corresponds to a `dataOut` port of an inner activity in a different branch.

Figure 3.17 shows an example `alt` activity *initSimCaseAlt* specified in the MeteoAG [159] workflow. The `alt` activity consists of two branches (Lines 3–10 and Lines 11–19). The first branch contains a single atomic activity *initSimCase1* (Line 4), while the second branch contains two atomic activities *conv* (Line 12) and *initSimCase2* (Line 13). The weights of these two branches (Lines 3 and 11) in this

```
1  <alt name="initSimCaseAlt">
2    <dataIn ... />
3    <branch weight="1">
4      <activity name="initSimCase1" ... >
5        <dataIns ... />
6        <dataOuts>
7          <dataOut name="seaSurface" ... />
8        </dataOuts>
9      </activity>
10   </branch>
11   <branch weight="2">
12     <activity name="conv" ... />
13     <activity name="initSimCase2" ... >
14       <dataIns ... />
15       <dataOuts>
16         <dataOut name="seaSurface" ... />
17       </dataOuts>
18     </activity>
19   </branch>
20   <dataOuts>
21     <dataOut name="seaSurface" source="initSimCase1/seaSurface,
             initSimCase2/seaSurface" ... />
22   </dataOuts>
23 </alt>
```

Fig. 3.17 The `alt` activity *initSimCaseAlt*

example indicate the number of activities in each branch. This means that the first branch is preferred. However, this does not mean the first branch will be executed, because the scheduler may find that the execution time of the second branch is shorter, or the execution of one branch failed at runtime, then the other branch has to be taken. The `dataOut` port *seaSurface* (Line 21) of the `alt` activity specifies either *initSimCase1/seaSurface* in the first branch or *initSimCase2/seaSurface* in the second branch as the output of the `alt` activity.

3.2.3 AWDL Data Flow

The data flow in AWDL is expressed by data flow links from *source data ports* (see Sect. 3.2.1) to *sink data ports* (see Sect. 3.2.1). A source data port can be an input data port of the whole workflow, an input data port of a compound activity, or an output data port of an atomic activity. A sink data port can be an output data port of the whole workflow, an output data port of a compound activity, or an input data port of an atomic activity. When a source data port is connected to a sink data port with data flow, the data produced at the source data port will arrive at the sink data port at runtime when the data are to be processed. One source data port may have

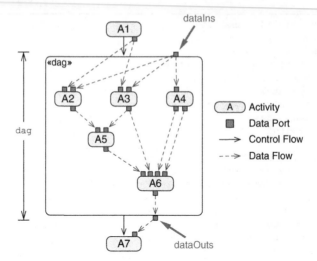

Fig. 3.18 Data flow in dag activity

multiple sink data ports, in which case each sink data port will receive a copy of the data produced at the source data port.

For each activity in AWDL, it must be guaranteed that whenever the control flow reaches the activity, all the dataIn ports of the activity have been assigned well-defined values. When the control flow leaves, all its dataOut ports must be well-defined as well. The data flow in the five compound activities introduced in the previous subsection is explored in the following.

3.2.3.1 Data Flow in DAG Activity

Figure 3.18 illustrates possible data flow in the dag activity. The data ports attaching to the top (or bottom) edge of an activity indicate the dataIn (or dataOut) ports of that activity. The control flow inside the dag activity is not shown to avoid overloading the figure. In the dag activity, the user can define an arbitrary complex acyclic data flow. It is assumed that activities associated with the data source are executed before those activities associated with the data sink in accordance with the defined control flow.

3.2.3.2 Data Flow in Conditional Activity and Alternative Activity

The data flow in the if activity is nontrivial. Figure 3.19a illustrates illegal data flow in the if activity. If *branch1* is executed, then the dataIn port of activity *A4* would be undefined. In order to ensure that data in AWDL workflow are always well defined, dataOut ports are defined for the if activity itself, as shown in

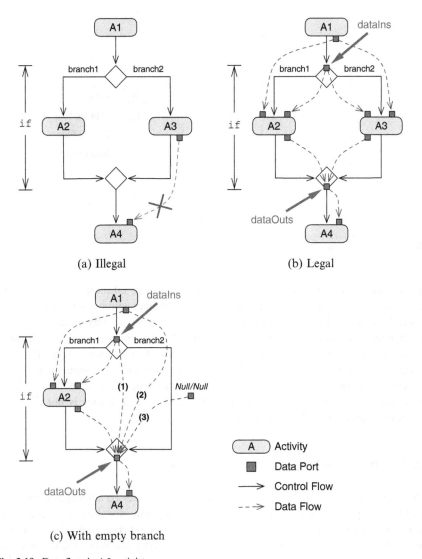

(a) Illegal

(b) Legal

(c) With empty branch

Fig. 3.19 Data flow in if activity

Fig. 3.19b. The purpose of using these dataOut ports is twofold: the source attributes of these dataOut ports specify the possible internal data flow from each branch, and these dataOut ports represent the output of the if activity, which is well defined whichever branch of the if activity is executed. The internal data flow for an empty branch can be specified in three ways, as indicated by the three data flow edges labeled with *(1)*, *(2)*, and *(3)* in Fig. 3.19c: from the dataIn ports of the if activity, from the data port that holds valid data before the execution of the if activity starts, or from the predefined dummy data port *Null/Null* indicating

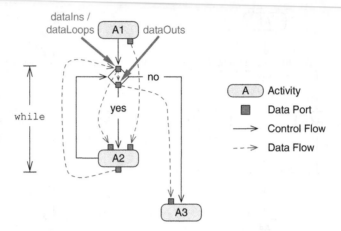

Fig. 3.20 Data flow in while activity

empty data. As a consequence, the dataIn ports of the subsequent activity *A4* is not allowed to be linked from a dataOut port of an inner activity of the if activity. Instead, it must be linked from a dataOut port of the if activity. In this case, it is ensured that each dataOut port is well defined for each possible execution path.

Similar to the if activity, the alt activity also has its own dataOut ports which are used to define internal data flow and represent the output of the alt activity to be further processed by subsequent activities. The data flow linking from inner activities of the alt activity to subsequent activities is not allowed. In addition, there is no empty branch in the alt activity.

3.2.3.3 Data Flow in Sequential Loop Activity

The data flow in sequential loop activities occurs in the while activity and the for activity with parallel = *"no"*. We explain the data flow model for sequential loop activities exemplified by the while activity with the loop condition to be evaluated before the loop body is executed. For the while activity, the flow of data from one iteration to the next one is required, i.e., the output of one iteration serves as the input of the subsequent iteration. To model the data flow for the while activity, we consider two cases: (a) the loop body is never executed if the loop condition never evaluates to *true*, and (b) the loop body is executed multiple times which implies a cyclic data flow. Figure 3.20 illustrates the data flow model for the while activity with the loop condition (indicated by a diamond) is evaluated before the execution of the loop body (i.e., activity *A2*):

(a) The dataIn ports of the while activity get their values through their source attributes or value elements. The dataLoop ports of the while activity are assigned initial values via their initSource attributes or value elements.

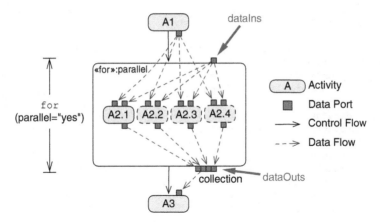

Fig. 3.21 Data flow in `for` activity with `parallel=`*"yes"*

(b) If the loop condition evaluates to *false*, the data flow continues at step (d). If *true*, the inner activity *A2* is executed. *A2* can obtain data from the `dataIn` ports of the `while` activity, the `dataLoop` ports of the `while` activity, or from some predecessor activities such as *A1*.

(c) Once *A2* has been executed, data from its `dataOut` ports can be transferred to the `dataLoop` ports of the surrounding `while` activity, specified by their `loopSource` attributes. Then the loop condition is evaluated again with the new data from the `dataLoop` ports.

(d) When the loop condition evaluates to *false*, the current data of the `dataLoop` ports are mapped to the `dataOut` ports of the `while` activity.

(e) Subsequent activities of the `while` activity, e.g., *A3*, can only obtain the data from the `dataOut` ports of the `while` activity.

For each possible execution path inside the `while` activity, it is ensured that the data flow is well defined and valid data are available at all `dataIn` and `dataOut` ports of all executed activities. In case that *A2* receives data from an activity outside of the `while` activity, these data remain constant and accessible for all iterations. Note that the number of possible `dataOut` ports of the `while` activity must be smaller than or equal to the number of its `dataLoop` ports because only `dataLoop` ports hold the final values of the `while` activity.

3.2.3.4 Data Flow in Parallel Loop Activities

The data flow in parallel loop activities occurs in the `for` activity with `parallel` =*"yes"* (Fig. 3.21). In contrast to sequential loop activities, there is no need to model cyclic data flow. Since in general it cannot be decided at compile time how many times the loop body will be executed, *data collections* are used to hold all result data produced by all the iterations when the `for` activity terminates.

```
 1  <activity name="name" type="type">
 2    <dataIns>
 3      <dataIn name="name" type="type" source="source"? >
 4        <value> constants </value>?
 5        <properties> ... </properties>
 6        <constraints> ... </constraints>
 7      <dataIn>*
 8    </dataIns>
 9    <properties> ... </properties>
10    <constraints> ... </constraints>
11    <dataOuts>
12      <dataOut name="name" type="type" saveto="saveto"? >*
13        <properties> ... </properties>
14        <constraints> ... </constraints>
15      </dataOut>
16    </dataOuts>
17  </activity>
```

Fig. 3.22 Properties and constraints

Before any iteration of the for activity is executed, the number of iterations is evaluated. Then all iterations are executed in parallel. For example, four iterations, indicated by *A2.1*, *A2.2*, *A2.3*, and *A2.4* in Fig. 3.21, are executed in parallel. Each iteration may receive an element from the data collection represented by the loopElement data port of the for activity. Every iteration may also receive some other input data from either the dataIn ports of the for activity or some predecessors such as *A1*. At the end of its execution, each iteration writes its results into the data collections specified by the dataOut ports of the for activity. Multiple data collections can be used to hold multiple output data from each iteration. The output data collections can then be accessed through the dataOut ports of the for activity by subsequent activities such as *A3*.

3.2.4 Properties and Constraints

In AWDL, properties and constraints can be defined by users to provide additional information to a workflow runtime environment to steer and to optimize the execution of workflow applications. Properties provide hints about the behavior of activities, e.g., the expected size of output data, the way input data is processed (*readonly* or *readwrite*), etc. Constraints must be fulfilled by the underlying workflow runtime environment, e.g., to execute an activity on a specific node, to provide at least 512 MB memory for the execution of an activity, to finish the execution of an activity in 30 min, etc. The user can define properties and constraints elements for activities (Lines 9 and 10) and for data ports (Lines 5, 6, 13, and 14), as illustrated in Fig. 3.22.

```
 1 <activity name="InitializeSimulation"
       type="actt://Meteorology/simulation_init">
 2   <constraints>
 3     <constraint name="awdl:node"
           value="karwendel.dps.uibk.ac.at"/>
 4   </constraints>
 5   <dataIns>
 6     <dataIn name="analyzedSurface" type="awdl:file"
           source="Meteo2/analyzedSurface">
 7       <properties>
 8         <property name="awdl:readonly" value="true"/>
 9       </properties>
10     </dataIn>
11   </dataIns>
12   <dataOuts>
13     <dataOut name="ramsMicrophysics" type="awdl:file">
14       <properties>
15         <property name="awdl:datasize" value="10.0MB"/>
16       </properties>
17     </dataOut>
18   </dataOuts>
19 </activity>
```

Fig. 3.23 Examples of properties and constraints

Figure 3.23 shows some examples of properties and constraints specified in activity *InitializeSimulation*. The constraint *awdl:node* (Line 3) specifies that this activity must be executed on the node *karwendel.dps.uibk.ac.at*. This could be a user specified requirement or a decision made by a workflow scheduler. The property *awdl:readonly* (Line 8) of the dataIn port *analyzedSurface* indicates whether the activity changes the input file represented by this dataIn port during its execution. The value *true* of this property could be a hint for a workflow enactment engine to consider data transfer optimization. The property *awdl:datasize* (Line 15) of the dataOut port *ramsMicrophysics* gives the estimated size of the output data represented by this dataOut port. This could be used by a data-aware workflow scheduler [93] to make a decision on whether to move data to a computation or move a computation to data.

3.2.5 The Structure of an AWDL Workflow

Figure 3.24 illustrates the complete structure of an AWDL workflow. It consists of the specification of the workflow metadata, the definition of sub-workflows, the definition of the workflow input and output, and the specification of the workflow body. The workflow metadata contains domain, name, version,

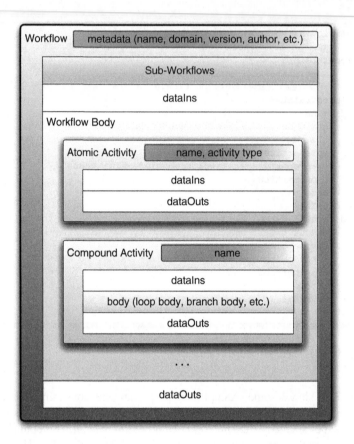

Fig. 3.24 The structure of an AWDL workflow

and `author`. Particularly, the `domain` attribute indicates the domain of this
workflow application, such as *Material Sciences*, *Meteorology*, and *Astrophysics*.
The workflow body is a sequence of activities, each of which can be an atomic
activity or a compound activity. The next section shows an excerpt of the AWDL
representation of the material science workflow application WIEN2k [25]. We will
discuss sub-workflows in Chap. 4.

3.3   AWDL Modeling: A Real-World Scientific Workflow Example

WIEN2k [25] is a program package for performing electronic structure calculations
of solids using density functional theory. The programs which compose the WIEN2k
package are typically organized in the workflow illustrated in Fig. 3.25. The activity

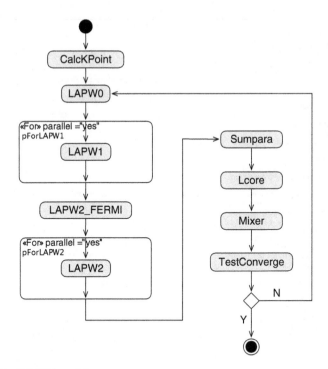

Fig. 3.25 The WIEN2k workflow

LAPW1 and the activity *LAPW2* can be executed in parallel, as specified by the parallel iterative constructs. The number of parallel loop iterations of each construct is determined by *kpoint* (atoms), which is the output integer of the activity *CalcKPoint*. A final task *TestConverge* is applied to several output files to test whether the problem convergence criterion is fulfilled. The number of iterations for the convergence loop is unknown at compile time. Note that with only about a dozen AWDL activities we can describe a WIEN2k workflow with several hundred activity instances (one for each *kpoint* in both parallel loops).

A representative excerpt of the AWDL representation for the workflow is given in Fig. 3.26. The Activity Types (ATs) such as *actt://MaterialScience/LAPW0*, *actt://MaterialScience/LAPW1*, etc. have been defined in the activity registry service GLARE. The workflow consists of an atomic activity *CalcKPoint* (Line 10), followed by a while loop (Line 16). In this while loop, the activity *LAPW0* (Line 23), the parallel for loop *pForLAPW1* (Line 32), the activity *LAPW2_FERMI* (Line 43), the parallel for loop *pForLAPW2* (Line 44), and the activities *Sumpara* (Line 45) *LCore* (Line 46), *Mixer* (Line 47), and *TestConverge* (Line 48) are executed sequentially. The value of the dataLoop port *val* (Line 19) of the while loop is changed after each loop iteration by the dataOut port of the activity *TestConverge*, which is referred by the loopSource attribute of the dataLoop port at Line 19. In the parallel for loop *pForLAPW1* and *pForLAPW2*, the inner

```
1   <workflow domain="MaterialScience" name="WIEN2k" version="1.0" author="junqin" >
2    <dataIns>
3     <dataIn name="val" type="xsd:boolean" >
4      <value> false </value>
5     </dataIn>
6     <dataIn name="in0File" type="awdl:file"
         source="gsiftp://karwendel.dps.uibk.ac.at/home/junqin/WIEN2k/in/atype.In0"/>
7     <!-- other dataIn ports -->
8    </dataIns>
9    <workflowBody>
10    <activity name="CalcKPoint" type="actt://MaterialScience/CalcKPoint" >
11     <dataIns .../>
12     <dataOuts>
13      <dataOut name="kpoint" type="xsd:integer" />
14     </dataOuts>
15    </activity>
16    <while name="doWhileConv">
17     <dataIns> ... </dataIns>
18     <dataLoops>
19      <dataLoop name="val" type="xsd:boolean" initSource="WIEN2k/val"
              loopSource="TestConverge/outVal" />
20      <!-- other dataLoop ports -->
21     </dataLoops>
22     <loopBody>
23      <activity name="LAPW0" type="actt://MaterialScience/LAPW0" >
24       <dataIns>
25        <dataIn name="in0File" type="awdl:file" source="Wien2K/in0File" />
26       </dataIns>
27       <dataOuts>
28        <dataOut name="outFileVsp" type="awdl:file" />
29        <!-- other dataOut ports -->
30       </dataOuts>
31      </activity>
32      <for name="pForLAPW1" parallel="yes">
33       <dataIns>
34        <dataIn name="fVsp" type="awdl:file" source="LAPW0/outFileVsp" />
35        <!-- other dataIn ports -->
36       </dataIns>
37       <loopCounter name="taskNumber" type="xsd:integer" from="1"
               to="CalcKPoint/kpoint"/>
38       <loopBody>
39        <activity name="LAPW1" ... />
40       </loopBody>
41       <dataOuts ... />
42      </for>
43      <activity name="LAPW2_FERMI" ... />
44      <for name="pForLAPW2" parallel="yes" ... />
45      <activity name="Sumpara" ... />
46      <activity name="Lcore" ... />
47      <activity name="Mixer" ... />
48      <activity name="TestConverge" ... >
49       <dataIns> ... </dataIns>
50       <dataOuts>
51        <dataOut name="outVal" type="xsd:boolean" />
52        <!-- other dataOut ports -->
53       </dataOuts>
54      </activity>
55     </loopBody>
56     <condition combinedWith="and">
57      <acondition data1="doWhileConv/val" data2="true" operator="=="/>
58     </condition>
59     <dataOuts>
60      <dataOut name="outVal" type="xsd:boolean" source="doWhileConv/outVal" />
61      <!-- other dataOut ports -->
62     </dataOuts>
63    </while>
64   </workflowBody>
65   <dataOuts>
66    <dataOut name="outVal" type="xsd:boolean" source="doWhileConv/outVal"
            saveto="gsiftp://karwendel.dps.uibk.ac.at/home/junqin/WIEN2k/out/conv.out"/>
67    <!-- other dataOut ports -->
68   </dataOuts>
69  </workflow>
```

Fig. 3.26 An excerpt of the AWDL representation of the WIEN2k workflow

activities are executed in parallel. Finally, the output *outVal* of the workflow *WIEN2k* is stored in a file as the result of the workflow execution.

3.4 Reification and Execution

Abstract workflows must be reified before they can be submitted for execution. This section explains in detail the reification and execution process (Fig. 3.27) in ASKALON with the example scientific workflow application WIEN2k.

First, the abstract WIEN2k workflow serves as an input to the Meta-Scheduler. The abstract workflow includes activities, control flow constructs like sequence, while and parallel for, as well as data flow links among activities. Each atomic activity in the abstract workflow is described by an Activity Type (AT). Figure 3.28 illustrates the activity *LAPW0* with the AT *actt://MaterialScience/LAPW0* in the abstract workflow. The activity *LAPW0* has four input data ports (see Lines 3–6) and four output data ports (see Lines 9–12). The data associated with the four input data ports, that is, one string and three files, are derived from the workflow input. Note that no concrete information such as where the activity will be executed and how data are transferred is encoded in the abstract workflow.

Next, for each atomic activity specified in the workflow, the Meta-Scheduler retrieves the corresponding Activity Deployments (ADs) from GLARE (included in the Resource Manager) based on the activity type of the atomic activity. For a given AT, there may be multiple ADs, each of which may be deployed on a different node and may differ in performance. The Meta-Scheduler can obtain the historical performance data for a given AD from the Performance Predictor. Based on the retrieved ADs and their performance data, the Meta-Scheduler can calculate a optimal schedule in which a specific AD is selected for each atomic activity specified in the workflow. In the absence of the historical performance data, the scheduling can also be made based on the hardware information of nodes (e.g., the number of CPUs, the memory size, network bandwidth, etc.) retrieved from the Resource Manager. A detailed explanation of the scheduling strategies and algorithms is out of the scope of this book. For more information on these topics, readers may refer to [51, 52, 200, 201]. Once the ADs are selected, the concrete information associated with these ADs is then inserted into the abstract workflow. At this point in time, the abstract workflow is transformed into a concrete workflow which can be submitted to the Enactment Engine for execution. Figure 3.29 illustrates the activity *LAPW0* in the transformed concrete workflow: the selected AD for the AT *actt://MaterialScience/LAPW0* is the executable *lapw0.sh* (Line 5) deployed in the directory */home/junqin/WIEN2k-DEPLOY* (Line 4) on the node *karwendel.dps.uibk.ac.at* (Line 3). The command line usage (Line 7) to run the executable, as well as the expected input and output file paths and names (specified via *awdl:fileloc* in Lines 13, 18, 24, 31, 36, 41, and 46) are also given in Fig. 3.29.

Concrete information of other types of computational entities such as Web services and Java classes can also be supported via properties. For Web services,

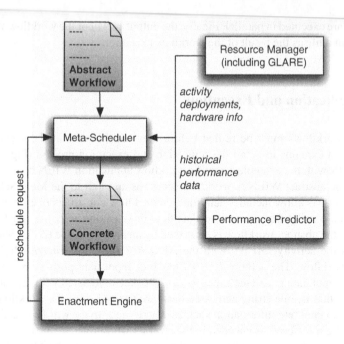

Fig. 3.27 Reification and execution

```
1  <activity name="LAPW0" type="actt://MaterialScience/LAPW0">
2    <dataIns>
3      <dataIn name="case" type="xsd:string"
             source="WIEN2K/case" />
4      <dataIn name="in0File" type="awdl:file"
             source="WIEN2K/in0File" />
5      <dataIn name="clmsumFile" type="awdl:file"
             source="WIEN2K/clmsumFile" />
6      <dataIn name="structFile" type="awdl:file"
             source="WIEN2K/structFile" />
7    </dataIns>
8    <dataOuts>
9      <dataOut name="defFile" type="awdl:file" />
10     <dataOut name="vspFile" type="awdl:file" />
11     <dataOut name="scf0File" type="awdl:file" />
12     <dataOut name="vnsFile" type="awdl:file" />
13   </dataOuts>
14 </activity>
```

Fig. 3.28 The activity *LAPW0* in the abstract workflow

```
1  <activity name="LAPW0" type="actt://MaterialScience/LAPW0">
2    <properties>
3      <property name="awdl:gridsite" value="karwendel.dps.uibk.ac.at" />
4      <property name="awdl:path" value="/home/junqin/WIEN2k-DEPLOY" />
5      <property name="awdl:executable" value="lapw0.sh" />
6      <property name="awdl:workingdir" value="." />
7      <property name="awdl:usage" value="${binDir} ${case}" />
8    </properties>
9    <dataIns>
10     <dataIn name="case" type="xsd:string" source="WIEN2K/case" />
11     <dataIn name="in0File" type="awdl:file" source="WIEN2K/in0File" >
12       <properties>
13         <property name="awdl:fileloc" value="${case}.in0" />
14       </properties>
15     </dataIn>
16     <dataIn name="clmsumFile" type="awdl:file" source="WIEN2K/clmsumFile" >
17       <properties>
18         <property name="awdl:fileloc" value="${case}.clmsum" />
19         <property name="awdl:readonly" value="true" />
20       </properties>
21     </dataIn>
22     <dataIn name="structFile" type="awdl:file" source="WIEN2K/structFile" >
23       <properties>
24         <property name="awdl:fileloc" value="${case}.struct" />
25       </properties>
26     </dataIn>
27   </dataIns>
28   <dataOuts>
29     <dataOut name="defFile" type="awdl:file">
30       <properties>
31         <property name="awdl:fileloc" value="lapw0.def" />
32       </properties>
33     </dataOut>
34     <dataOut name="vspFile" type="awdl:file">
35       <properties>
36         <property name="awdl:fileloc" value="${case}.vsp" />
37       </properties>
38     </dataOut>
39     <dataOut name="scf0File" type="awdl:file">
40       <properties>
41         <property name="awdl:fileloc" value="${case}.scf0" />
42       </properties>
43     </dataOut>
44     <dataOut name="vnsFile" type="awdl:file">
45       <properties>
46         <property name="awdl:fileloc" value="${case}.vns" />
47       </properties>
48     </dataOut>
49   </dataOuts>
50 </activity>
```

Fig. 3.29 The activity *LAPW0* in the concrete workflow

the properties may include *wsdl* (the URL of the WSDL [35] document of a
Web service), *operation* (the operation of the service), etc. For Java classes, the
properties may include *jarfile*, *class*, and *method*. Properties can be defined similarly
for software components. These properties need to be understood by workflow
enactment engines such that ADs can be correctly executed. We will focus on
executables in the remainder of this book, because (a) executables are one of

most common types of scientific applications deployed in distributed systems; (b) other types of scientific applications can be easily supported by adding required properties; and (c) this book presents the idea of scientific workflow programming at a high level of abstraction where the low level complexity such as ADs are shielded from users.

Finally, the concrete workflow is submitted to the Enactment Engine for execution on a distributed system. Based on the execution order specified by the control flow in the concrete workflow, the Enactment Engine executes the atomic activities contained in the concrete workflow sequentially, in parallel, iteratively or conditionally. To execute an atomic activity on a node, the Enactment Engine first retrieves the job submission protocol of the node from the Resource Manager, then encodes the activity specific information (e.g., working directory, command line parameters) given in the concrete workflow into the corresponding format such as the Globus Resource Specification Language (RSL) [70] or the Job Submission Description Language (JSDL) [132], and then finally executes the activity on the node. Once the execution of an atomic activity is finished, the Enactment Engine registers the output data of the activity either internally or into a data catalog service such that the output data can be made available when needed. If the execution of an atomic activity fails, the Enactment Engine can give it a retry. If the Enactment Engine is still not able to execute the activity, it can ask the Meta-Scheduler for rescheduling. Data flow links among the activities are dealt with intelligently by the Enactment Engine in three ways: (a) if the data associated with the source data port and the sink data port are on two different nodes, the Enactment Engine transfers the data from one node to another based on the specifications of both the data ports (e.g., in which directory the source data exists or is produced, to which directory the data is expected to be transferred, the name of the file expected by the sink data port) and the supported file transfer protocols on both nodes; (b) if the data associated with the source data port and the sink data port are on the same node or two different nodes among which a shared file system is used for data storage, the Enactment Engine uses a local operating system *copy*; (c) similar as the case in (b), except that the activity containing the sink data port reads the data without modifying its content. Such information can be obtained from the property *awdl:readonly* of input data ports of the activity. For example, Line 19 in Fig. 3.29 indicates that the activity *LAPW0* (actually the executable *lapw0.sh*) reads the input file *clmsumFile* without modifying the content of the file. In this case, making an alias of the file (e.g., with the unix command *ln*) in the directory where the activity is expected to read the file is used by the Enactment Engine in order to reduce unnecessary data transfer or copy.

3.5 Summary

In this chapter, we presented our work on the Abstract Workflow Description Language (AWDL), which is a novel XML-based language for the specification of scientific workflow applications at a high level of abstraction. AWDL allows the user to concentrate on describing scientific workflows without dealing with implementation specific or low-level details of the underlying distributed infrastructure. AWDL provides a rich set of constructs such as dag, if, for, while, alt, and subWorkflow, to facilitate the specification of scientific workflows and to modularize and reuse scientific workflows. AWDL supports basic data types which is a subset of the XML Schema Datatypes, as well as advanced data types *file* and *collection* which are frequently used in scientific workflows. Properties and constraints can be specified to steer and optimize workflow execution by the underlying middleware. As part of the ASKALON development and runtime environment for workflows on distributed systems, AWDL has been extensively used for the specification of scientific workflow applications in the field of material science, river modeling, astrophysics, and finance modeling. The AWDL representation of the material science workflow application WIEN2k demonstrates the basic capability of AWDL.

In the next chapter, we will present the workflow modularization mechanism of AWDL, including the definition and the invocation of sub-workflows, as well as workflow libraries.

Chapter 4
Workflow Modularization

4.1 Introduction

As more scientific workflows are built, workflow modularization mechanisms become essential for workflow languages or systems. For example, a domain scientist in one research group wants to run a workflow constructed by another group and to obtain results useful for his own research, but without knowing how to construct a scientific workflow application. In another case, domain scientists want to invoke a workflow multiple times within their own workflows (e.g., via a for loop). However, who creates the invoked workflow is not important, the workflow may have been composed by the same scientist or some other scientists, and it may have been defined inside or outside the workflow being composed. In addition, manually keeping track of the relationships among different versions of a workflow is a challenging task. Sharing workflows via email or file copying is also error prone. Therefore, workflow modularizations are important and must be supported by modern scientific workflow systems.

Following the specification of AWDL presented in the previous chapter, this chapter presents the workflow modularization mechanism of AWDL. It includes the definition and invocation of sub-workflows, as well as workflow libraries. An algorithm for detecting infinite recursive sub-workflow invocations is also presented. With the workflow modularization mechanism, domain scientists are no longer required to build every workflow from scratch. The workflow development time is significantly reduced and the quality of workflows is also improved by reusing established and validated workflows.

4.2 Sub-workflows

The informal XML grammar of subWorkflow in AWDL is illustrated in Fig. 4.1. The subWorkflow is similar to a procedure in other high-level programming languages. It is used to modularize, encapsulate, and reuse a code region.

J. Qin and T. Fahringer, *Scientific Workflows*, DOI 10.1007/978-3-642-30715-7__4,
© Springer-Verlag Berlin Heidelberg 2012

```
1  <subWorkflow name="name">
2    <dataIns>
3      <dataIn name="name" type="type" />*
4    </dataIns>
5    <subWorkflowBody>
6      <activity .../>+
7    </subWorkflowBody>
8    <dataOuts>
9      <dataOut name="name" type="type" source="source"/>*
10   </dataOuts>
11 </subWorkflow>
```

Fig. 4.1 subWorkflow

Sub-workflows are organized in AWDL workflows. In an AWDL workflow, the name of each subWorkflow is unique.

A sub-workflow is invoked in the enclosing workflow which specifies the data to be processed in the sub-workflow through the data flow specification of the workflow. Therefore, there is no source attribute for the input data ports of the subWorkflow. This is one difference between a sub-workflow and a workflow. Inside a sub-workflow, only data flow among the sub-workflow and its inner activities is allowed. Such a data flow mechanism enables safe invocations of sub-workflows anywhere in the enclosing workflow, as well as publishing sub-workflows in a workflow library (see Sect. 4.3) as stand-alone workflows for further reuse. This is another difference between a sub-workflow and a workflow: a sub-workflow in a workflow is not visible outside of that workflow. Therefore, it cannot be invoked from another workflow unless it is published in a workflow library. An example of subWorkflow is illustrated in Sect. 4.5.

4.3 Workflow Library

In order to facilitate workflow sharing and reuse, as well as workflow version tracking, we put forward the concept of *workflow library*. By analogy to *unix libraries*, a workflow library is a set of established workflows and the corresponding management tool. Users can publish workflows in a workflow library, or mark workflows in a workflow library as deprecated. The workflows in a workflow library can be shared among research groups and can be invoked in other workflows. The functionalities provided by a workflow library are as follows:

- To publish workflows in the workflow library.
- To associate workflows with metadata, especially, workflow versions can be generated automatically based on the latest version in the workflow library.
- To search workflows by their metadata.

- To show workflow graphs, including graphs of its sub-workflows.
- To run workflows with a single click.
- To mark a workflow as deprecated for discouraging their use because, for example, a better alternative exists.

We have developed a workflow library called ASKALON Workflow Hosting Environment (AWHE) which will be demonstrated in Sect. 5.5.

The use of workflow libraries enables the categorization of ASKALON users into three classes. *Workflow Executors* execute existing, validated workflows by means of workflow libraries. *Workflow Developers* compose workflows by dragging and dropping activities, sub-workflows, and workflows into new workflows. Workflow developers can publish their workflows with the default input data (via the `source` attributes or the `value` elements of `dataIn` ports) and the default locations to save output data (via the `saveto` attributes of `dataOut` ports, see Sect. 3.2.1). Workflow developers can also leave the information empty for (potential) users to execute the published workflows with their own input data and their own locations for output data. *Application Providers* deploy binary executables, Web services, etc. into distributed systems and associate them with activity types via an activity registry service such as GLARE.

Users can run workflows directly from a workflow library without modifications, or with specifications of their own input data and locations for their output data. However, for the former to happen, users must have the necessary permissions to read the input data specified via the `source` attributes as well as to write the output data to the locations specified via the `saveto` attributes. Note that changes of back-end resources, e.g., the location of binary executables, are transparent to users because AWDL workflows are abstract, i.e., no concrete information such as the location of binary executables is encoded in AWDL workflows.

4.4   Invocation of (Sub-)workflows

As we described in Sect. 3.2.1, each atomic activity in AWDL has a `type` attribute which refers to an activity type. Figure 4.2 illustrates such an atomic activity referring to AT *actt://mathematics/Matrix-Multiplication*, i.e., *MatrixMultiplication* in the *mathematics* domain. The execution of this activity means the execution of the specific AD mapped from the AT. Since the AT is abstract, i.e., implementation independent, the atomic activity can be reused in other workflows. This is called AT invocation. The invocation of (sub-)workflows is done similarly in AWDL. If an atomic activity in a workflow has a type referring to a sub-workflow defined in the workflow or a workflow published in a workflow library, executing this activity invokes the corresponding sub-workflow or workflow. Figure 4.3 illustrates an example of sub-workflow invocation: the workflow *w* defines a sub-workflow *subW1* (Line 2) which is invoked at Line 5 by the activity *a*. Figure 4.4 illustrates a workflow invocation: the workflow is referred by its domain, name, and version in a

```
1 <activity name="a"
      type="actt://mathematics/MatrixMultiplication">
2   <dataIns> ... </dataIns>
3   <dataOuts> ... </dataOuts>
4 </activity>
```

Fig. 4.2 Activity type invocation

```
1 <workflow name="w">
2   <subWorkflow name="subW1" .../>
3   <dataIns> ... </dataIns>
4   <workflowBody>
5     <activity name="a" type="subw://subW1">
6         <dataIns> ... </dataIns>
7         <dataOuts> ... </dataOuts>
8     </activity>
9   </workflowBody>
10   <dataOuts> ... </dataOuts>
11 <workflow>
```

Fig. 4.3 Sub-workflow invocation

```
1 <activity name="a"
      type="wlib://domain/workflow/version">
2   <dataIns> ... </dataIns>
3   <dataOuts> ... </dataOuts>
4 </activity>
```

Fig. 4.4 Workflow invocation

workflow library. In summary, the value of the type attribute of an atomic activity can be as follows:

- *actt://domain/activitytype*, referring to an activity type registered in an activity registry service.
- *subw://subworkflow*, referring to a sub-workflow that is specified as part of the workflow containing the atomic activity.
- *wlib://domain/workflow/version*, referring to a workflow published in a workflow library.

When an atomic activity refers to an AT, a sub-workflow, or a workflow, the types and the numbers of the input and output data ports are determined by the AT, the sub-workflow, or the workflow. As we will see in Sects. 5.4 and 5.5, the input and output data ports of the atomic activity are added automatically when the type attribute is determined.

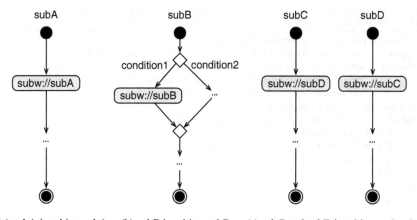

(a) subA invoking subA   (b) subB invoking subB   (c) subC and subD invoking each other

Fig. 4.5 Examples of incorrect recursive sub-workflow invocations

In order to support alternative execution, the value of the `type` attribute of an atomic activity can also refer to multiple ATs, multiple sub-workflows, multiple workflows, or any combination of them. Obviously, this requires that the referenced ATs, sub-workflows, and workflows must have the same input and output data structure.

4.4.1 Detection of Infinite Sub-workflow Invocation

As mentioned, sub-workflows can be invoked when executing an atomic activity by referencing the sub-workflows in the `type` attribute of the atomic activity. This enables recursive sub-workflow invocations in the case where the atomic activity is defined in the sub-workflow. As in high-level programming languages (e.g., Java or C++), improperly designed recursive sub-workflow invocations can lead to infinite recursion. While some infinite sub-workflow invocations can be detected at composition time by analyzing the model of a workflow without actually running it, others, for example, depending on specific data being processed, can only be found at runtime. We deal with the former, i.e., the infinite sub-workflow invocations detectable at composition time, in this section. Figure 4.5 illustrates three examples of incorrect recursive sub-workflow invocations. In Fig. 4.5a, *subA* will cause infinite recursion because the first activity in *subA* invokes the sub-workflow itself. This is also the case with *subB* (Fig. 4.5b) if the branch at the left-hand side is executed at runtime. Finally, Fig. 4.5c shows a case of incorrect recursive sub-workflow invocations involving different sub-workflows invoking each other.

To address this problem, incorrect recursive sub-workflow invocations are detected by traversing workflow models while workflows are being composed and

---

Algorithm 4.1: Find incorrect recursive sub-workflow invocation

---

1 *Method 1: detectIncorrectRecursiveInvocation()*
   Input   : workflow w to detect incorrect recursive sub-workflow invocation
   Output : ordered list p, indicating sub-workflow invocation path, with the last element
              being the sub-workflow that is incorrectly recursively invoked, $p = \emptyset$ means
              no incorrect recursive sub-workflow invocation found.
2 Initialize the sub-workflow invocation path $p = \emptyset$
3 **forall** *sub-workflow sub invoked in the workflow w* **do**
4   detectRecursiveSubWorkflowInvocation(p, sub)
5   **if** $p \neq \emptyset \wedge \neg\ isCorrectRecursiveInvocation(p)$ **then**
6   **return** p
7   **end**
8 **end**
9 **return** $\emptyset$

10 *Method 2: detectRecursiveSubWorkflowInvocation()*
   Input   : sub-workflow invocation path p;   sub-workflow sub to be invoked next
   Output : **true**, if a recursive sub-workflow invocation is found; **false**, otherwise
11 **if** *contains(p, sub)* **then**
12   append(p, sub)
13   **return true**
14 **end**
15 append(p, sub)
16 **forall** *activity a in the sub-workflow sub such that a has a type referring to a sub-workflow s* **do**
17   isRecursion = detectRecursiveSubWorkflowInvocation(p, s) *// recursively call Method 2*
18   **if** *isRecursion* **then**
19   **return true**
20   **end**
21 **end**
22 removeLastElement(p)
23 **return false**

24 *Method 3: isCorrectRecursiveInvocation()*
   Input   : sub-workflow invocation path p with the last element being the sub-workflow
              being recursively invoked
   Output : **true** if correct, **false** otherwise
25 **if** *there are activities between two invocations of the last sub-workflow* **then**
26   **return true**
27 **else**
28   **return false**
29 **end**

---

before they are submitted for execution on distributed systems. Our approach for detecting incorrect sub-workflow invocations is described by Algorithm 4.1. *Method 1* is the entry point of the algorithm and for each sub-workflow invoked from the *main* workflow, it detects recursive sub-workflow invocations (*Method 2*) and, when found, it evaluates whether the recursive sub-workflow invocation is correct (*Method 3*). Specifically, *Method 2* detects recursive invocations by recursively checking all possible sub-workflow invocation paths. The return *boolean* value of *Method 2* is used by itself to check whether it should continue expanding the sub-workflow invocation path p. The detected recursive sub-workflow invocation path p is then evaluated in *Method 1* by calling *Method 3* (p is shared by the three methods). *Method 3* evaluates the correctness of a recursive sub-workflow invocation path by checking whether there are data processing steps (i.e., activities) between two invocations of the same sub-workflow. If there are no activities in between, the sub-workflow invocation path is considered to be incorrect because it will cause infinite recursion. Otherwise, if there are some activities executed between two invocations of the same sub-workflow, it is considered to be a "correct" (from the workflow composition point of view) recursive sub-workflow invocation. Note that, in the latter case, we assume that in the second invocation of the sub-workflow, the input data of the sub-workflow comes from the output data of these activities and the output data of these activities are different from their input data. This is reasonable because it does not make sense for an activity to have output data identical to its input data.

4.4.2 Workflow Invocation

As presented in Sect. 4.3, to facilitate workflow execution, *Workflow Developers* may publish their workflows into a workflow library with predetermined or commonly used input data (via the source attributes or the value elements of dataIn ports) and locations of output data (via the saveto attributes of dataOut ports). However, workflow invocation frequently requires that the invoked workflow process the data in the invoking workflow. To address this issue, the source attributes or the value elements of dataIn ports, and the saveto attributes of dataOut ports of the invoked workflow are simply ignored by the workflow engine. Instead, the data in the invoking workflow can be passed to the invoked workflow through the data flow between the two workflows.

For workflow invocation, we support two kinds of AWDL code generation mechanisms: (a) embedding the AWDL code of the invoked workflows as sub-workflows into the invoking workflow so that the workflow engine can execute the invoking workflow directly without retrieving the AWDL code of sub-workflows from workflow libraries. With this approach, we convert the workflow invocations into sub-workflow invocations; and (b) using the references of the invoked workflows in the invoking workflow without embedding the AWDL code of the invoked workflows. The workflow runtime system can obtain the code of the invoked workflows from workflow libraries when needed. This is the so-called late binding mechanism. This is also the distinction between sub-workflow invocation and workflow invocation as the AWDL code for sub-workflows is always embedded while the code for external workflows is not. Examples of the two code generation mechanisms are demonstrated in the next section.

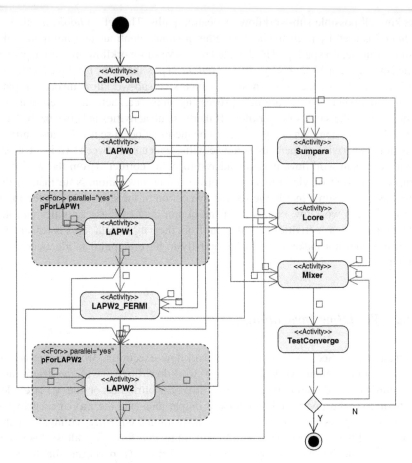

Fig. 4.6 The WIEN2k workflow

4.5 Case Study: WIEN2k

The UML Activity Diagram representation of the workflow WIEN2k [25] is
illustrated in Fig. 4.6, where arrows without small squares are control flow edges
and arrows with small squares are data flow edges. Control flow and data flow edges
may overlap. For the reason of simplicity, multiple data flow edges between any pair
of activities are represented with a single data flow edge. The workflow consists of
a while loop (represented by a DecisionNode and a control flow edge connecting
backwards to a predecessor, i.e., the activity *LAPW0*. See Chap. 5 for the details
on UML-based scientific workflow modeling). At the end of each loop iteration
an output value is evaluated against a threshold to see whether the computation is
converged. The workflow can be reorganized by extracting the body of the while

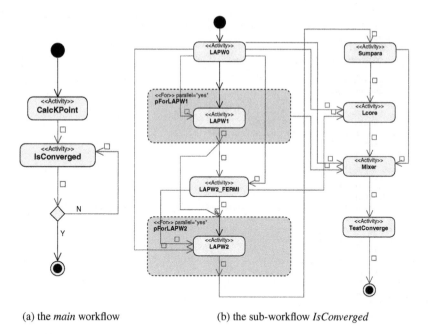

(a) the *main* workflow   (b) the sub-workflow *IsConverged*

Fig. 4.7 The WIEN2k workflow using sub-workflows

loop as a sub-workflow *IsConverged* (Fig. 4.7b) and then invoking the sub-workflow from the `while` loop in the *main* workflow (Fig. 4.7a).

The corresponding AWDL representation of the WIEN2k workflow using sub-workflows is illustrated in Fig. 4.8. The sub-workflow *IsConverged* is specified at Lines 2–21. The *main* workflow is specified at Lines 22–53 which invokes the sub-workflow at Lines 36–45. The data in the *main* workflow are passed to the sub-workflow through the `dataIn` ports (e.g., the `dataIn` port *in0File* at Line 38) of the activity *IsConverged*. The output data of the sub-workflow are passed back to the *main* workflow through the `dataOut` ports (e.g., the `dataOut` port *val* at Line 42) of the activity *IsConverged*.

Note that if the sub-workflow is published as a workflow *wlib://MaterialSicences /IsConverged/1.0* in a workflow library, the AWDL representation shown in Fig. 4.8 can be considered the case where the AWDL code of the invoked workflow *wlib://MaterialSicences/IsConverged/1.0* is embedded in the invoking workflow (i.e., the *main* workflow). If we remove Lines 2–21 and then change the `type` of the activity *IsConverged* to *wlib://MaterialSicences/IsConverged/1.0*, Fig. 4.8 would show the case of late binding code generation mechanism. In this case, the workflow runtime system can obtain the AWDL code of the workflow *wlib://MaterialSicences/IsConverged/1.0* from the workflow library when needed.

As a consequence of using sub-workflows, the workflow model is simplified in terms of the number of control and data flow connections. The modularization of this workflow is also improved: the extracted sub-workflow can be reused (i.e., invoked)

```
1   <workflow domain="MaterialScience" name="WIEN2k" ... />
2     <subWorkflow name="IsConverged">
3       <dataIns>
4         <dataIn name="in0File" type="awdl:file" />
5         <!-- other dataIns ports -->
6       </dataIns>
7       <subWorkflowBody>
8         <activity name="LAPW0" ... />
9         <for name="pForLAPW1" parallel="yes" ... />
10        <activity name="LAPW2_FERMI" ... />
11        <for name="pForLAPW2" parallel="yes" ... />
12        <activity name="Sumpara" ... />
13        <activity name="Lcore" ... />
14        <activity name="Mixer" ... />
15        <activity name="TestConverge" ... />
16      </subWorkflowBody>
17      <dataOuts>
18        <dataOut name="val" type="xsd:boolean" source="TestConverge/outVal"/>
19        <!-- other dataOut ports -->
20      </dataOuts>
21    </subWorkflow>
22    <dataIns>
23      <dataIn name="val"... />
24      <dataIn name="in0File" ... />
25      <!-- other dataIn ports -->
26    </dataIns>
27    <workflowBody>
28      <activity name="CalcKPoint" ... />
29      <doWhile name="doWhileConv">
30        <dataIns> ... </dataIns>
31        <dataLoops>
32          <dataLoop name="val" type="xsd:boolean" initSource="WIEN2k/val"
                      loopSource="IsConverged/val" />
33          <!-- other dataLoop ports -->
34        </dataLoops>
35        <loopBody>
36          <activity name="IsConverged" type="subw://IsConverged" >
37            <dataIns>
38              <dataIn name="in0File" type="awdl:file" source="Wien2K/in0File"/>
39              <!-- other dataIns ports -->
40            </dataIns>
41            <dataOuts>
42              <dataOut name="val" type="xsd:boolean"/>
43              <!-- other dataOut ports -->
44            </dataOuts>
45          </activity>
46        </loopBody>
47        <condition combinedWith="and">
48          <acondition data1="doWhileConv/val" data2="true" operator="=="/>
49        </condition>
50        <dataOuts ... />
51      </doWhile>
52    </workflowBody>
53    <dataOuts ... />
54  </workflow>
```

Fig. 4.8 The AWDL representation of the WIEN2k workflow using sub-workflows

anywhere in the *main* workflow. If the extracted sub-workflow has been published into a workflow library, it can be reused in other workflows as well. In this case, only the *main* workflow (Fig. 4.7a) needs to be composed, which significantly reduces the user effort needed for composing scientific workflows. Using sub-workflows also facilitates workflow maintenance and evolution as any change to the sub-workflow will be automatically reflected in any activity, sub-workflow, or workflow that has a reference to the sub-workflow.

4.6 Summary

As more and more scientific workflows are being designed and built, workflow sharing and reuse becomes important and necessary for enhancing scientists' productivity. In this chapter, we presented the AWDL modularization mechanism for workflow sharing and reuse in ASKALON. A sophisticated algorithm for the detection of incorrect sub-workflow invocation at composition time is also presented. The mechanism provides a simple and consistent way for reusing workflows, sub-workflows, and workflow activities. We demonstrated the effectiveness of our approach by applying it to a real-world scientific workflow application.

In the next chapter, we will present our approach for UML-based scientific workflow modeling which supports the visual composition of scientific workflows.

Chapter 5
UML-Based Scientific Workflow Modeling

5.1 Introduction

In recent years, significant research efforts have been involved in the development of tools support for scientific workflow modeling. Many of them are text-oriented (e.g., XML or self-defined scripts). Compared with text-based modeling, graph-based modeling, which allows users to graphically define a scientific workflow through dragging and dropping the modeling elements of interest, is a promising approach. However, most of the graph-based scientific workflow modeling tools are based on user-defined notations, which hinders the collaboration among different projects. Much remains to be done to streamline the task of scientific workflow modeling.

The Unified Modeling Language (UML) [177] is a standardized general-purpose modeling language. In this chapter, we present our approach for modeling scientific workflows based on the standard UML Activity Diagram [176]. Following the formal definitions of UML Activity Diagram, we discuss the relationship between an UML Activity Diagram and a scientific workflow and describe how UML Activity Diagram can be extended to model AWDL constructs. The corresponding UML Activity Diagram based tool for scientific workflow composition is presented in Sect. 5.4.

5.2 UML Activity Diagram

The UML Activity Diagram [177] is used for *flow modeling* of various types of systems independently from their implementation (software or hardware). The hierarchical modeling capabilities of the UML Activity Diagram support modeling at arbitrary levels of detail and complexity. An *activity diagram* is a flow graph, which consists of a set of *nodes* interconnected by directed *edges*. There are three types of nodes: *action nodes*, *control nodes*, and *object nodes*. *Action nodes* are basic units of the behavior specification (see Fig. 5.1a). Actions may contain *pins*,

J. Qin and T. Fahringer, *Scientific Workflows*, DOI 10.1007/978-3-642-30715-7__5,
© Springer-Verlag Berlin Heidelberg 2012

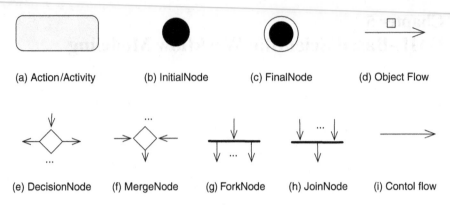

Fig. 5.1 A subset of modeling elements of UML activity diagram

which represent inputs and outputs. *Control nodes* steer the control and data along the flow graph (see Fig. 5.1b, c, e–h). *Object nodes* contain the data that flows through the graph. An edge of an activity diagram indicates either a control flow or an object flow. A *control flow edge* specifies the precedence relationship between two interconnected nodes (see Fig. 5.1i). An *object flow edge* specifies the flow of objects along interconnected *action nodes* (see Fig. 5.1d). Formally, an activity diagram is defined as follows:

Definition 5.1. An activity diagram λ is a pair $(\mathcal{N}, \mathcal{E})$, where

- $\mathcal{N}$ is a set of nodes, and
- $\mathcal{E}$ is a set of directed edges. Every directed edge $e \in \mathcal{E}$ is associated with an ordered pair of nodes (n_k, n_j), where $n_k, n_j \in \mathcal{N}$.

5.3 Modeling Scientific Workflows with the UML Activity Diagram

A scientific workflow is a flow of a set of activities. The formal definition of a scientific workflow is given by Definition 2.5. The relationship between a scientific workflow $w = (A, \overrightarrow{D})$ and an activity diagram $\lambda = (\mathcal{N}, \mathcal{E})$ is defined by relations $R' = \{(a_i, n_i) \mid \forall i, a_i \in A \wedge n_i \in \mathcal{N}\}$ and $R'' = \{(\overrightarrow{d_j}, e_j) \mid \forall j, \overrightarrow{d_j} \in \overrightarrow{D} \wedge e_j \in \mathcal{E}\}$. This means that each activity a_i of a scientific workflow is associated with a node n_i of a UML Activity Diagram, and each dependence $\overrightarrow{d_j}$ of a scientific workflow is associated with an edge e_j of a UML Activity Diagram.

In order to be able to model different types of systems, the UML specification provides several extension mechanisms to specialize semantics of modeling elements for a particular domain. For example, UML may be extended by defining new modeling elements, *stereotypes*, based on existing elements, *base classes* (i.e., metaclasses). A stereotype is defined as a subclass of an existing UML metaclass,

Table 5.1 Extending UML activity diagram to model AWDL constructs

Base class	Stereotype and tags	Description	Notation
Action	«Activity» *type*: string	Indicates that the Action represents an atomic activity, i.e., an indecomposable computation unit in scientific workflows.	Figure 5.2b
Structured-ActivityNode	«DAG»	Indicates that the StructuredActivityNode represents a group of activities that are executed based on the order specified in DAG.	Figure 5.3a
LoopNode	«For» *parallel*: boolean; *collection*: awdl:collection	Indicates that the LoopNode represents a for loop that iterates over a range of integer or float numbers sequentially or in parallel depending on the value of the *parallel* tag.	Figure 5.3e
ExpansionRegion	«For» *parallel*: boolean; *collection*: awdl:collection	Indicates that the ExpansionRegion represents a for loop that iterates over elements of data collections sequentially or in parallel depending on the value of the *parallel* tag.	Figure 5.3f

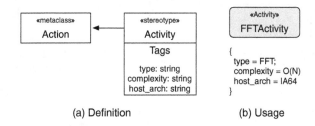

(a) Definition   (b) Usage

Fig. 5.2 The definition and usage of the stereotype *Activity*

with the associated *tagged values* (i.e., meta attributes) and *constraints*. Stereotypes are notated by the stereotype name enclosed in guillemets «StereotypeName», or by a graphic icon. Based on this mechanism, we have extended the UML Activity Diagram by defining some new *stereotypes* with associated *tagged values* based on existing elements, each corresponding to a specific AWDL construct (see Table 5.1). Figure 5.2 depicts an instance of the procedure, where we define a model element *Activity* by stereotyping the base class *Action* to model an AWDL *atomic activity*, which refers to an indecomposable computational task. The tagged value *type* specifies the *activity type* (e.g., Fast Fourier Transform (FFT)), which is an abstract description of a group of Activity Deployments (ADs) (concrete computational entities) implementing the same functionality and having the same input and output data structure. Other elements are defined in an analogous manner to the *Activity*.

The AWDL control flow constructs which are not listed in Table 5.1, i.e., sequence, parallel, if, while, and alt are modeled using UML Activity

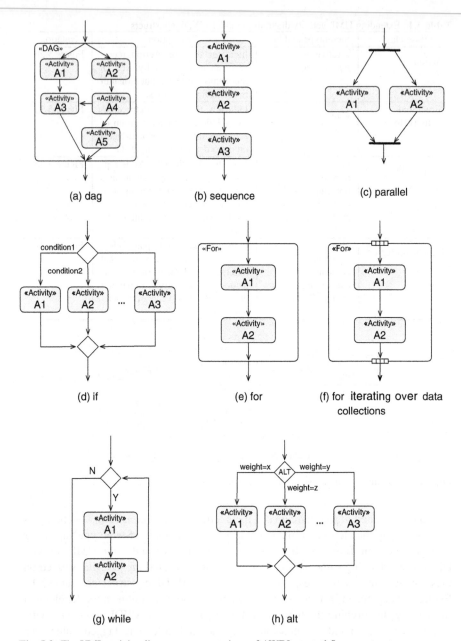

Fig. 5.3 The UML activity diagram representations of AWDL control flow constructs

Diagram modeling elements such as *DecisionNode*, *MergeNode*, *ForkNode*, and *JoinNode*, as well as the extended stereotype *Activity*. The corresponding UML Activity Diagram representations are illustrated in Fig. 5.3, where atomic activity *A1, A2, A3, A4*, and *A5* can be substituted with any compound activity.

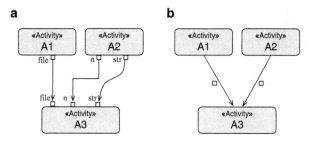

Fig. 5.4 Modeling data flow

We use the *object flow* in UML Activity Diagrams to model the data flow in scientific workflows and *pins* to model input and output data ports. Connecting an output data port of an activity to an input data port of another activity constitutes a data flow. The data contained in data flow can be any data type which is supported in AWDL. Figure 5.4a illustrates three data flow links. The output file *file* of activity *A1*, as well as the output number *n* and the output string *str* of activity *A2* serves as the inputs of the activity *A3*. Based on our experiences in multiple domains such as material science, meteorology, hydrology, and astrophysics, an activity often contains tens of inputs and/or outputs. In order to reduce clutter in diagrams of scientific workflows, we use the data flow notation with pins elided (Fig. 5.4b), as recommended by the UML Activity Diagram specification [176]. An additional simplification employed in Fig. 5.4b is to show only one data flow between two activities if there are multiple ones between them.

Properties and constraints are modeled by tagged values. Figure 5.2b shows an example of adding properties and constraints to an *Activity* using UML tagged values. Expected properties include data size (for data flow), estimated computational complexity, etc. Expected constraints include minimizing execution time, executing on a specific host architecture, etc.

Sub-workflows in AWDL are modeled in separate activity diagrams. The *main* workflow (caller) provides input data to sub-workflows and gets output data from them. The input data are processed in sub-workflows (callee).

5.4   Graphical Scientific Workflow Composition Tool

Based on the approach for modeling scientific workflows with the UML Activity Diagram presented in the previous section, we have developed a graphical scientific workflow composition tool for the composition of scientific workflows. We implement our graphical workflow composition tool in Java and thus independent of platform because we expect that users will compose scientific workflow applications on various different platforms. The tool is implemented based on Model-View-Controller (MVC) paradigm. The main components are: the *Graphical User*

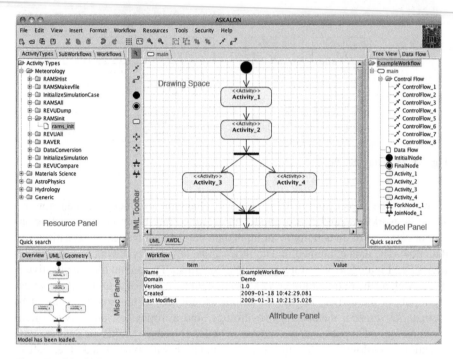

Fig. 5.5 Main GUI

Interface   (GUI), the *Model Traverser*, and the *Model Checker*. The tool has
been integrated into ASKALON as a front end for composition, execution, and
monitoring of numerous real-world scientific workflow applications from multiple
scientific domains.

5.4.1   Graphical User Interface

Figure 5.5 illustrates the GUI of the workflow composition tool. The GUI consists
of a menu bar, a standard toolbar, a UML toolbar, a resource panel, a drawing
space, a model panel, a attribute panel, a misc panel, etc. The UML toolbar contains
basic modeling elements of the UML Activity Diagram, including, from top to
bottom, Control Flow edge, Data Flow edge, InitialNode, FinalNode, Activity,
DecisionNode, MergeNode, ForkNode, JoinNode. Users can compose scientific
workflows by dragging and dropping modeling elements into the drawing space.
The resource panel provides a list of Activity Types (ATs) deployed in the activity
registry service GLARE, a list of sub-workflows defined in the workflow being
composed, and workflows published in a workflow library in three tabbed panels
ActivityTypes, *SubWorkflows*, and *Workflows*, respectively. Dragging and dropping

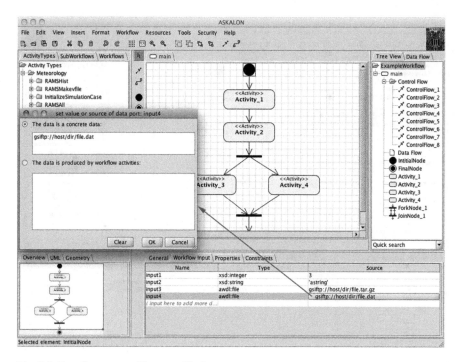

Fig. 5.6 Data flow composition: specific data

an AT, a sub-workflow, or a workflow from the corresponding list into the drawing place creates an activity with associated input and output data ports as specified by the AT, the sub-workflow or the workflow. The drawing space consists of a tabbed panel which contains an activity diagram in each tab, corresponding to a (sub-)workflow. As an illustrative example, the workflow shown in the drawing place in Fig. 5.5 is a `sequence` activity which consists of two atomic activities *Activity_1* and *Activity_2* followed by a `parallel` activity. In the `parallel` activity, *Activity_3* and *Activity_4* are executed in parallel. Other AWDL control flow constructs can be created with the elements in the UML toolbar as well. Their appearance in the GUI would be exactly like the corresponding ones shown in Fig. 5.3. In order to avoid redundancy, we do not show them here. The model panel shows *tree views* of scientific workflows. The attribute panel is used to specify activity names, activity types, properties, and constraints, as well as data flow.

Data flow composition is done by setting `source` attributes of data ports. The `source` of an input data port of a workflow is typically specific data, e.g., a specific value, a specific file (see Fig. 5.6), etc. The `source` of an input data port of an activity can be an output data port (called *source data port*) of a predecessor of this activity. In this case, the model traverser is invoked to find predecessors. The data ports of the predecessors are then filtered based on the data type of the *sink data port*). Figure 5.7 illustrates the data flow composition for the input data port

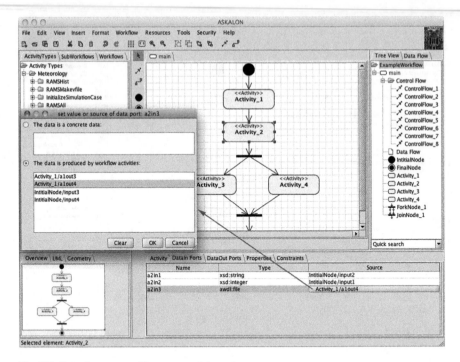

Fig. 5.7 Data flow composition: source data port

Activity	DataIn Ports	DataOut Ports	Properties	Constraints		
Name				Value		
awdl:node				karwendel.dps.uibk.ac.at		
(input here to add more constraint)						

Fig. 5.8 Activity constraint: *awdl:node*

a2in3 of *Activity_2*. The predecessors of *Activity_2* are *InitialNode* (representing the initial inputs of the workflow) and *Activity_1*. Both predecessors have four data ports with data type *awdl:file*, matching the data type of the sink data port *a2in3*. Users can select one among the four source data ports as the source of the sink data port *a2in3*. With the help of semantic technologies, we have further improved the data flow composition mechanism in the graphical tool by an automatic data flow composition algorithm which compares data semantics, instead of data types, of sink and source data ports. The details are discussed in Chaps. 7 and 8.

Properties and constraints of activities and data ports can also be set through the attribute panel. Figure 5.8 illustrates the constraint *awdl:node* of an activity

Activity \ DataIn Ports ` DataOut Ports \ Properties \ Constraints \					
Name	Type	SaveTo		Properties \ Constraints \	
a2out1	awdl:file			Name	Value
				awdl:datasize	100MB
				(input here to add more property)	

Fig. 5.9   Data port property: *awdl:datasize*

which indicates that the activity must be executed on the specified node. Figure 5.9 illustrates the property *awdl:datasize* of a data port which indicates the estimated data size of the data represented by this data port.

The workflow composition tool can be also extended through *plugins*. A plugin is a Java class that defines a set of callback methods that are called when the appropriate event occurs, e.g., a new activity is added/removed/selected, etc. A plugin can also have a GUI component which can be added as a tab in the resource panel, the model panel, the attribute panel, or the misc panel. The tabs in the panels shown in Fig. 5.5 are all built-in plugins.

5.4.2   Model Traverser

The *Model Traverser* provides the possibility to walk through scientific workflow models, visit each modeling element by retrieving its attributes and its incoming and outgoing connections, and capture AWDL constructs. The result of the model traverser is AWDL representations of scientific workflows, which serve as the input for ASKALON. By clicking the *AWDL* tab of each diagram, the model traverser is invoked and the AWDL representation of the corresponding (sub-)workflow is generated (Fig. 5.10). Error messages are shown when errors occur. The AWDL representation of the entire scientific workflow, including its sub-workflows, can be generated automatically by clicking the menu *File | Export to AWDL file*.

5.4.3   Model Checker

The Model Checker is developed to assist users in creating valid scientific workflows. The Model checker consists of two parts: the static model checker and the dynamic model checker. The static model checker validates workflow models against static rules which are defined in configuration files. These rules include the maximum number of incoming (or outgoing) control flow edges that can connect

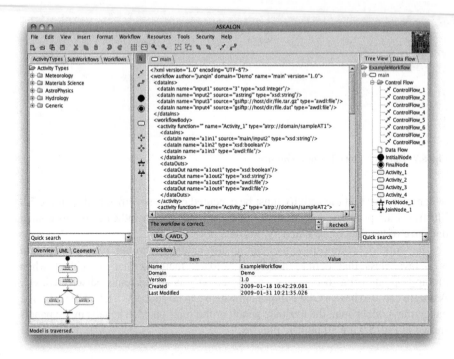

Fig. 5.10 Model traverser

to (or from) a certain node (see Definition 5.1), what kinds of nodes a certain node can connect to (or be connected from), etc. Figure 5.11 illustrates such a static connection rule which specifies that InitialNode can have at most *one* outgoing ControlFlow connecting to an Action (including its stereotype Activity), DecisionNode, ForkNode, LoopNode, ExpansionRegion, StructuredActivityNode, or ActivityFinalNode. It also specifies that a ControlFlow connecting from an InitialNode to a MergeNode or a JoinNode is not allowed (because these targets are not present in the rules). Connection rules for other type of nodes can also be specified similarly. Figure 5.12 illustrates some errors which can be detected by the static model checker.

The dynamic model checker detects control flow errors, data flow errors, and runtime errors which cannot be captured by static connection rules but can be captured by workflow traversing. Example of these errors include a ForkNode without a corresponding JoinNode, a DecisionNode not matching any of the two cases illustrated in Fig. 5.3d, g, the source attribute of an input data port of an atomic activity referring to a successor of this activity, the source attribute of an input data port of an atomic activity in a branch of an if construct referring to activities in a different branch of the if construct, the activity type of an atomic activity not being defined in the GLARE service, etc. These kinds of control flow, data flow, and runtime errors are captured with the help of the model traverser.

```
1  <connectionRules>
2    <connection name="ControlFlow">
3      <source="InitialNode"  max="1">
4        <target name="Action" />
5        <target name="DecisionNode" />
6        <target name="ForkNode" />
7        <target name="LoopNode" />
8        <target name="ExpansionRegion" />
9        <target name="StructuredActivityNode" />
10       <target name="ActivityFinalNode" />
11     </source>
12     <!-- other Control Flow connection rules -->
13     <source .../>
14   </connection>
15   <!-- Data Flow connection rules -->
16   <connection name="DataFlow" ... />
17 </connectionRules>
```

Fig. 5.11 Connection rules

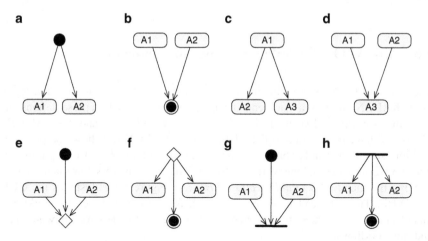

Fig. 5.12 Error examples detectable by the static model checker. (**a**): too many control flow edges from InitialNode; (**b**): too many control flow edges to FinalNode; (**c**): too many control flow edges from Activity *A1*; (**d**): too many control flow edges to Activity *A3*; (**e**): control flow from DecisionNode to FinalNode is not allowed; (**f**): control flow from DecisionNode to FinalNode is not allowed; (**g**): control flow from InitialNode to JoinNode is not allowed; (**h**): control flow from JoinNode to FinalNode is not allowed

Figure 5.13 illustrates some errors which can be detected by the dynamic model checker.

The model checker validates scientific workflow models while users are drawing a workflow, before a workflow is saved, after a workflow is loaded, before a

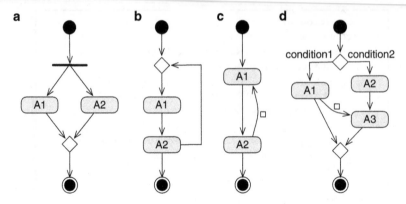

Fig. 5.13 Error examples detectable by the dynamic model checker. (**a**): no JoinNode found for ForkNode; (**b**): one control flow edge missing from DecisionNode; (**c**): data flow referring to predecessors is not allowed; (**d**): data flow referring between branches is not allowed

workflow is submitted for execution, and on user request. If an error is detected by either the static or the dynamic model checker, the corresponding error message is given.

5.5 ASKALON Workflow Hosting Environment

The ASKALON Workflow Hosting Environment (AWHE) is a *workflow library* in ASKALON. It uses a back-end database to store AWDL representations of scientific workflows. Two menu items *"Open from AWHE..."* and *"Publish into AWHE..."* have been added to the GUI of the ASKALON workflow composition tool for users to load and publish workflows. A sub-workflow can also be published into AWHE as a stand-alone workflow by selecting the sub-workflow diagram and clicking the menu item *"Publish into AWHE..."*. Figure 5.14 illustrates the GUI of AWHE. Through AWHE, users can search for workflows based on workflow metadata (e.g., domain, author, version, etc., see Fig. 5.15), view workflow graphs, and run workflows.

AWHE also provides a plugin in the workflow composition tool, i.e., the *Workflows* tab in the resource panel. The plugin shows a list of workflows published in AWHE. Users can drag a workflow from the list and drop it into the drawing place. This will create a new activity whose activity type, input data ports, and output data ports will be set automatically based on the dragged workflow. The execution of this activity invokes the dragged workflow. This functions similarly to dragging and dropping a sub-workflow from the *SubWorkflows* list of the resource panel (see Fig. 5.5), or an activity type from the *ActivityTypes* list of the resource panel (see Fig. 5.5).

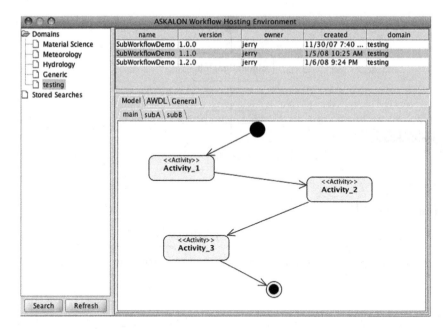

Fig. 5.14 ASKALON workflow hosting environment (AWHE)

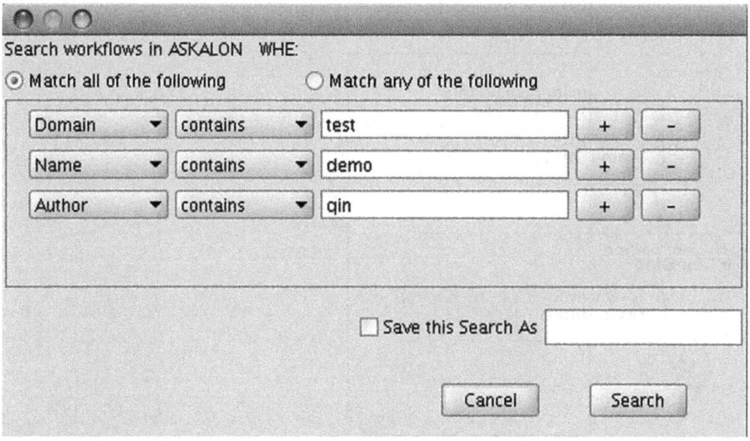

Fig. 5.15 Searching scientific workflows in AWHE

5.6 Real-World Scientific Workflow Modeling and Code Generation

MeteoAG [159] is a scientific workflow application for meteorology simulations based on the numerical model RAMS [38]. The simulations conducted in the workflow produce precipitation fields of heavy precipitation cases over the western

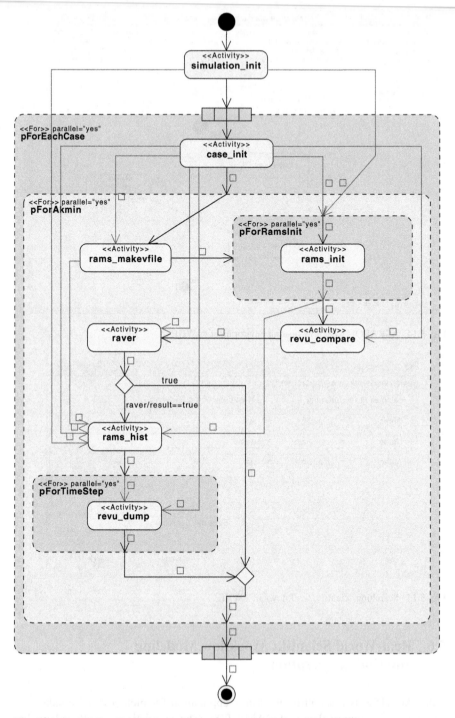

Fig. 5.16 The UML activity diagram representation of the MeteoAG workflow

part of Austria, at a spatial and temporal grid, in order to resolve most alpine watersheds and thunderstorms. Figure 5.16 illustrates the UML Activity Diagram representation of the workflow which consists of two levels of nested parallel loops to calculate multiple simulation cases in parallel. The loop body of the parallel `for` construct *pForEachCase* is the parallel `for` construct *pForAkmin* which consists of a sequence of atomic activities, parallel loops, and an `if` construct required for simulating a single case.

In addition, Figs. 4.6 and 4.7 discussed in Chap. 4 are the UML Activity Diagram representations of the WIEN2k workflow. In this case, the sub-workflow *isConverged* is represented in a separate diagram (Fig. 4.7b).

The generation of the corresponding AWDL code of a scientific workflow is done by traversing the activity diagrams of the scientific workflow. This is done in the following steps: (a) assemble the activities (either atomic or compound) in the *main* diagram into a Java object, namely *AWDLWorkflow*; (b) assemble the activities (either atomic or compound) in each *sub* diagram into a Java object, namely, *AWDLSubWorkflow*; (c) put *AWDLSubWorkflows* into *AWDLWorkflow*; and (d) call the *toXml()* method of the object *AWDLWorkflow* to generate the corresponding AWDL representation in XML which can then be submitted for execution. See Sect. 3.4 for details on how AWDL workflows can reified and executed on distributed systems.

5.7 Summary

Most of the existing scientific workflow modeling tools are text-based or based on user-defined notations. Lack of standards hinders the collaboration among different projects. To address this problem, we proposed an approach to model scientific workflows based on the widely adopted standard UML Activity Diagram. We presented the UML Activity Diagram representations of AWDL control flow and data flow constructs. Some control flow constructs are modeled through extending the UML Activity Diagram by defining some new *stereotypes* with associated *tagged values* based on existing elements. We demonstrated our graphical workflow composition tool, which mainly consists of a GUI, model traverser, and model checker. The model traverser and checker are responsible for the correctness of scientific workflows and the generation of AWDL representations of scientific workflows. The workflow composition tool supports extensions through plugins. We demonstrated our approach for several real-world scientific workflow applications.

In the next chapter, we discuss data flow optimization supported in AWDL in the context of data collections.

Part III
Optimization

Chapter 6
Collection-Oriented Data Flow Support for Scientific Workflows

6.1 Introduction

Control flow constructs have been identified and developed in many workflow frameworks and tools to enable users to define the exact execution order of tasks. These constructs can be divided into four categories: *sequential, parallel, conditional*, and *iterative* constructs. With each of these constructs, different data flow can be specified. Data flow in scientific workflow applications are commonly complex because datasets are involved. For instance, a scientific application consumes a portion of a dataset produced by another application, a parallel iterative construct consumes multiple datasets, and each of its loop iteration processes a variable number of elements in the datasets. However, how datasets and the corresponding data elements can be specified in data flow links, especially how datasets can be distributed onto the parallel loop iterations, is a problem not sufficiently addressed by most scientific workflow languages. A naive solution is to replicate the entire dataset in each activity or loop iteration, or to restrict file names used in datasets which reduces the workflow reusability. Figure 6.1 illustrates the problem (indicated by the question marks) through an example of a parallel `for` loop construct which accepts a dataset consisting of six data elements as input to its four loop iterations. Each loop iteration produces an output data element. The parallel `for` construct has a subsequent task A which requires only the output data elements produced by iterations 0 and 2. Obviously, more flexible dataset-oriented data flow mechanisms are needed to avoid redundant data transfers.

In this chapter we present a sophisticated approach as part of AWDL to solve the problem by introducing the concept of *data collection* and the corresponding collection distribution constructs, which are inspired by High Performance Fortran (HPF) [92]. The corresponding runtime support has been implemented as part of ASKALON. By using our approach, data flow can be modeled and controlled more accurately which allows sophisticated data transfer optimizations. The efforts to port scientific applications onto distributed systems can also be reduced.

J. Qin and T. Fahringer, *Scientific Workflows*, DOI 10.1007/978-3-642-30715-7_6,

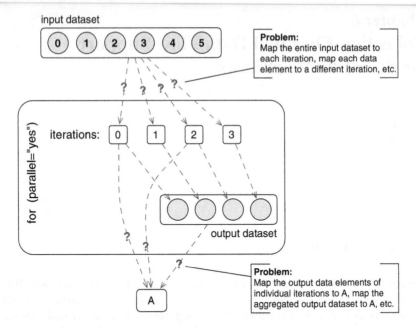

Fig. 6.1 Data flow problems

6.2   Data Collections and Collection Distribution Constructs

Scientific workflows usually involve large and complex dataset processing. For instance, a scientific application consumes a portion of a dataset produced by another application, a parallel iterative construct produces datasets based on their input, or a parallel iterative construct consumes multiple datasets and each of its loop iteration processes a variable number of data elements of different datasets. In this section, we describe AWDL *data collections* and explain how *data collections* can be mapped to activities or distributed onto loop iterations by using collection distribution constructs.

6.2.1   Data Collections

Datasets in scientific workflows may contain static or dynamic (unknown at composition time) number of data elements. Modeling each element in datasets with a logical data port at the scientific workflow language level can be awkward and often impossible. To solve this problem, AWDL introduces the concept of *data collection* to model datasets in scientific workflows at a high level of abstraction.

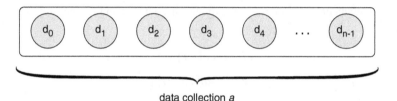

data collection a

Fig. 6.2 A data collection a with n data elements

An AWDL *data collection* (Fig. 6.2) is a logical data representation of physical data. It is defined as a data type *awdl:collection* in AWDL, where *awdl* is the namespace used in XML representations of AWDL workflows. A data port with type *awdl:collection* represents a list of data elements provided by domain users as the initial input of a workflow or produced by workflow activities as an intermediate result. The number of the data elements contained in a data collection may be dynamic. The data elements in a data collection are logical representations of physical data, which can be files in a file system, data retrieved from a relational database, or primitive data such as *integers* or *strings* in the memory of the underlying workflow runtime system. Files will be used in the following sections to demonstrate our approach. Data elements can be accessed with their indices in the enclosing data collection.

To port scientific applications, especially the ones producing dynamic output datasets, onto distributed systems, one of the common approaches is to write some wrapping code such as to *tar* a set of output files into a *tar* file. This kind of wrapping code is not flexible in the case where only a portion of the dataset is required in subsequent activities. The reusability of the wrapping code is also limited. In contrast, the AWDL data collection presented here provides a more flexible solution and avoids this kind of wrapping code. Thus our approach is a valuable contribution to simplify porting workflow applications onto distributed systems.

6.2.2   Collection Distribution Constructs

AWDL provides two built-in constraints for specifying collection distribution constructs: *awdl:element-index* and *awdl:distribution*. The namespace *awdl* is omitted in the following text to avoid redundancy. The constraint *element-index* is used to specify portions of data collections and it can be used for data ports of activities. The constraint *distribution* is used to partition data collections into blocks which are then distributed onto loop iterations. While the constraint *distribution* can be used for both sequential and parallel iterative constructs, we only focus on the parallel iterative constructs in the remainder of this chapter.

The value of the constraint *element-index* is a list of comma separated colon expressions. The syntax is defined by the following grammar, where ei denotes the constraint *element-index*, *ce* a colon expression, *sa* a start index, *so* a stop index, *sr* a stride:

$$ei ::= ce[, ce] *$$

$$ce ::= sa[: so[: sr]]$$

For example, the constraint *element-index=1,3,6:10:2* specifies the data elements associated with index 1, 3, 6, 8, 10 in a data collection. Note that in the absence of the constraint *element-index*, the entire data collection is specified.

To distribute data collections onto parallel loop iterations, we reused ideas from High Performance Fortran (HPF) [92], where some directives are used to map a data array into a processors array. In AWDL, a data collection is a list of data elements, i.e., a one-dimensional array. Parallel loop iterations can also be considered a one-dimensional array, which we denote by *iteration array*. Thus the problem can be formulated as how to map a one-dimensional array of data elements (a data collection) to another one-dimensional array of iterations (an iteration array). AWDL supports the following collection distribution constructs: *BLOCK*, *BLOCK(b)*, *BLOCK(b, l)* and *REPLICA(r)*, which are specified through the constraint *distribution* of input data ports of parallel iterative constructs. These four collection distribution constructs are processed at runtime to determine which elements of a data collection are distributed onto which iteration. We explain these four collection distribution constructs in detail in the following sections with the assumption that all data elements in data collections are distributed onto at least one iteration. It is possible that some iterations may not be assigned to any data element. In the case where not all data elements in a data collection are required to be distributed onto parallel loop iterations, a subset of the data collection can be obtained through the constraint *element-index*. The constraint *element-index* has higher precedence than the constraint *distribution* when both of them are specified for the same data port.

In order to express collection distributions, we assume that any collection C with $|C|$ data elements is associated with an *index domain* J^C which is defined by a set of integers $\{i \mid 0 \leqslant i < |C|\}$. The index domain J^C provides an unambiguous *name* for the data elements in the data collection. Let J^C denote an index domain of a data collection C, K^I an index domain of an iteration array I, the collection distribution problem can be further formulated as how to map J^C to K^I. The notations used in the explanation of the four collection distribution constructs are summarized in Table 6.1.

6.2.2.1 BLOCK Distribution

BLOCK distribution partitions a data collection C into equal sized, contiguous blocks and distributes each of them onto a different iteration of an iteration array I. The size of each iteration's block is determined by the element number $|C|$ and the iteration number $|I|$.

Table 6.1 Notations

Symbols	Description
C	a Data collection
$\|C\|$	The element number of C
J^C	The index domain of C
I	An iteration array
$\|I\|$	The iteration number of I
K^I	The index domain of I
i	An element index
$[i_1 : i_2]$	A set of element indices, defined by $[i_1 : i_2] := \{i \mid i_1 \leq i \leq i_2\}$
$\theta(i)$	a function mapping indices of C to indices of I

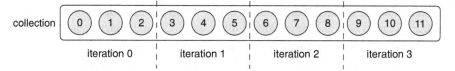

collection

iteration 0   iteration 1   iteration 2   iteration 3

Fig. 6.3 The *BLOCK* distribution

Definition 6.1. *BLOCK distribution* of a data collection C is a function $\theta: J^C \rightarrow K^I$ that partitions the data collection C into $n = \left\lfloor \dfrac{|C|}{\left\lceil \frac{|C|}{|I|} \right\rceil} \right\rfloor$ contiguous blocks of size $b = \left\lceil \dfrac{|C|}{|I|} \right\rceil$ which are distributed onto the first n iterations, with $0 \leq n < |I|$, and, if $|C| \bmod b \neq 0$, one additional block with $|C| \bmod b$ elements which are distributed onto the last iteration with index n. The function is given by:

$$\theta(i) = \left\{ \left\lfloor \frac{i}{\left\lceil \frac{|C|}{|I|} \right\rceil} \right\rfloor \,\middle|\, 0 \leq i < |C| \right\}$$

Figure 6.3 illustrates the distribution of a data collection with $|C| = 12$ data elements onto $|I| = 4$ loop iterations based on the collection distribution construct *BLOCK*, where each iteration is assigned to a block of three data elements.

6.2.2.2   BLOCK(b) Distribution

While *BLOCK* distribution partitions a data collection into equal sized blocks (except that the last one may have a smaller size) based on the iteration number, it is more common in scientific applications to partition a data collection into fixed sized blocks. For example, three files are produced in each time step of a simulation process, and the three files of one time step are required by the subsequent computation which is enclosed in the loop body of a parallel loop

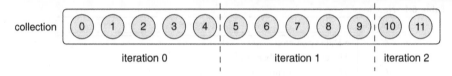

Fig. 6.4 The *BLOCK(5)* distribution

construct. *BLOCK(b)* is provided for this purpose, with the integer parameter b specifying the fixed block size.

Definition 6.2. *BLOCK(b) distribution* of a data collection C is a function θ: $J^C \rightarrow K^I$ that partitions the data collection C into $n = \left\lfloor \frac{|C|}{b} \right\rfloor$ contiguous blocks of size b which are distributed onto the first n iterations, with $0 \leq n < |I|$, and, if $|C| \bmod b \neq 0$, one additional block with $|C| \bmod b$ elements which are distributed onto the next iteration with index n. We require $b \geq \left\lceil \frac{|C|}{|I|} \right\rceil$ to ensure that all data elements in the collection C are distributed onto at least one iteration. All other iterations (if any) are not assigned to any data elements. The function is given by:

$$\theta(i) = \left\{ \left\lfloor \frac{i}{b} \right\rfloor \mid 0 \leq i < |C| \wedge b \geq \left\lceil \frac{|C|}{|I|} \right\rceil \right\}$$

Figure 6.4 illustrates the distribution of a data collection with $|C| = 12$ elements onto $|I| = 3$ iterations based on the collection distribution construct *BLOCK(5)*, where iteration 0 is assigned to a block of five data elements with index $[0 : 4]$, iteration 1 a block of five data elements with index $[5 : 9]$, and the last iteration a block of two data elements with index $[10 : 11]$, respectively.

6.2.2.3   BLOCK(b,l) Distribution

BLOCK distribution and *BLOCK(b)* distribution partition a data collection into equal sized, contiguous blocks (except that the last one may have a smaller size) which does not involve replication. For some applications, an overlap between neighboring blocks is required. For example, an application which processes the files of a certain time step may also need the files from the previous time step. For this purpose, *BLOCK(b,l)* is provided with the integer parameter b specifying the block size, and the integer parameter l specifying the size of the overlapped part between neighboring blocks.

Definition 6.3. *BLOCK(b,l) distribution* of a data collection C is a function θ: $J^C \rightarrow K^I$ that partitions the data collection C into $n = \left\lfloor \frac{|C|-l}{b-l} \right\rfloor$ overlapped blocks of size b (with an overlap of size l between each two neighboring blocks) which are distributed onto the first n iterations, with $0 \leq n < |I|, l < b$, and, if $(|C| - l) \bmod (b - l) \neq 0$, one additional block with $|C| - n \times (b - l)$ elements

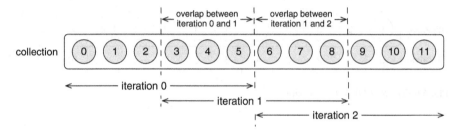

Fig. 6.5 The *BLOCK(6,3)* distribution

are distributed onto the next iteration with index n. We require $\left\lceil \frac{|C|-l}{b-l} \right\rceil \leqslant |I|$ to ensure that all data elements in the collection C are distributed onto at least one iteration. All other iterations (if any) are not assigned to any data elements. The function returning a set of iteration indices is given by:

$$\theta(i) \quad = \left\{ [\theta(i)_{min} : \theta(i)_{max}] \,\middle|\, 0 \leqslant i < |C| \,\wedge\, l < b \,\wedge\, \left\lceil \frac{|C|-l}{b-l} \right\rceil \leqslant |I| \right\}$$

where

$$\theta(i)_{min} = \left\{ \max\left(0, \left\lfloor \frac{i-l}{b-l} \right\rfloor \right) \,\middle|\, 0 \leqslant i < |C| \,\wedge\, l < b \,\wedge\, \left\lceil \frac{|C|-l}{b-l} \right\rceil \leqslant |I| \right\}$$

$$\theta(i)_{max} = \left\{ \min\left(\left\lfloor \frac{i}{b-l} \right\rfloor, |I|-1 \right) \,\middle|\, 0 \leqslant i < |C| \,\wedge\, l < b \,\wedge\, \left\lceil \frac{|C|-l}{b-l} \right\rceil \leqslant |I| \right\}$$

Figure 6.5 illustrates the distribution of a data collection with $|C| = 12$ elements onto $|I| = 3$ iterations based on the collection distribution construct *BLOCK(6,3)*, where iteration 0 is assigned to a block of six data elements with index $[0 : 5]$, iteration 1 a block of six data elements with index $[3 : 8]$, and iteration 2 a block of six data elements with index $[6 : 11]$. The data elements with index 3, 4, 5 are distributed onto both iteration 0 and iteration 1, and the data elements with index 6, 7, 8 are distributed onto both iteration 1 and iteration 2.

6.2.2.4 REPLICA(r) Distribution

The *BLOCK*, *BLOCK(b)*, and *BLOCK(b,l)* distributions are normally used when $|C| \geq |I|$. However, in some cases, a smaller number of data elements are needed to be replicated onto a larger number of loop iterations. To support this kind of data distribution, the *REPLICA(r)* distribution (we consider it as a special distribution) is provided with the integer parameter r specifying onto how many iterations each data element in a data collection should be replicated.

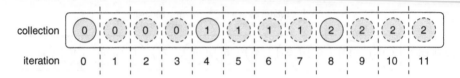

Fig. 6.6 The *REPLICA(4)* distribution

Definition 6.4. *REPLICA(r) distribution* of a data collection C is a function θ: $J^C \rightarrow K^I$ that replicates each data element in the data collection C, r times which are distributed onto the first $n = r \times |C|$ iterations, with $0 \leqslant n < |I|$. We require $r \leqslant \left\lfloor \frac{|I|}{|C|} \right\rfloor$ to ensure that all replicated data elements are distributed onto at least one iteration. All other iterations (if any) are not assigned to any data elements. The function returning a set of iteration indices is given by:

$$\theta(i) = \left\{ \left[r \times i : r \times (i+1) - 1 \right] \mid 0 \leqslant i < |C| \wedge r \leqslant \left\lfloor \frac{|I|}{|C|} \right\rfloor \right\}$$

Figure 6.6 illustrates the distribution of a data collection with $|C| = 3$ elements onto $|I| = 12$ iterations based on the collection distribution construct *REPLICA(4)*, where iterations with index $[0 : 3]$ are assigned to the data element with index 0, iterations with index $[4 : 7]$ the data element with index 1, iterations with index $[8 : 11]$ the data element with index 2, respectively.

Note that both the constraint *element-index* and the constraint *distribution* can be specified for an input data port of a parallel iterative construct, and a parallel iterative construct can have as many input data ports as needed. Thus, AWDL supports processing of multiple collections with one parallel iterative construct, and each collection, which may have different number of data elements, can be processed independently based on the associated collection distribution constructs.

6.3 Case Study

In this section, we apply the collection distribution constructs presented in Section 6.2 to four real-world scientific workflow applications: (1) the material science application WIEN2k [25], (2) the meteorology application MeteoAG [159], (3) the astrophysics application AstroGrid [158], and (4) the astrophysics application GRASIL [166].

6.3.1 WIEN2k

Figure 6.7 shows the *awdl:collection* involved data flow in the material science workflow WIEN2k [25]. A detailed explanation of the whole workflow can be found

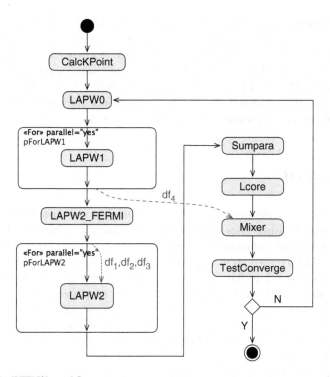

Fig. 6.7 The WIEN2k workflow

in Sect. 3.3. In this workflow, the parallel `for` construct *pForLAPW1* produces three data collections: *energyFileCol*, *vectorFileCol*, and *scf1 FileCol*. The atomic activity *LAPW2_FERMI* consumes the data collection *energyFileCol* and produces another data collection *weighFileCol*. The four data flow links (the labeled dashed lines in Fig. 6.7) with their associated collection distribution constructs specify how these data collections are consumed by subsequent activities. The data flow links df_1, df_2, and df_3 each has a constraint *distribution = BLOCK(1)* in its source data port. These constraints specify that for each loop iteration of the parallel `for` construct *pForLAPW2*, only one data element of the corresponding data collection (*energyFileCol*, *vectorFileCol* or *weighFileCol*) is required. This example shows how a parallel `for` construct can process multiple data collections. Note that, in this case, it is not required that all data collections must have the same number of data elements. The iteration number of the parallel `for` construct *pForLAPW2* is decided neither by the iteration number of the parallel `for` construct *pForLAPW1* nor by the element number of the data collection *weighFileCol*. Instead, the parallel `for` construct *pForLAPW2* has its own loop counter for this purpose. We believe this approach is more flexible than those described in related work. The data flow link df_4 has a constraint *element-index=0* in its sink data port because the activity *Mixer* only requires the first data element in the data collection *scf1 FileCol*.

Note that without the constraint *distribution*, all data elements in the collections *energyFileCol*, *vectorFileCol*, and *weighFileCol* would have to be transferred at runtime to the computer where each activity *LAPW2* will be executed, which would result in redundant data transfers. The same holds for the data collection *scf1Collection*. The AWDL representation of the WIEN2k workflow with focus on collection-oriented data flow, and the performance improvement with these collection distribution constructs are discussed in Sect. 6.4.1.

6.3.2   MeteoAG

Figure 6.8 illustrates the structure of the meteorological workflow MeteoAG [159] with two labeled dashed lines showing the interesting data flow links. Examining the data flow link df_1 in this workflow, the activity *rams_hist* produces in each time step two *grid* files (based on the input parameter *NGRID* which is specified in the input file, NGRID = 2 in this case) and one *head* file, which we denote by two data collections: *gridFiles*, *headFiles*. For each run of an iteration of the parallel `for` construct *pForREVUDump*, the activity *revu_dump* requires the files of one time step (two *grid* files and a *head* file) produced by the activity *rams_hist*. The collection distribution constructs *BLOCK(2)* and *BLOCK(1)* are used here to fulfill the data flow requirements.

The data flow link df_2 in this workflow is a good example to demonstrate *BLOCK(b,l)* distribution. Like the activity *rams_hist*, the activity *rams_makevfile* produces two *grid* files and one *tag* file in each time step. Again, we denote them by two data collections: *gridFiles* and *tagFiles*. For each run of an iteration of the parallel `for` construct *pForRAMSInit*, the activity *rams_init* requires not only the files of the current time step but also those of the previous time step. Therefore, the collection distribution constructs *BLOCK(4,2)* and *BLOCK(2,1)* can be used respectively for the distribution of the two data collections *gridFiles* and *tagFiles* onto the parallel loop iterations.

Both examples in the workflow MeteoAG also show that how multiple data collections can be processed by one parallel iterative construct independently in terms of how many data elements of each data collection are processed in one loop iteration. The performance from these collection distribution constructs is discussed in Sect. 6.4.2.

6.3.3   AstroGrid

The AstroGrid [158] scientific workflow application is about numerical simulations of the movements and interactions of galaxy clusters based on N-Body systems. The computation starts with the state of the universe at some time in the past

Fig. 6.8 The MeteoAG
workflow

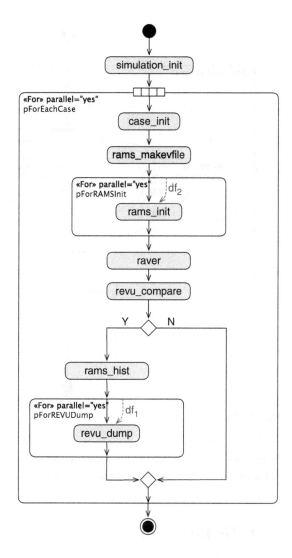

and continues to the current time. Galaxy potentials are computed for each time
step. Then the hydrodynamic behavior and processes are calculated. The workflow
structure is illustrated in Fig. 6.9. Examining the data flow link illustrated with the
dashed line, the activity *nbody* produces two data collections: *t00Files*, consisting
of multiple *t00* files, and *dataFiles*, consisting of multiple *data* files. One *t00*
file is produced at each time step. One *data* file is produced whenever four *t00*
files are available. For each run of an iteration of the parallel for construct
pForEachPoten, the activity *poten* requires one *t00* file and the corresponding *data*
file. While the data collection *t00Files* is iterated over by the parallel for construct
pForEachPoten, the data collection *dataFiles* is distributed based on the collection

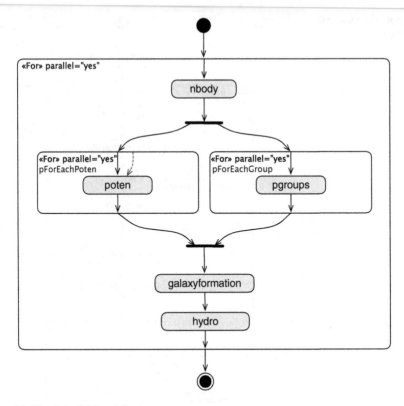

Fig. 6.9 The AstroGrid workflow

distribution construct *REPLICA(4)*, which specifies that every *data* file should be replicated four times then distributed onto the corresponding loop iterations.

6.3.4 GRASIL

GRASIL [166] is an application to calculate the spectral energy distribution (SED) of galaxies lying in a certain field of view (light cone) ranging from now back to shortly after the beginning of the universe. The workflow structure is very simple and is illustrated in Fig. 6.10. The activity *init* produces a data collection, in which each data element corresponds to the data about a specific galaxy. The data collection is then processed by a parallel `for` construct *pForGalaxy*, which uses the constraint *distribution = BLOCK* to distribute the input collection onto its loop iterations. The activity *grasil* is designed to accept a data collection with a variable number of galaxies and calculates each of them, which make the workflow immune to the changes of the element number of the data collection produced by the activity *init*. Thus the workflow reusability is improved.

Fig. 6.10 The GRASIL
workflow

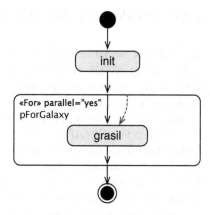

Table 6.2 The nodes used for the experiments of collection distribution

Node	CPU	Num of CPU	GHz	JobManager	Location
karwendel	Dual Core AMD Opteron	8	2.4	SGE	Innsbruck
c703-pc2201	Pentium 4	8	2.8	Torque	Innsbruck
c703-pc2509	Pentium 4	8	2.8	Torque	Innsbruck
schafberg	Itanium 2	8	1.4	PBS	Salzburg
altix1	Itanium 2	8	1.4	PBS	Innsbruck
c703-pc450	Pentium 4	8	1.8	Torque	Innsbruck
hydra	AMD Athlon	8	1.67	Torque	Linz

6.4 Experimental Results

We have implemented all collection distribution constructs described in this chapter
and integrated them in ASKALON. With our UML-based scientific workflow modeling tool [150], the domain users can develop AWDL-based scientific workflow
applications, including the selection of correct collection distribution constructs.
We have conducted experiments with the WIEN2k workflow and the MeteoAG
workflow on a distributed system with nodes installed on various sites in Austria.
The sizes of the files in the data collections used in our experiments range from
several kilobytes to several megabytes. In both experiments, we measured the
number of file transfers and the execution time and compared them for two cases:
(1) without collection distribution constructs specified (denoted by *without data
collection distribution*), and (2) with collection distribution constructs specified
(denoted by *with data collection distribution*). The corresponding results are
presented in the following sections. A subset of the computational resources which
have been used for the experiments is summarized in Table 6.2.

6.4.1 Results of the WIEN2k Workflow

The WIEN2k workflow structure is illustrated in Fig. 6.7 in Sect. 6.3.1, and the corresponding AWDL representation is depicted in Fig. 6.11 where collection distribution constructs are specified at Lines 34, 39, 44, and 60. For simplicity, details not related to collections are omitted. Since the integer data port *kpoint* produced by the activity *LAPW0* determines the iteration number of the parallel for constructs *pForLAPW1* and *pForLAPW2* (Line 14 and Line 48), which further determines the size of the data collections mentioned in Sect. 6.3.1, we performed two series of experiments for the WIEN2k workflow, corresponding to two different problem sizes: *kpoint = 116* and *kpoint = 252*. The experiments were conducted on six nodes: *karwendel, c703-2201, c703-2509, schafberg, c703-pc450,* and *hydra*. For each problem size, we first executed the workflow on the fastest node *karwendel*. Then, we incrementally added new nodes to investigate whether we could improve the performance of the workflow application by increasing the available computational resources.

As shown in Fig. 6.12, we significantly improved the performances for both problem sizes by using collection distribution constructs. Specifically, when executing the workflow with *kpoint = 116* on 6 nodes, the number of file transfers was reduced by 67% and the execution time was reduced by 30% compared with the execution without collection distribution. Accordingly, we achieved the speedup of 2.60 on 6 nodes, compared with the maximum speedup of 1.96 achieved on 4 nodes when no collection distribution constructs are used. Similarly, in the case where *kpoint* is 252, there was a 68% reduction in the number of file transfers and a 42% reduction in the execution time when executing on 6 nodes. And the corresponding speedup was 2.58 on 6 nodes, compared with the maximum speedup of 1.74 achieved on 4 nodes without collection distribution. By using the collection distribution constructs, the scalability of the workflow was also improved: because of redundant file transfers, the workflow did not scale for more than 4 nodes for experiments without collection distribution. Furthermore, the reduction of the number of file transfers and the execution time was even greater with an increased number of nodes, especially when *kpoint* is 252. This is because when no collection distribution constructs are used, the entire collections must be transferred to any additional node for the execution of the loop iterations on that node. However, if we use the corresponding collection distribution constructs for the data collections in the workflow, only the files required by the iterations scheduled on that node need to be transferred. When increasing the problem size to *kpoint = 252*, the number of file transfers and the corresponding execution time were further reduced due to an increased collection size for increasing problem size.

Figure 6.13 illustrates two stacked bar charts that show the performance analysis of the execution of the parallel for construct *pForLAPW2* on 5 nodes when *kpoint = 252*. The horizontal axis is the time and the vertical axis represents Activity Instances (AIs) (see Sect. 3.2.1). For each AI, the time consumed at different stages (e.g., Queuing, DataStageIn, Active, etc.) is illustrated in a horizontal bar.

```
1  <workflow name="WIEN2k" ... >
2    <dataIns ... />
3    <workflowBody>
4      <activity name="CalcKPoint" ... >
5        <dataIns ... />
6        <dataOuts> <dataOut name="kpoint" type="xsd:integer"/> </dataOuts>
7      </activity>
8      <doWhile name="doWhileConv">
9        <dataIns ... />
10       <dataLoops ... />
11       <loopBody>
12         <activity name="LAPW0" ... />
13         <for name="pForLAPW1" parallel="yes">
14           <loopCounter name="taskNumber" type="xsd:integer" from="1"
                     to="CalcKPoint/kpoint" />
15           <loopBody>
16             <activity name="LAPW1" ... />
17           </loopBody>
18           <dataOuts>
19             <dataOut name="engergyFileCol" type="awdl:collection"/>
20             <dataOut name="vectorFileCol" type="awdl:collection"/>
21             <dataOut name="scf1FileCol" type="awdl:collection"/>
22           </dataOuts>
23         </for>
24         <activity name="LAPW2_FERMI" ... >
25           <dataIns ... />
26           <dataOuts>
27             <dataOut name="weighFileCol" type="awdl:collection"/>
28           </dataOuts>
29         </activity>
30         <for name="pForLAPW2" parallel="yes">
31           <dataIns>
32             <dataIn name="energyFileCol" type="awdl:collection"
                       source="pForLAPW1/engergyFileCol">
33               <constraints>
34                 <constraint name="distribution" value="BLOCK(1)"/>
35               </constraints>
36             </dataIn>
37             <dataIn name="vectorFileCol" type="awdl:collection"
                       source="pForLAPW1/vectorFileCol">
38               <constraints>
39                 <constraint name="distribution" value="BLOCK(1)"/>
40               </constraints>
41             </dataIn>
42             <dataIn name="weighFileCol" type="awdl:collection"
                       source="LAPW2_FERMI/weighFileCol">
43               <constraints>
44                 <constraint name="distribution" value="BLOCK(1)"/>
45               </constraints>
46             </dataIn>
47           </dataIns>
48           <loopCounter name="taskNumber" type="xsd:integer" from="1"
                     to="CalcKPoint/kpoint" />
49           <loopBody>
50             <activity name="LAPW2" ... />
51           </loopBody>
52           <dataOuts ... />
53         </for>
54         <activity name="Sumpara" ... />
55         <activity name="Lcore" ... />
56         <activity name="Mixer" ... >
57           <dataIns>
58             <dataIn name="scf1FileCol" type="awdl:collection"
                       source="pForLAPW1/scf1FileCol">
59               <constraints>
60                 <constraint name="element-index" value="1"/>
61               </constraints>
62             </dataIn>
63           </dataIns>
64           <dataOuts ... />
65         </activity>
66         <activity name="TestConverge" ... />
67       </loopBody>
68       <condition ... />
69       <dataOuts ... />
70     </doWhile>
71   </workflowBody>
72   <dataOuts ... />
73 </workflow>
```

Fig. 6.11 Collection distribution constructs used in the WIEN2k workflow

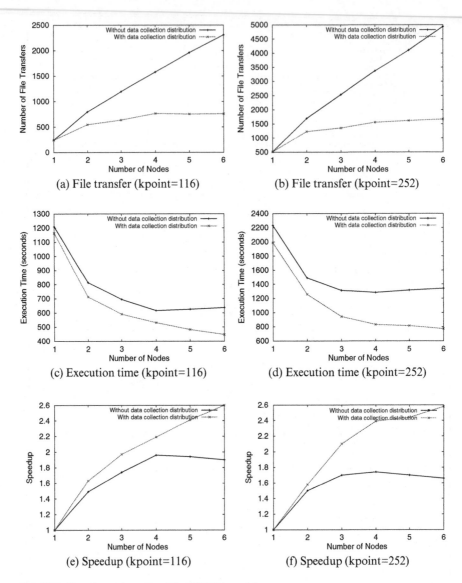

Fig. 6.12 Experimental results of the WIEN2k workflow

As illustrated in Fig. 6.13a, there exists significant DataStageIn time for the parallel for construct *pForLAPW2*, which results in a total execution time of 713.61 s. The total execution time of *pForLAPW2* is only 231.70 s when using collection distribution constructs (see Fig. 6.13b). The bottom-left dim gray parts in the two charts represent the time consumed by the AIs of the activity *LAPW2* while waiting in the job queue of the workflow enactment engine due to the lack of CPU resources.

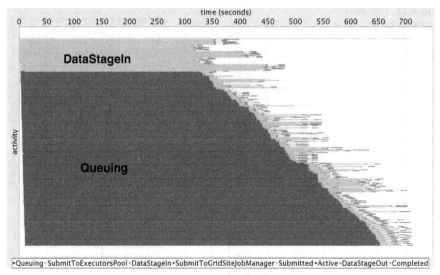

(a) Without data collection distribution

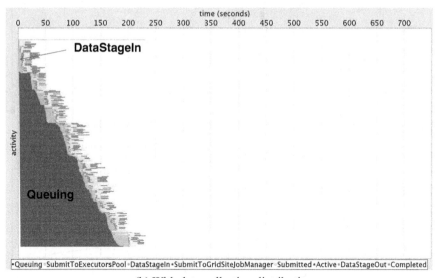

(b) With data collection distribution

Fig. 6.13 Performance analysis of the execution of *pForLAPW2* with kpoint=252 on 5 nodes

6.4.2 Results of the MeteoAG Workflow

The MeteoAG workflow structure is illustrated in Fig. 6.8. The corresponding AWDL representation is omitted here to avoid redundancy. In this experiment,

Fig. 6.14 The MeteoAG
experimental results

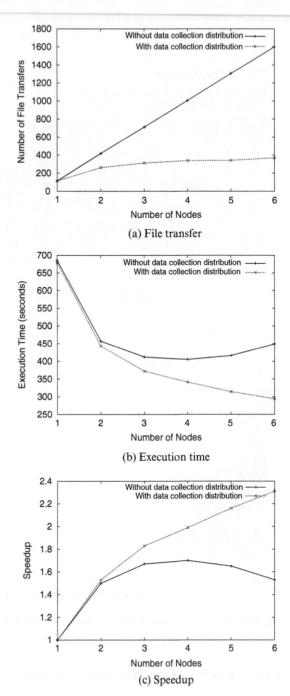

(a) File transfer

(b) Execution time

(c) Speedup

we ran the parallel for construct *pForEachCase* with two parallel loop iterations (corresponding to two simulation cases), each of which has two parallel for constructs with 48 parallel loop iterations (corresponding to 48 simulation time steps). The experiments were conducted on six nodes: *karwendel, altix1, schafberg, c703-2201, c703-pc450,* and *hydra.* We conducted the experiments in the same way as for the WIEN2k workflow: first running the workflow on the fastest nodes, then incrementally adding the slower nodes.

As illustrated in Fig. 6.14, we significantly improved the performance of this workflow application when using collection distribution constructs. Compared with the execution on 6 nodes without collection distribution, the number of file transfers was reduced by 77% and the execution time was reduced by 53% when using collection distribution constructs. Accordingly, we achieved the speedup of 2.31 on 6 nodes, compared with the maximum speedup of 1.70 achieved on 4 nodes without collection distribution. The workflow scalability was also improved when using collection distribution constructs.

By using collection distribution constructs, the total number of file transfers is reduced and thus the performance is improved. We observed similar behavior for the other two applications, which are omitted here to avoid redundancy.

6.5 Summary

Existing work does not provide a flexible dataset-oriented data flow mechanism to meet the complex data flow requirements of scientific workflow applications. In this chapter, we presented an approach as part of AWDL to solve this problem by introducing the concept of *data collection* and the sophisticated collection distribution constructs. A data collection is used to model a static or dynamic dataset at a high level of abstraction. The collection distribution constructs are used to map data collections to activities and to distribute data collections onto loop iterations. The collection distribution constructs are specified through AWDL constraints *awdl:element-index* and *awdl:distribution*. Five collection distribution constructs, i.e., comma separated colon expressions, *BLOCK, BLOCK(b), BLOCK(b,l),* and *REPLICA(r),* were discussed. With this approach, AWDL enables the specification of more flexible and accurate dataset-oriented data flow in various scientific workflow domains, such as mapping portions of data collections to activities, distribution of data collections onto loop iterations, processing multiple data collections with one parallel iterative construct independently in terms of how many data elements of each collection are processed in one loop iteration. Our approach reduces data duplication, optimizes data transfers between workflow activities, and thus improves workflow performance. It also simplifies the effort to port scientific applications onto distributed systems. We demonstrated our approach by applying it to four real-world scientific workflow applications and reported the experimental results.

Part IV
Synthesis

Chapter 7
Semantic-Based Scientific Workflow Composition

7.1 Introduction

Scientific workflow composition is a challenging task for domain scientists. To simplify scientific workflow composition, some scientific workflow development environments [42, 51, 60, 77, 110] enable users to compose scientific workflow applications at a high level of abstraction based on Activity Types (ATs). Others [23,77,110,133,155] adopt a knowledge-based process to help users build scientific workflows. However, there are still two problems with existing approaches: (a) users still have to understand the data type systems used by scientific workflow runtime environments to select correct ATs for their workflows, and (b) users need to know how to specify data flow among workflow activities, especially in a workflow where many data ports have the same data type (e.g., *string*, *file*).

As an illustrating example, let us assume that users are offered two ATs: *RAMSInitA* and *RAMSInitB* (Fig. 7.1a). Both ATs represent the same functionality, that is, to evolve the physical representation of the atmosphere from an earlier RAMS model to the specified initial simulation time. The AT *RAMSInitA* requires an input integer in the range from 1 to 12 indicating *Month* and a zipped input file indicating *SeaSurface*, and produces *RAMSModeledAtmosphere* as a collection of files. The AT *RAMSInitB* requires and produces similar kinds of data, except that the input data *Month* must be a string with one value from the set {*Jan, Feb, . . . , Dec*}, the input data *SeaSurface* must be a collection of files, and the output data *RAMSModeledAtmosphere* is a *.tar.gz* file. All the other data ports of both ATs are omitted for the reason of simplicity. In this case, users have to choose between *RAMSInitA* and *RAMSInitB* for their workflow based on the data types of the data produced by predecessor ATs in the workflow. Once one of the two ATs is selected, users also have to make decision on the successor ATs in the workflow so that the successor ATs can correctly process the data produced by the previously selected AT.

When all ATs are selected and connected with control flow, data flow composition is another complex task for users, as illustrated in Fig. 7.1b which shows part

J. Qin and T. Fahringer, *Scientific Workflows*, DOI 10.1007/978-3-642-30715-7__7,

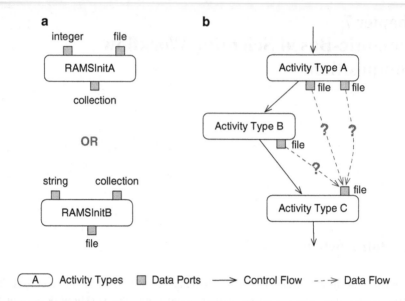

A) Activity Types   ▢ Data Ports   ⟶ Control Flow   - - ➤ Data Flow

Fig. 7.1 Two scientific workflow composition problems. (**a**): Two Activity Types (ATs) with the same functionality but different input and output data structures; (**b**): Data flow composition among three data ports having the same data type *file*

of a workflow. In this workflow, AT *A* produces two files and AT *B* produces one file (indicated by the data type *file*) and AT *C* requires a file as input. The problem here is where the input file of AT *C* should come from: from one of the two outputs of AT *A* or from the output of AT *B* (as illustrated by three data flow links with question marks in Fig. 7.1b). The data flow composition could be even worse in a real-world scientific workflow application because (a) there may be hundreds of data ports with the same data type that are available for a successor AT, and (b) the closer the successor AT is positioned to the end of the workflow, the more data ports are available. The process to determine which data ports have to be connected by data flow is error prone and requires extensive user expertise.

In this chapter, we present a novel semantic approach to solve the two aforementioned problems as part of AWDL [53] with the help of ontology technologies (see also Sect. 2.4.1). Ontology [75] technologies have been used by researchers [23, 77, 102, 104, 155, 205] to provide knowledge support for scientific workflow composition. We have developed a generic AWDL ontology which consists of three top level concepts (or classes): *Function*, *Data*, and *DataRepresentation*. The ontology can be extended by domain-specific ontologies such as the meteorology ontology illustrated in this chapter. With the help of these ontologies, we separate concerns between data semantics (*Data* class, hereafter abbreviated as DC and used exchangeable with *data semantics*) and data representation (*DataRepresentation* class), as well as between Activity Function (AF) and Activity Type (AT) in AWDL. The separation allows users to compose workflows at the level of Data

Classes (DCs) and Activity Functions (AFs) and leaves the task of dealing with Data Representations (DRs) and Activity Types (ATs) to the scientific workflow composition tool (thus solving the first problem), and enables automatic data conversion between different Data Representations (DRs). The separation also provides a foundation for our automatic scientific workflow composition algorithm presented in Chap. 8 where the automatic data flow composition algorithm provides a solution for the second problem.

The contributions of this chapter are as follows:

- We introduce the concept of *DataRepresentation* in scientific workflows, and some comprehensive properties associated with the concept.
- We separate concerns between Data Class (DC) and Data Representation (DR) and between Activity Function (AF) and Activity Type (AT), which makes AWDL more abstract which in turn leads to an easier to use scientific workflow composition tool for domain scientists.
- With the help of the generic AWDL ontology and the extended domain ontologies, scientific workflows in three different levels (semantic, syntactic, and concrete) of abstraction can be described with one single scientific workflow language.
- We applied our approach to a real-world meteorology scientific workflow application.

7.2 Ontologies

Based on our experiences in collaborating with scientists from multiple domains, such as meteorology, material science, and astrophysics [147], we have identified some questions raised by users when they compose scientific workflows. Among others, the following questions are frequently asked:

- Which activity provides a solution for a requested task, e.g., to evolve the physical representation of the atmosphere?
- Which activity produces or consumes given data, e.g., SeaSurface, LandCover?

To answer these questions, we have developed an upper ontology which is shown in Fig. 7.2. It is motivated by the need to ease scientific workflow composition. There are three main concepts in the upper ontology: *Function, Data,* and *DataRepresentation* which are described as follows.

Data is a superclass of any kind of workflow data. It provides a high-level description of workflow data, that is, the semantics of workflow data. *Data* can be extended by a *GenericData* (e.g., Month). *Data* can also be extended for domain-specific data. For example, *MeteorologyData* can be defined as a subclass of *Data* and a superclass of all kinds of meteorological data. *Data* is the input to or the output of *Function*. Users can search *Functions* based on input and output *Data*.

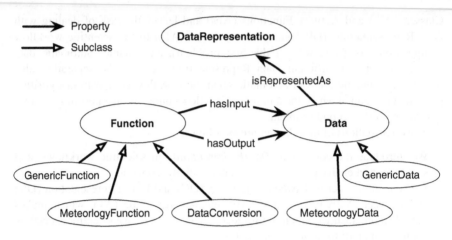

Fig. 7.2 The upper ontology

Function is a superclass of both generic and domain-specific functions which are implemented by Web services, executables, Java classes, etc. *Function* has properties *hasInput* and *hasOutput* which indicate input and output data of *Function*. The values of the properties *hasInput* and *hasOutput* are *Data*. This enables domain users to search AFs based on input and output data classes. In addition to these two properties, *Function* also has a *hasDescription* property, whose value is a textual description on what exact functionality it represents. This enables domain users to search *Functions* based on free text. For example, a user may input "*atmosphere evolution*" to find *Functions* which can simulate the evolution of the atmosphere. We adopted the *string-matching* algorithm presented by Cardoso et al. in [31] to match free text against the descriptions of *Functions* in our approach. To follow the IOPE (Input, Output, Precondition, and Effect, i.e., four properties to semantically describe capabilities of Web Services) pattern [184] of modern semantic technologies, we also associated the properties *hasPrecondition* and *hasEffect* with *Function*. However, we defer the *Precondition* and *Effect* related research to future work since we do not observe much need of this from the scientific domains where we are involved. *Function* can also be extended by domain-specific function concepts such as *MeteorologyFunction*. Specific meteorological functions can then be defined by subclassing *MeteorologyFunction*. The subclass *DataConversion* of the class *Function* in Fig. 7.2 will be explained in Sect. 7.3.2.

DataRepresentation describes storage-related information of *Data*, that is, how data are stored in computer systems. While *Data* specifies the semantic information of workflow data that is easy to understand by human beings, *DataRepresentation* indicates additional storage-related information (syntactic information) of workflow data that is required by services or executables to correctly process the data. We define some comprehensive properties for the concept *DataRepresentation* which are shown in Fig. 7.3. Table 7.1 shows the descriptions and the possible values of these properties. While the property *hasStorageType* is easy to understand, the

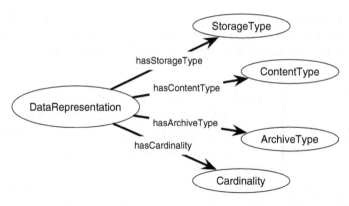

Fig. 7.3 Ontology for DataRepresentation

Table 7.1 DataRepresentation properties

Property	Description	Possible value
hasStorageType	Where the *Data* is stored	Memory, FileSystem, Database
hasContentType	Which format the *Data* is stored in	XML Schema Datatypes, File Types
hasArchiveType	Whether and how the *Data* is archived	zip, gzip, bz2, tar, rar, none, etc.
hasCardinality	What is the cardinality of the *Data*	single, multiple

property *hasContentType* indicates the format in which *Data* is stored. Its value indicates data types, including simple or complex data types supported by the XML Schema Datatype specification, and file types such as BinaryFile, TextFile, CSVFile (a subclass of TextFile), XMLFile (a subclass of TextFile), CDFFile (a scientific data format that can include scalar, vector, and multi-dimensional data arrays, a subclass of BinaryFile), etc. The value *none* of the property *hasArchiveType* indicates that *Data* is not archived. This could be the case for unarchived files or for data stored in memory like *strings* or *integers*. The property *hasCardinality* describes whether *Data* is a single data element or a collection of data elements. Obviously, *DataRepresentation* is a broader concept than data types and provides richer information required by scientific applications. The same exact data can have alternative *DataRepresentations*, such as a *string* stored in memory, a record in a database table, or a set of files each structured either as a table, an XML structure, or a labeled list (Gil [65] has proposed similar ideas).

The separation of data semantics (*Data*) and data representation (*DataRepresentation*) enables scientists to compose scientific workflow applications semantically without dealing with specific data representations including data types. This is the main difference between our approach and existing semantic approaches, most of which still present data types (e.g., *string*, *integer*, etc.) to users when composing scientific workflows.

For the reasons of convenience, ⊏ will be used in the remainder of this chapter to denote the *subclass* relation between two classes specified in ASWO. For example,

$C' \sqsubseteq C$ means the class C' is a subclass of C. A data representation DR' can also be a subclass of another data representation DR if their storageType, archiveType, and cadinality are same, and the contentType of DR' is a subclass of the contentType of DR. That is,

$$DR' \sqsubseteq DR = \begin{cases} true \ DR'.\text{hasStorageType} = DR.\text{hasStorageType} \\ \quad \wedge\ DR'.\text{hasContentType} \sqsubseteq DR.\text{hasContentType} \\ \quad \wedge\ DR'.\text{hasArchiveType} = DR.\text{hasArchiveType} \\ \quad \wedge\ DR'.\text{hasCardinality} = DR.\text{hasCardinality} \\ false \ \text{otherwise} \end{cases}$$

In the remainder of this book, we will refer to the generic AWDL ontology and the extended domain-specific ontologies as Abstract Scientific Workflow Ontologies (ASWO).

7.3   Ontology-Based Scientific Workflow Representation

In this section, we explain how ASWO are used to describe scientific workflow activities and how a semantic scientific workflow representation can be mapped to the corresponding syntactic representation.

7.3.1   Activity Function

An *Activity Function (AF)* is an abstract concept to describe workflow activities at the semantics level. It describes input and output data with Data Classes (DCs). An AF is formally defined as follows:

$$AF = \langle F, \mathcal{I}, \mathcal{O} \rangle$$

where F indicates the function, $\mathcal{I}$ is an ordered set of input DCs, and $\mathcal{O}$ is an ordered set of output DCs. The function refers to the ontology class *Function* or one of its subclasses defined in ASWO. The input and output DCs are *Data* or its subclasses defined in ASWO. No data representation is defined in an AF. For example, in the meteorology domain, an AF *RAMSInit*, to evolve the physical representation of the atmosphere from an initial state preprocessed by RAMS to the specified initial simulation time, is shown in Fig. 7.4. The functionality is specified through the attribute function at Line 1. The DC of each data port is specified through the attribute semantics at Line 3, Line 4, and Line 8, where *SeaSurface* indicates water body properties, e.g., temperature, ice cover, etc. and *RAMSModeledAtmosphere* is the forecasted atmosphere based on an RAMS model.

```
 1  <activity function="RAMSInit">
 2    <dataIns>
 3      <dataIn name="month" semantics="Month"/>
 4      <dataIn name="sst" semantics="SeaSurface"/>
 5      <!-- other input data -->
 6    </dataIns>
 7    <dataOuts>
 8      <dataOut name="rma"
              semantics="RAMSModeledAtmosphere"/>
 9      <!-- other output data -->
10    </dataOuts>
11  </activity>
```

Fig. 7.4 Activity function *RAMSInit*

AFs can be extracted from ASWO because the ontology specifies knowledge about which *Function hasInput* or *hasOutput* which *Data*.

7.3.2 Activity Type

We also extend the concept of AT in AWDL. An AT describes a workflow activity at the syntax level. An AT is specified as:

$$AT = \langle F, T, \mathcal{I}, \mathcal{DR}_{\mathcal{I}}, \mathcal{O}, \mathcal{DR}_{\mathcal{O}} \rangle$$

where F, $\mathcal{I}$, and $\mathcal{O}$ are same as they are defined in an AF, T is a Uniform Resource Identifier (URI) indicating the type, $\mathcal{DR}_{\mathcal{I}}$ is an ordered set of DRs of input data $\mathcal{I}$, and $\mathcal{DR}_{\mathcal{O}}$ is an ordered set of DRs of output data $\mathcal{O}$. ATs can be deployed in an AT repository. In our case, the GLARE service (see Sect. 2.5.2) in ASKALON is used for this purpose. An AT is associated with an AF through the functionality of the AT, i.e., $AT.F$. If $AT.F = AF.F$, then $AT.\mathcal{I} \cong AF.\mathcal{I} \wedge AT.\mathcal{O} \cong AF.\mathcal{O}$, where the relation $\cong$ indicates *semantically compatible*. Given two ordered sets $\mathcal{DC}$ and $\mathcal{DC}'$ each containing n DCs, $\mathcal{DC} \cong \mathcal{DC}'$ is defined as follows:

$$\mathcal{DC} \cong \mathcal{DC}' = \begin{cases} true & i \in [1, n] : \mathcal{DC}_i = \mathcal{DC}'_i \\ & \text{or } \mathcal{DC}_i \text{ is a subclass of } \mathcal{DC}'_i \text{ based on ASWO} \\ false & \text{otherwise} \end{cases} \quad (7.1)$$

Multiple ATs with semantically compatible input and output data but different data representations can be associated with one AF. In other words, one AF can be mapped to multiple ATs. If one wants to define an AT to be associated with an AF which has non-semantically compatible input and output data, then a subclass of the corresponding functionality should be defined in ASWO and the AT should be

```
 1  <activity function="RAMSInit"
        type="actt://Meteorology/rams_init_c">
 2    <dataIns>
 3      <dataIn name="month" semantics="Month">
 4        <dataRepresentation>
 5          <storageType>Memory</storageType>
 6          <contentType>xsd:string</contentType>
 7          <archiveType>none</archiveType>
 8          <cardinality>one</cardinality>
 9        </dataRepresentation>
10      </dataIn>
11      <dataIn name="sst" semantics="SeaSurface">
12        <dataRepresentation>
13          <storageType>FileSystem</storageType>
14          <contentType>awdl:file</contentType>
15          <archiveType>none</archiveType>
16          <cardinality>one</cardinality>
17        </dataRepresentation>
18      </dataIn>
19      <!-- other input data -->
20    </dataIns>
21    <dataOuts>
22      <dataOut name="rma" semantics="RAMSModeledAtmosphere">
23        <dataRepresentation>
24          <storageType>FileSystem</storageType>
25          <contentType>awdl:file</contentType>
26          <archiveType>zip</archiveType>
27          <cardinality>multiple</cardinality>
28        </dataRepresentation>
29      </dataOut>
30      <!-- other output data -->
31    </dataOuts>
32  </activity>
```

Fig. 7.5 Activity type *rams_init_c*

associated with the AF extracted from the ontology based on the subclass. Figure 7.5 illustrates an AT *rams_init_c* which is associated with the AF *RAMSInit* illustrated in Fig. 7.4. Besides containing the same information as the AF, the AT also specifies the name of the activity type through the `type` attribute (Line 1) and the data representation for each data port (Lines 4–9, Lines 12–17 and Lines 23–28).

There is a special kind of AT called *Data Conversion AT (dcAT)*. Their functionality is *DataConversion*, i.e., $dcAT.F = DataConversion$ (see Fig. 7.2). A dcAT can convert *Data* from one representation to another. For example, Fig. 7.6 illustrates a dcAT *month-str-int* which converts *Month* from a *string* in the set $\{Jan, Feb, \dots, Dec\}$ to an *integer* in the range from 1 to 12.

Instead of using ATs, users compose scientific workflows using AFs with their domain knowledge only. The scientific workflow composition tool can then help

```
1  <activity function="DataConversion"
       type="actt://Generic/month-str-int">
2    <dataIns>
3      <dataIn name="strMonth" semantics="Month">
4        <dataRepresentation>
5          <storageType>Memory</storageType>
6          <contentType>xsd:string</contentType>
7          <archiveType>none</archiveType>
8          <cardinality>one</cardinality>
9        </dataRepresentation>
10     </dataIn>
11   </dataIns>
12   <dataOuts>
13     <dataOut name="intMonth" semantics="Month">
14       <dataRepresentation>
15         <storageType>Memory</storageType>
16         <contentType>xsd:integer</contentType>
17         <archiveType>none</archiveType>
18         <cardinality>one</cardinality>
19       </dataRepresentation>
20     </dataOut>
21   </dataOuts>
22 </activity>
```

Fig. 7.6 Activity type *month-str-int*

establish data flow among AFs by providing a list of semantically compatible data sources for users to select. Let us refer to AF-based scientific workflow representations as semantic scientific workflow representations and to AT-based scientific workflow representations as syntactic scientific workflow representations. Semantic scientific workflow representations must be mapped to the corresponding syntactic representation before they are submitted for scheduling and execution. Depending on the selection of ATs, the source data ports and the sink data ports of some data flow links may have different data representations. The conversion between different data representations can be done automatically by the insertion of dcATs. This is explained in detail in the following section.

7.3.3   From Semantics to Syntax

The process to map semantic scientific workflows to syntactic ones is to map all AFs in the semantic workflows to ATs. Because an AF can be mapped to multiple ATs which differ in their input and output data representations, the data representations of the selected ATs must satisfy the established data flow. For example, for a given data flow link, if the *source AF* (i.e., the AF containing the source data port) is mapped to an AT which produces an XMLFile, the AT mapped from the

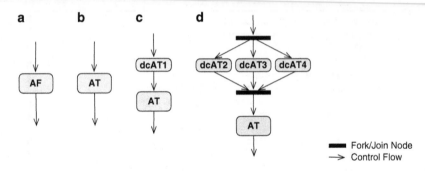

Fig. 7.7 Mapping an AF to ATs

sink AF (i.e., the AF containing the sink data port) must be able to accept the XMLFile as input by the AT itself or with the help of data conversion ATs. This is a typical Constraint Satisfaction Problems (CSPs). Our solution to this problem is a *backtracking* algorithm which is explained in the following.

Let us first have a look that how an AF can be mapped to an AT. Assuming the input data representations of the AF are determined (either given or derived from predecessors), we retrieve a set of ATs that are associated with the AF from the AT repository and compare the input data representations of the ATs with that of the AF. If there exist an AT that can accept the input data representations of the AF, i.e., each input data representation of the AF is same or subclass of (see Sect. 7.2) the corresponding input data representation of the AT, the AT is a *candidate* AT of the AF, and the mapping from the AF to the AT is a *direct match*. In some cases, if some input data representations of the AF are converted to other data representations by data conversion ATs, there may exist an AT that can accept the converted data representations. The AT, together with the corresponding data conversion ATs, is also considered to be a *candidate* AT of the AF. The mapping from the AF to such an AT is an *indirect match*. An AF *can be mapped* if there exists at least one candidate AT. A semantic workflow *can be mapped* if all of the included AFs can be mapped. Figure 7.7 illustrates scenarios of a direct match and two indirect matches: (a) mapping from (a) to (b) indicates a direct match; (b) mapping from (a) to (c) indicates the case where one data representation is converted; and (c) mapping from (a) to (d) indicates the case where more than one data representations are converted. *dcAT1*, *dcAT2*, *dcAT3*, and *dcAT4* in the figure are data conversion ATs. A `parallel` compound activity is used in Fig. 7.7d to enable parallel execution of data conversions. The effect of the mapping process is twofold: semantic activities become syntactic activities (because data representations are included), and data representations are converted automatically if necessary.

To map a semantic scientific workflow to a syntactic one, all candidate ATs for AFs have to be identified, and a candidate AT for each AF has to be selected such that the data flow specified in the semantic scientific workflow is still satisfied in terms of data representations. This is a nontrivial task due to the fact that the

---

Algorithm 7.1: Workflow mapping: mapping()

Input	: ordered set of AFs $\mathcal{AF}$	
	ordered set of mapped ATs $\mathcal{AT}$	*// empty in the first call*
Output	: set of possible mapping solutions $\mathcal{S}$	

```
 1  S ← ∅                                        // initialize the solution set
 2  AF ← AF[ |AT| ]                              // the AF to be mapped in this call
 3  C ← set of candidate ATs of AF              // set of candidate ATs of AF
 4  if C ≠ ∅ then
 5      if |AT| = |AF| − 1 then                 // mapping the last AF
 6          forall AT ∈ C do
 7              AT' ← append AT to AT
 8              S ← S ∪ AT'
 9          end
10      else                                    // not the last AF, then do depth-first mapping
11          forall AT ∈ C do
12              AT' ← append AT to AT
13              S ← S ∪ mapping(AF, AT')         // recursive call for mapping the next AF
14          end
15      end
16  end
17  return S
```

---

selection of candidate ATs of an AF has an influence on the mapping of subsequent AFs, because different candidate ATs may have different output data representations from which the input data representations of the subsequent AF are derived. For example, the selection of a candidate AT of an AF could result in no candidate ATs available for a subsequent AF. Therefore, a backtracking mechanism is required to find all possible mapping solutions. To do this, we have implemented a backtracking algorithm (Algorithm 7.1) through recursive invocation.

The principle of Algorithm 7.1 is as follows. A semantic scientific workflow is considered to be an ordered set of AFs, i.e.,

$$\{AF_0, AF_1, \ldots\}$$

where each AF is associated with an index, and the source AF always has a smaller index than the sink AF for any data flow dependence specified in the workflow. This is to ensure that the source AF is always mapped before the sink AF. A mapping solution is an ordered set of ATs, i.e.,

$$\{AT_0, AT_1, \ldots\}$$

where each of the AT is a selected candidate AT (including the corresponding data conversion ATs if required) of the corresponding AF. Algorithm 7.1 accepts an ordered set of AFs (with zero-based indices) and an ordered set of mapped ATs (is empty in the first call) as inputs, and returns all possible mapping solutions through depth-first mapping. $|\mathcal{AT}|$ and $|\mathcal{AF}|$ in the algorithm are the cardinalities of $\mathcal{AT}$ and $\mathcal{AF}$, respectively.

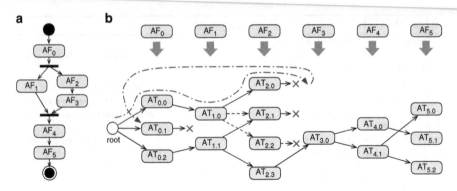

Fig. 7.8 Workflow mapping process

Figure 7.8 illustrates the workflow mapping process through an example workflow (Fig. 7.8a). First, the AFs in the workflow are put into an ordered set as shown in the top part of Fig. 7.8b. Since AF_1, as well as AF_2 and AF_3 are executed in parallel, the order among these AFs can also be slightly different, e.g., $\{AF_2, AF_3, AF_1\}$ or $\{AF_2, AF_1, AF_3\}$. However, this does not affect the final mapping solutions returned by the algorithm. Then, the mapping process starts with the *root* node of the mapping tree at the bottom part of Fig. 7.8b and maps each AFs in the depth-first manner. The other nodes in the mapping tree are the candidate ATs (data conversion ATs are not shown for the reasons of simplicity) with the corresponding AF above them. The cross signs in the mapping tree indicate that no candidate ATs available with the current partial mapping solution. For example, when AF_0, AF_1, and AF_2 are respectively mapped to $AT_{0.0}$, $AT_{1.0}$, and $AT_{2.0}$, there is no candidate AT found for AF_3. A complete mapping solution is a path from the root node of the mapping tree to one of the candidate ATs of AF_5. The mapping tree shown in Fig. 7.8b contains three mapping solutions:

$$\{AT_{0.2}, AT_{1.1}, AT_{2.3}, AT_{3.0}, AT_{4.0}, AT_{5.1}\}$$
$$\{AT_{0.2}, AT_{1.1}, AT_{2.3}, AT_{3.0}, AT_{4.1}, AT_{5.0}\}$$
$$\{AT_{0.2}, AT_{1.1}, AT_{2.3}, AT_{3.0}, AT_{4.1}, AT_{5.2}\}$$

While the backtracking algorithm for workflow mapping always goes up one level in the mapping tree if all candidate ATs of an AF have been checked or there is no candidate AT available for the AF, we can also use the *backjumping* technique to reduce mapping space. Let us take the mapping tree in Fig. 7.8 as an example and assume that AF_3 has one input data port DP_{sink} with its source referring to an output data port DP_{source} of AF_0. When AF_0, AF_1, and AF_2 are mapped to $AT_{0.0}$, $AT_{1.0}$, and $AT_{2.0}$, we check the ATs which are associated with AF_3. If none of them can be a candidate AT of AF_3 because the data representation of DP_{source} does not match that of DP_{sink} of these ATs, and nor data conversion ATs can do the corresponding conversion, the algorithm can directly *backjump* to try to map AF_0 to its next candidate AT, i.e., $AT_{0.1}$ (as indicated by the dash dotted line in Fig. 7.8) and skip the dashed paths. This is a *safe jump* because the output data port DP_{source} of $AT_{0.0}$ cannot be processed by any ATs that is associated with AF_3. In other words, any partial mapping solution starting with $AT_{0.0}$ cannot lead to a complete solution.

It is known that a backtracking algorithm can find all possible solutions for a constraint satisfaction problem. Therefore, our algorithm can also find all possible solutions for workflow mapping. With different mapping solutions, different syntactic workflows can be generated. These syntactic workflows can be assembled into difference branches of an `alt` activity. This provides a possibility for the workflow scheduler to schedule (without actual execution) all of these syntactic workflows and select the best one (e.g., with minimum execution time or minimum cost) for the actual execution. If the execution of the selected syntactic workflow fails, the workflow runtime system can recover from the failure by executing another syntactic workflow.

When syntactic scientific workflows are scheduled and executed, based on the scheduling decision, the concrete information such as the node, the specific service or executable on that node, the working directory, the executable usage, and the input file name patterns, etc. are determined for each AT. Such concrete information is stored in the `properties` and `constraints` of activities (Fig. 3.23 in Chap. 3 illustrates such an example). At this point of time, ATs become ADs. From this point of view, we can say that we describe scientific workflows at three different levels (semantic, syntactic, and concrete) of abstraction with a single scientific workflow language, AWDL.

7.4 Implementation

We have extended the generic AWDL ontology with an ontology for meteorology simulation with the aim to ease the composition of scientific workflows in this domain. We designed the ontology using the Protege-OWL editor [146] and implement a prototype of our approach using the Jena APIs [85]. Figure 7.9 shows the main *Data* classes of the meteorology ontology. All meteorological data classes are defined as subclasses (represented with "is-a") of the class *MeteorologyData*. For example, *AnalyzedSurface* means "the status of the surface and the interface between surface and atmosphere," *SeaSurface* means "water body properties, including temperature, ice cover etc." Figure 7.10 shows the main *Function* classes. All meteorological functionalities are defined as subclasses of the class *MeteorologyFunction*. For example, *RAMSInit* means "to evolve atmosphere starting from an initial state preprocessed by RAMS," *RAVER* means "to verify model results against a set of observations or ouput from a different model." Some classes are hidden in the two figures (indicated by small triangles) for the reason of simplicity. The hierarchy of these classes is visualized by the OWLViz plugin for Protege.

These *Data* and *Function* classes are used as a search space to guide users to compose the workflow Meteo2 [151], a scientific workflow application for

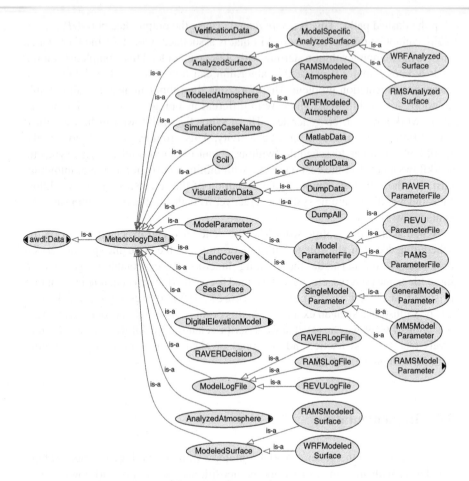

Fig. 7.9 The main data classes of the meteorology ontology

meteorology simulations based on the numerical model RAMS [38]. To compose the workflow, users can search AFs either by free text or based on input and output DCs. When a free text is given, we first build a list of keywords by eliminating the common words (e.g., *a*, *an*, *and*, *by*, etc.) from the given text, then examine each AF to see whether the description of the AF and its input and output DCs contain all the keywords in the list. If so, the AF is considered to be a matching AF. For example, the AF *REVUGnuplot* can be located by searching "*REVU output visualized by gnuplot.*" In the case of searching AFs based on input and output DCs, a AF which consumes all given input DCs and produces all given output DCs is considered to be a matching AF. Note that the list of given input or output DCs do not have to be complete, that is, a matching AF may consume or produce additional DCs. For example, searching with two input DCs "*LandCover*" and "*SeaSurface*" and one output DC "*RAMSModeledAtmosphereAndSurface*", we

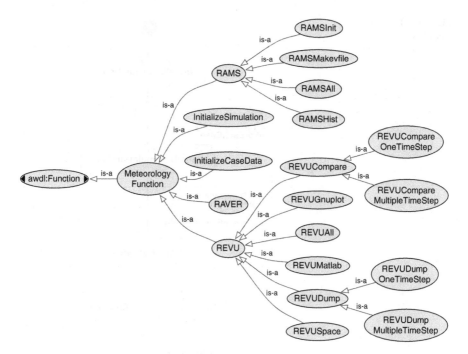

Fig. 7.10 The main function classes of the meteorology ontology

can get two AFs: *RAMSInit*, which has ten input DCs and three output DCs, and *RAMSHist* which has eleven input DCs and two output DCs. Once users have located an AF, they can drag and drop it into the drawing place and connect it with other located AFs with control and data flow. Note that the establishment of data flow is now easier for domain users because it can be done solely based on domain knowledge without considering any data representation. Since we have data semantics associated with data ports, data flow can also be established automatically based on the output DCs of predecessor activities and input DCs of successor activities. Such an algorithm is presented in detail in Chap. 8.

Figure 7.11 illustrates the UML Activity Diagram representation of the composed workflow which consists of eight AFs connected with several control flow constructs, e.g., parallel for and dag. As the first step in the workflow, the parameters for the entire simulation are initialized (*InitializeSimulation*). Then the simulation is split into several cases (*InitializeSimulationCase*). In each simulation case, for each value of the horizontal diffusion coefficient, several RAMS modeling steps are performed: creating an initial state from raw analyzed data (*RAMSMakevfile*), evolving the physical representation of the atmosphere starting from an earlier RAMS model for an specified initial simulation phase and for all simulation phases in parallel (*RAMSInit* and *RAMSAll*). Once the RAMS results of the initial phase is compared and verified (*REVUCompare* and *RAVER*), all RAMS results are dumped (*REVUAll*) to be viewed by meteorologists.

Fig. 7.11 The Meteo2
workflow

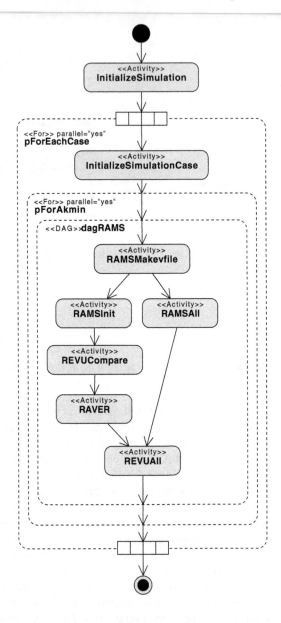

The prototype of our approach is implemented in ASKALON. The architecture of the prototype is shown in Fig. 7.12. When the ASKALON scientific workflow composition GUI is started, the ontologies are loaded from a shared URL and the AFs are extracted and saved in the memory of the GUI. Then users can search AFs based on free text or input and output data and construct a scientific workflow. For each AF put into the workflow, the *Workflow Analyzer* analyzes the control flow dependences and provides a list of semantically compatible *data sources* for

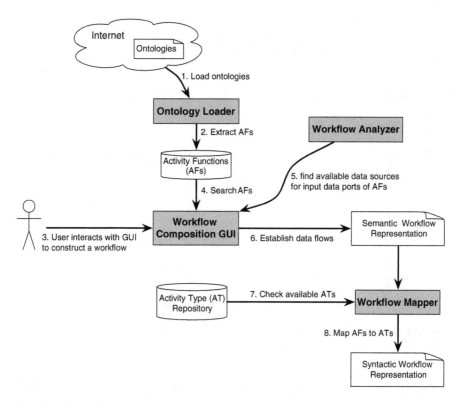

Fig. 7.12 The architecture of the prototype

each input data port of this AF. Users then establish data flow by selecting data sources for the input data ports of this AF from the provided data source lists. Once the scientific workflow is constructed, the *Workflow Mapper* maps the semantic scientific workflow representation to the corresponding syntactic representation by consulting the AT repository. When the mapping is done, the syntactic scientific workflow representation is ready to be submitted to the ASKALON runtime system for scheduling and execution.

Note that the meteorology ontologies represent the knowledge of the meteorology domain, it can also be used to compose other workflows in the domain. We believe that our approach can be adapted for other scientific domains by developing the corresponding ontologies for those domains, as we demonstrated in the previous sections for the meteorology simulation domain.

7.5 Experimental Results

We conducted two experiments to evaluate our scientific workflow composition approach presented in this chapter: (a) how much time it takes to find a requested AF, and (b) how fast a semantic scientific workflow representation can be mapped to the

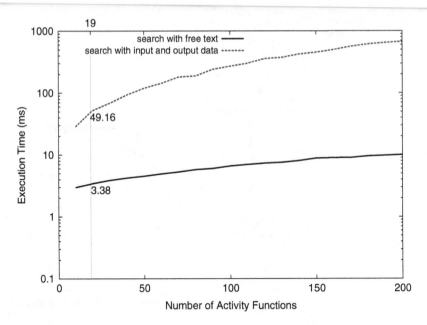

Fig. 7.13 Execution time of searching for AFs based on free text and based on input and output data

corresponding syntactic scientific workflow representation. The computer used to run the experiments is a normal desktop computer with 2 GB RAM and one 2.4 GHz Intel Core 2 Duo CPU. The Java runtime environment used is JRE 1.5.0_13. The scientific workflow application used in the experiments is Meteo2 (see Sect. 7.4).

The number of the subclasses of the class *MeteorologyFunction* defined in ASWO is 19, which means 19 AFs can be extracted and used for the composition of the scientific workflow Meteo2. To evaluate the performance of searching AFs in the case where there are hundreds of AFs available, we manually duplicate the defined AFs to 200 AFs and examine the performance behavior while the number of AFs increases. Two curves in Fig. 7.13 illustrate the execution time of searching for an AF based on free text and based on input and output data, respectively. The horizontal axis indicates the number of available AFs. The vertical axis (in logarithmic scale) shows the execution time. With 200 AFs, searching based on free text costs a few milliseconds, and searching AFs based on input or output data costs lightly more than half a second (673.05 ms). The execution time for searching AFs based on input and output data is longer because all given input and output data used as search criteria have to be compared with all defined input and output data of the AFs. Note that when the number of the available AFs is 19, the execution time for searching AFs based on free text and based on input and output data are 3.38 ms and 49.16 ms, respectively. We can conclude that the overhead is reasonably small and the workflow composition tool can respond fast enough to search requests of users.

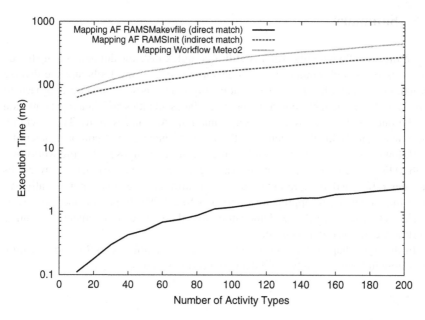

Fig. 7.14 Execution time of mapping AF *RAMSMakevfile* (direct match), mapping AF *RAMSAll* (indirect match), and mapping the entire workflow Meteo2

When AFs are put in a workflow and connected with control flow, data flow among the AFs can be established automatically based on the semantics of data ports. We show such experimental results in the next chapter together with our automatic data flow composition algorithm.

To map an AF in the workflow to ATs, we compare the *input source data representations* of the AF with the input data representations of those ATs in the AT repository which are associated with the AF. Figure 7.14 illustrates the execution time of mapping AF *RAMSMakevfile* (direct match), mapping AF *RAMSAll* (indirect match), and mapping the entire workflow Meteo2. The vertical axis is shown in logarithmic scale. In the case of a direct match, the maximum average execution time is less than 3 ms. In the case of an indirect match, the execution time is 274.50 ms when 200 ATs are associated with the same AF. The execution time for an indirect match is longer because an indirect match is attempted only when the search for a direct match fails. In the case where 200 ATs are available for each given AF, the execution time for mapping the entire scientific workflow Meteo2 is 449.70 ms which consists of the execution time of two indirect matches and six direct matches. Since Meteo2 consists of eight AFs and two levels of nested parallel loops, we can draw the conclusion that a few seconds are enough to map a moderate sized scientific workflow application to the corresponding syntactic representation. Note that the number of AFs specified in the scientific workflow is not the number of activities to be actually executed on distributed systems, which is usually much larger because a workflow may have parallel loops.

7.6   Summary

Scientific workflow composition is still a complex task for domain scientists due to a lack of enough domain knowledge support in existing tools and the diverse structures of scientific data. This chapter presents a novel semantic approach to alleviate this problem by separating between data semantics and data representation on the one hand and between Activity Function (AF) and Activity Type (AT) on the other hand. With this approach, the effort to manage and compose scientific workflows is significantly reduced because: (a) users compose scientific workflows with AFs, which requires domain knowledge only; and (b) data conversions between different data representations of workflow data are done automatically. We have implemented our approach as part of ASKALON. Experiments with a real-world meteorology workflow demonstrate that the overhead of semantic scientific workflow composition is negligible.

In the next chapter, we present our automatic scientific workflow composition algorithm in terms of control and data flow composition.

Chapter 8
Automatic Scientific Workflow Composition

8.1 Introduction

One of the tasks involved in the composition of scientific workflows is the selection of workflow activities. Extensive research [42, 60, 77, 105] has proposed abstract descriptions of workflow activities which are independent of the changes of distributed resources. Since an abstract activity represents a group of concrete computational entities (e.g., software components, Web services) which have the same functionality and the same input and output data structure, the number of abstract activities is usually considerably smaller than the number of concrete computational entities. Consequently, the efforts required for the selection of workflow activities is reduced, and the process of scientific workflow composition is simplified. However, the selection of abstract activities is still a challenging and time-consuming process for domain scientists, especially when there are hundreds or thousands of such abstract activities available for selection.

Automatic workflow composition has been widely studied in several areas like Business Process Management, Semantic Web Services, and distributed computing. Compared with other areas, automatic workflow composition in the distributed computing area usually requires that the composed scientific workflows should be (a) *portable* or adaptable to the changes of distributed resources, i.e., the scientific workflows should be abstract and can be concretized when they are actually executed on distributed systems; (b) *fault tolerant*, e.g., scientific workflows should contain alternative execution paths, if available. If an activity is not available or fails at runtime due to the dynamic nature of distributed systems, an alternative execution path should be adopted; and (c) *optimized*: scientific workflows should be optimized for execution time. We call portable, fault tolerant and optimized scientific workflows *high quality scientific workflows*.

To the best of our knowledge, there is still a lack of a general and efficient approach for automatic composition of high quality scientific workflows. Based on the idea of semantic scientific workflows presented in Chap. 7, this chapter presents our algorithm for automatic composition of high quality scientific workflows at the

J. Qin and T. Fahringer, *Scientific Workflows*, DOI 10.1007/978-3-642-30715-7_8,
© Springer-Verlag Berlin Heidelberg 2012

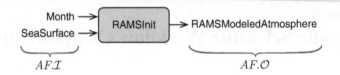

Fig. 8.1 The activity function *RAMSInit*

semantic level. The algorithm consists of two sub-algorithms dealing with control and data flow composition, respectively. The control flow composition algorithm is a planning-based algorithm for automatic scientific workflow composition using an AF Data Dependence (ADD) graph. The algorithm employs progression to create an ADD graph, and regression to extract workflows, including alternative ones if available. The algorithm also optimizes the extracted workflows by analyzing data flow dependences among AFs. Once control flow is established, the data flow composition algorithm composes data flow of scientific workflows in two steps: locating possible source data ports of each sink data port through backwards control flow traversing, and matching source data ports against sink data ports based on data semantics.

Our approach has been implemented as part of ASKALON [51]. In contrast to existing approaches (see Sect. 9.4), our control flow composition algorithm is general, i.e., not limited to any workflow modeling notation such as Petri Nets, and can efficiently and automatically compose high quality scientific workflows. The complexity of the algorithm is quadratic in the number of AFs. With the help of semantic technologies, about 93% data flow links of a real-world scientific workflow can be established by our data flow composition algorithm. A series of experimental results illustrate the effectiveness and efficiency of our approach.

8.2   Activity Function

As presented in Chap. 7, an AF, as a semantic description of a group of ATs, is formally defined as a triple $\langle F, \mathcal{I}, \mathcal{O} \rangle$, where F indicates the function, $\mathcal{I}$ and $\mathcal{O}$ are two ordered set of Data Classes (DCs) indicating the input data and the output data. Figure 8.1 shows an example AF *RAMSInit* in the meteorology domain, where $AF.\mathcal{I} = \{Month, SeaSurface\}$ and $AF.\mathcal{O} = \{RAMSModeledAtmosphere\}$ respectively denotes the input and output data of the AF *RAMSInit*. Other input and output data are omitted for the reason of simplicity.

This chapter aims to compose scientific workflows automatically at the semantic level. The semantic scientific workflows can be mapped to the syntactic ones based on the approach presented in Chap. 7 and then be reified and executed on distributed systems based on the ideas illustrated in Chap. 3. For the purpose of describing our scientific workflow composition algorithm in this chapter, we focus only on AFs and

DCs, instead of ATs, Data Representations (DRs) or concrete data (e.g., a specific value or file). In the remainder of this chapter, the availability of a data class (DC) means that of the corresponding concrete data. The terms *data* and *data class* will be used interchangeably for convenience.

8.3 Definition of the Scientific Workflow Composition Problem

Our control flow composition algorithm is a planning-based algorithm. Before the explanation of the algorithm, we first give a formal definition of the scientific workflow composition problem based on the STRIPS [55], a base language for expressing automated planning problems in Artificial Intelligence.

STRIPS divides its representational scheme into three components, namely, *an initial state, a goal state,* and *actions.* A plan for such a planning problem is a sequence of actions that can be executed from the initial state and that leads to the goal state. We use STRIPS as the basis for the definition of the scientific workflow composition problem, where *states* and *actions* are defined as follows:

- *State*: A state is a set of DCs, indicating the availability of data. The *initial state* indicates the user provided data which can be consumed by workflow activities. The *goal state* indicates the user required data which must be produced by the composed scientific workflow.
- *Action*: AFs are the actions. AFs can consume and produce DCs, thereby states can be changed and the goal state can be reached. Note that in the domain of scientific workflow composition, the consumption of data does not make it unavailable because AFs can work on copies of data.

For a given state s_i, an AF can be included (i.e., applied) in a workflow when s_i entails $AF.\mathcal{I}$, denoted by $s_i \models AF.\mathcal{I}$. The relation $\models$ between two DCs D' and D, between a set of DCs $\mathcal{DC}'$ and a DC D, and between two sets of DCs $\mathcal{DC}'$ and $\mathcal{DC}$ are defined respectively as follows (see Sect. 7.2 for the definition of $\sqsubset$):

$$D' \models D = \begin{cases} true & D' = D \vee D' \sqsubset D \\ false & \text{otherwise} \end{cases} \tag{8.1}$$

$$\mathcal{DC}' \models D = \begin{cases} true & \exists D' \in \mathcal{DC}' : D' \models D \\ false & \text{otherwise} \end{cases} \tag{8.2}$$

$$\mathcal{DC}' \models \mathcal{DC} = \begin{cases} true & \forall D \in \mathcal{DC} : \mathcal{DC}' \models D \\ false & \text{otherwise} \end{cases} \tag{8.3}$$

$\mathcal{DC}' \models \mathcal{DC}$ is *true* if and only if for any $D \in \mathcal{DC}$, $\mathcal{DC}'$ entails D, that is, $\mathcal{DC}'$ subsumes D or $\mathcal{DC}'$ subsumes a subclass of D. For example, if $\mathcal{DC} = \{D_1, D_{2.1}, D_3\}$,

$\mathcal{DC}'_1 = \{D_1, D_3\}$, $\mathcal{DC}'_2 = \{D_2, D_3\}$ and $\mathcal{DC}'_3 = \{D_1, D_4\}$ (D_i or $D_{i,j}$ indicates a data class, and $D_{i,j}$ is a subclass of D_i for any integer i and j), then both $\mathcal{DC} \models \mathcal{DC}'_1$ and $\mathcal{DC} \models \mathcal{DC}'_2$ are *true*, and $\mathcal{DC} \models \mathcal{DC}'_3$ is *false*, i.e., $\mathcal{DC} \nvDash \mathcal{DC}'_3$. For example, if we ignore the omitted input and output DCs, the AF *RAMSInit* in Sect. 8.2 can be applied in the state $s_i = \{SimulationCaseName, Month, SeaSurface\}$, where *SimulationCaseName*, *Month* and *SeaSurface* are either the initial input data provided by users or the output data produced by any AF which is already included in the workflow. The new state after applying the AF to s_i is $s_{i+1} = s_i \cup AF.\mathcal{O}$, i.e., $\{SimulationCaseName, Month, SeaSurface, RAMSModeledAtmosphere\}$.

We consider a scientific workflow composition problem as an Artificial Intelligence planning problem which is defined by the function

$$f : (s_{init}, s_{goal}, \mathcal{AF}) \rightarrow w$$

where each component is described as follows:

- s_{init} is the initial state.
- s_{goal} is the goal state.
- $\mathcal{AF}$ is the set of AFs among which some AFs will be selected for the composition of the scientific workflow w.
- w is a DAG of AFs connected by control flow edges. The AFs in the DAG fulfill the following restrictions:

  1. $s_{init} \models AF.\mathcal{I}$ for any AF which has no incoming control flow edges.
  2. $s_{init} \cup \left(\bigcup_{AF' \in \mathcal{AF}'} AF'.\mathcal{O} \right) \models AF.\mathcal{I}$ for any AF which has incoming control flow edges. Here $\mathcal{AF}'$ is the set of predecessors of this AF.
  3. $s_{init} \cup \left(\bigcup AF.\mathcal{O} \right) \models s_{goal}$

We assume $s_{init} \nvDash s_{goal}$, because otherwise no workflow need to be composed. Automatic composition of scientific workflows with loops and branches is explained in Sect. 8.5.5.

8.4 ADD Graph and Notations

This section defines the ADD graph and the notation used for the explanation of our control flow composition algorithm. The notation is explained through the example ADD graph illustrated at the top part of Fig. 8.2, where rectangles labeled with $D_0, D_1, \ldots$ are different DCs and round cornered rectangles labeled with $AF_0, AF_1, \ldots$ are different AFs. The edge connecting from D_j to AF_i indicates that the AF requires D_j as input. The edge connecting from AF_i to D_k indicates that the AF produces D_k as output. The dashed line with a hollow arrow connecting from $D_{i,j}$ to D_i indicates the former is a subclass of the latter according to ASWO. The initial state s_{init} and the goal state s_{goal} are $\{D_0, D_1\}$ and $\{D_9, D_{10}\}$, respectively. The dotted round cornered rectangles are used to group a set of AFs to improve

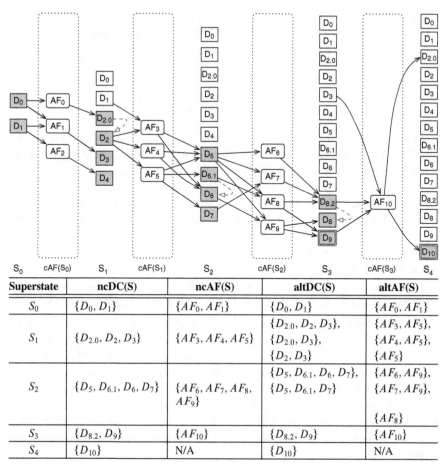

Superstate	ncDC(S)	ncAF(S)	altDC(S)	altAF(S)
S_0	$\{D_0, D_1\}$	$\{AF_0, AF_1\}$	$\{D_0, D_1\}$	$\{AF_0, AF_1\}$
S_1	$\{D_{2.0}, D_2, D_3\}$	$\{AF_3, AF_4, AF_5\}$	$\{D_{2.0}, D_2, D_3\}$, $\{D_{2.0}, D_3\}$, $\{D_2, D_3\}$	$\{AF_3, AF_5\}$, $\{AF_4, AF_5\}$, $\{AF_5\}$
S_2	$\{D_5, D_{6.1}, D_6, D_7\}$	$\{AF_6, AF_7, AF_8, AF_9\}$	$\{D_5, D_{6.1}, D_6, D_7\}$, $\{D_5, D_{6.1}, D_7\}$	$\{AF_6, AF_9\}$, $\{AF_7, AF_9\}$, $\{AF_8\}$
S_3	$\{D_{8.2}, D_9\}$	$\{AF_{10}\}$	$\{D_{8.2}, D_9\}$	$\{AF_{10}\}$
S_4	$\{D_{10}\}$	N/A	$\{D_{10}\}$	N/A

Fig. 8.2 An Activity Function Data Dependence (ADD) graph and its $ncDC(S)$, $ncAF(S)$, $altDC(S)$, and $altAF(S)$

the readability of the ADD graph. Some notations and their values are shown in the bottom part of Fig. 8.2 for the reasons of convenience.

Contributing AF (cAF): For a given state s_i, an AF is said to be a *contributing AF* if and only if $(s_i \vDash AF.\mathcal{I}) \wedge (AF.\mathcal{O} - s_i \neq \emptyset)$. That is, s_i entails $AF.\mathcal{I}$ and $AF.\mathcal{O}$ includes some DCs which are not in s_i. In other words, the AF can be applied in state s_i and applying the AF to s_i can produce new DCs. For example, in Fig. 8.2, AF_0, AF_1 and AF_2 are three cAFs of the superstate S_0 (explained below).

Superstate: Applying all cAFs of a state s_i to this state causes the transition to a new state. We call the new state a *superstate* (analogy to *superset* in *set* theory) because it is a union of all possible states which can be reached from s_i by applying any of these cAFs. Let us denote a superstate by S, the initial superstate by S_0 and let $S_0 = s_{init}$. Let us also denote the set of all cAFs of a superstate S by $cAF(S)$. For example, in Fig. 8.2, $cAF(S_0) = \{AF_0, AF_1, AF_2\}$, $cAF(S_1) = \{AF_3, AF_4, AF_5\}$, $cAF(S_2) = \{AF_6, AF_7, AF_8, AF_9\}$, and $cAF(S_3) = \{AF_{10}\}$. Applying $cAF(S_i)$ to S_i causes the transition to S_{i+1} which is defined as:

$$S_{i+1} = S_i \cup \left(\bigcup_{AF \in cAF(S_i)} AF.\mathcal{O} \right) \tag{8.4}$$

Contributed DC (cDC): It is obvious that S_{i+1} always contains some newly contributed (i.e., produced) DCs which are not in S_i. Let us denote the set of all cDCs in a superstate S by $cDC(S)$. Then, $cDC(S_{i+1}) = S_{i+1} - S_i$. For example, in Fig. 8.2, $cDC(S_1) = \{D_{2.0}, D_2, D_3, D_4\}$, $cDC(S_2) = \{D_5, D_{6.1}, D_6, D_7\}$, $cDC(S_3) = \{D_{8.2}, D_8, D_9\}$, and $cDC(S_4) = \{D_{10}\}$, as indicated by the rectangles with gray background in Fig. 8.2. Note that we include D_2 in $cDC(S_1)$ although D_2 is not directly contributed by any AF in $cAF(S_0)$. This is because $D_{2.0}$ entails D_2 and D_2 is input to AFs in $cAF(S_1)$. We also consider all DCs in S_0 are cDCs, that is, $cDC(S_0) = S_0 = \{D_0, D_1\}$.

ADD Graph: An ADD graph γ is a triple $\langle \mathcal{A}, \mathcal{D}, \overrightarrow{\mathcal{D}} \rangle$, where $\mathcal{D}$ is an ordered list of superstates (namely, $S_0, S_1, \ldots, S_n$). For each superstate $S_{i \in [0,n)} \in \mathcal{D}$, $cAF(S_i) \in \mathcal{A}$. $\overrightarrow{\mathcal{D}}$ is a set of dependences each connecting either from a DC in S_i to a cAF in $cAF(S_i)$ or from a cAF in $cAF(S_i)$ to a DC in S_{i+1}, where $i \in [0,n)$. The dependences connecting to (or from) a cAF indicate the corresponding input (or output) DCs of the cAF. Note that n will be used to indicate the index of the final superstate of an ADD graph in the remainder of the explanation of our control flow composition algorithm. In the example ADD graph illustrated Fig. 8.2, $n = 4$, $\mathcal{D} = \{S_0, S_1, \ldots, S_4\}$, $\mathcal{A} = \{cAF(S_0), cAF(S_1), \ldots, cAF(S_3)\}$. All dependences in $\overrightarrow{\mathcal{D}}$ are represented as directed edges in Fig. 8.2. An ADD graph has the following properties:

(a) For any $i, j \in [0,n) \land i \neq j$, $cAF(S_i) \cap cAF(S_j) = \emptyset$. That is, all $cAF(S)$ are disjoint. This is obvious because if an AF is a cAF of S_i, (1) it cannot be a cAF of any later superstate S_j, where $i < j < n$, due to the fact that applying the AF cannot produce any new DC, and (2) the AF also cannot be a cAF of any earlier superstate S_k, where $0 \leqslant k < i$, because otherwise it would not be a cAF of S_i. Therefore, the AF cannot be a cAF of any other superstate, that is, all $cAF(S)$ are disjoint.
(b) For any $i, j \in [0,n] \land i < j$, $S_i \subsetneq S_j$. That is, each superstate contains at least one more DC than any previous superstate. This is illustrated by Eq. 8.4.
(c) For any AF in $cAF(S_i)$, $AF.\mathcal{O} \cap cDC(S_{i+1}) \neq \emptyset$. That is, any cAF in $cAF(S_i)$ must produce at least one cDC in S_{i+1}. This is obvious based on the definition of cAF.
(d) For any AF in $cAF(S_i)$, $AF.\mathcal{I} \cap cDC(S_i) \neq \emptyset$. That is, any cAF in $cAF(S_i)$ must consume at least one cDC in S_i. This is because otherwise the AF would be included in one of the previous $cAF(S_j)$, where $j < i$.

Dependence: In an ADD graph, a node N can be either a DC or a cAF. Node N_j depends on node N_i, denoted by $N_i \, \delta \, N_j$, if there exists a path from N_i to N_j in the ADD graph. Note that the edge connecting from a subclass of a DC to the DC is also considered as part of a path. For example, in Fig. 8.2, $D_1 \, \delta \, D_3$, $AF_0 \, \delta \, D_7$, $AF_5 \, \delta \, AF_7$, and $D_3 \, \delta \, AF_{10}$. Obviously, $D_{8.2}$ does not depend on D_4, and D_{10} does not depends on D_8. In addition, we also say that a node N depends on itself, that is, $N \, \delta \, N$. It is obvious that the dependence relation is transitive. For the reasons of simplicity, $N_i \, \delta \, s_{goal}$, i.e., s_{goal} depends on N_i, will be used to indicate that $\exists D \in s_{goal} : N_i \, \delta \, D$.

Necessary cAF (ncAF): A cAF AF_i in an ADD graph is said to be necessary if and only if s_{goal} depends on this cAF, i.e., $AF_i \, \delta \, s_{goal}$. Let us denote all ncAFs in $cAF(S)$ by $ncAF(S)$. Then, $ncAF(S) = \{AF | AF \in cAF(S) \land AF \, \delta \, s_{goal}\}$. For the reasons of convenience, $ncAF(S)$ of each superstate is shown in the table at the bottom of Fig. 8.2. In particular, AF_2 is not included in $ncAF(S_0)$ because AF_2 is not necessary.

Necessary cDC (ncDC): Similarly, a cDC D_i in an ADD graph is said to be necessary if and only if $D_i \, \delta \, s_{goal}$. The set of all ncDCs in $cDC(S)$ is $ncDC(S) = \{D | D \in cDC(S) \land D \, \delta \, s_{goal}\}$. $ncDC(S)$ of each superstate is also shown in the table at the bottom of Fig. 8.2. In particular, $ncDC(S_1) = \{D_2, D_3\}$ because D_4 is not necessary. $ncDC(S_3) = \{D_{8.2}, D_9\}$ because D_8 is not necessary.

Alternative DC/AF Combination: According to the definition of ncDC and ncAF, the DCs in $ncDC(S_i)$ serve as input to the AFs in $ncAF(S_i)$. In some cases, due to the existence of subclass DCs, to satisfy the input of the AFs in $ncAF(S_i)$, not *all* of the ncDCs in $ncDC(S_i)$ are necessary. Instead, some of those ncDCs (i.e., an DC combination) may be sufficient. And there may also exist multiple alternatives of such DC combinations. Furthermore, for each of such DC combination, it is also possible that not *all* AFs in $ncAF(S_{i-1})$ are necessary to produce all ncDCs in the DC combination. In other words, there may also exists multiple alternatives of such AF combinations in $ncAF(S_{i-1})$, and each of those AF combination is sufficient to produce *all* ncDCs in a DC combination of $ncDC(S_i)$. Let us denote the set of all alternative DC combinations in $ncDC(S)$ by $altDC(S)$, and the set of all alternative AF combinations in $ncAF(S)$ by $altAF(S)$.

$altDC(S)$ and $altAF(S)$ of each superstate in the example ADD graph are shown in the table at the bottom of Fig. 8.2. Because $D_{6.1}$ is a subclass of D_6, there exist two alternative DC combinations: $\{D_5, D_{6.1}, D_6, D_7\}$ and $\{D_5, D_{6.1}, D_7\}$. To produce the first DC combination $\{D_5, D_{6.1}, D_6, D_7\}$, there exist two alternative AF combinations in $ncAF(S_1)$: $\{D_3, D_5\}$ and $\{D_4, D_5\}$. Although other AF combinations such as $\{AF_3, AF_4, AF_5\}$ can also produce $\{D_5, D_{6.1}, D_6, D_7\}$, we consider this AF combination redundant and will ignore it in our control flow composition algorithm because all ncDCs which can be produced by AF_3 (or AF_4) can also be produced by AF_4 (or AF_3). To produce the second DC combination $\{D_5, D_{6.1}, D_7\}$, there exist three alternative AF combinations: $\{D_3, D5\}$, $\{D_4, D_5\}$, and $\{D_5\}$. Therefore, in total, there are three alternatives AF combinations in $ncAF(S_1)$. Similarly, $\{AF_6, AF_9\}$, $\{AF_7, AF_9\}$ and $\{AF_8\}$ are three alternative AF

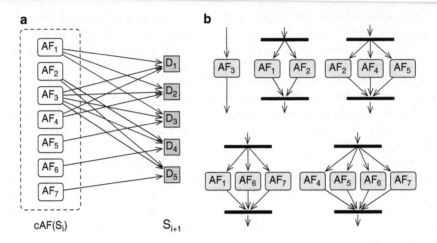

Fig. 8.3 Alternative AF combinations

combinations in $ncAF(S_2)$ each of which can produce $\{D_{8.2}, D_9\}$. $\{D_{8.2}, D_9\}$ is the only DC combination in $ncDC(S_3)$ because D_8 is not an ncDC.

We calculate the alternative DC combinations in $ncDC(S)$ by enumerating all possibilities that DCs in $ncDC(S)$ can be replaced with their subclass DCs in $ncDC(S)$. For example, assuming $D_0, D_{1.0.2}, D_{1.0}, D_1$, and D_2 are all ncDCs, $D_{1.0}$ is a subclass of D_1, and $D_{1.0.2}$ is a subclass of $D_{1.0}$, there exist four alternative DC combinations: $\{D_0, D_{1.0.2}, D_{1.0}, D_1, D_2\}$, $\{D_0, D_{1.0.2}, D_{1.0}, D_2\}$, $\{D_0, D_{1.0.2}, D_1, D_2\}$, and $\{D_0, D_{1.0.2}, D_2\}$. The calculation of alternative AF combinations is exemplified by part of an ADD graph shown in Fig. 8.3a, assume that $\{D_1, D_2, D_3, D_4, D_5\}$ is one alternative DC combination. In this case, there are in total five alternative AF combinations which can produce $\{D_1, D_2, D_3, D_4, D_5\}$, as illustrated in Fig. 8.3b, where ForkNode and JoinNode (each represented as a thick line segment) are UML Activity Diagram notations and used to indicate parallel execution.

Simple ADD Graph: A simple ADD graph is an ADD graph where all AFs are ncAFs, all DCs are ncDCs, and each $cAF(S_i)$ contains only a single AF combination, i.e., $\forall i \in [0, n) : |altAF(S_i)| = 1$. The ADD graph (Fig. 8.7) discussed in Sect. 8.5.5 is an example of a simple ADD graph. Note that the DCs in some superstates (the ones without gray background) are actually cDCs in previous superstates and they are necessary. Comparing Fig. 8.7 with Fig. 8.2, AF_2, D_4, and D_8 are eliminated because they are not necessary. Only AF_5 is kept in $cAF(S_1)$ because $\{AF_5\}$ is one of the alternative AF combinations in $cAF(S_1)$. AF_8 is kept for similar reasons. Because AF_7 and AF_9 are not included, D_6 and D_7 are not necessary any more, therefore they are eliminated as well. As we will see later, a simple ADD graph contains only a single workflow.

8.5 Control Flow Composition Algorithm

In order to solve a STRIPS-like problem, Artificial Intelligence planners typically use techniques such as progression, regression, and partial-ordering. Our control flow composition algorithm employs both progression to create an ADD graph and regression to extract workflows, including alternative workflows if available. The algorithm also optimizes control flow dependences of the extracted workflows in order to deal with the heterogeneous nature of distributed systems and workflow activities. This constitutes three phases of the algorithm: ADD graph creation, workflow extraction, and workflow optimization each of which is explained in the following.

8.5.1 ADD Graph Creation

The pseudocode of ADD graph creation is illustrated by Algorithm 8.1. The ADD graph is built starting from the initial superstate S_0 (Line 1). Before expanding the ADD graph to the next superstate S_{i+1}, the algorithm checks whether the current superstate S_i entails s_{goal} (Line 3). If so, the creation of the ADD graph is finished and the algorithm returns with the created ADD graph (Line 12). Otherwise, the algorithm searches for AFs in $\mathcal{AF}$ which are not cAF of all previous superstates and calculates $cAF(S_i)$ (Line 4). If $cAF(S_i) = \emptyset$, the algorithm returns *null* (Line 6), i.e., *no solution found*. If $cAF(S_i) \neq \emptyset$, the algorithm expands the ADD graph to the next superstate S_{i+1} (Line 8) and evaluates the superstate S_{i+1} again as illustrated above.

When the ADD graph is expanded to S_1, all AFs in $\mathcal{AF}$ have been accessed once, thereby $\bigcup_{AF \in \mathcal{AF}} AF.\mathcal{O} \models s_{goal}$ is determined. If it evaluates to *false* (i.e., some DCs in s_{goal} cannot be produced by any AF in $\mathcal{AF}$), the entire control flow composition algorithm returns *null* immediately. For the reasons of simplicity, this part is not shown in Algorithm 8.1.

Figure 8.2 is an ADD graph where the initial state $s_{init} = \{D_0, D_1\}$, the goal state $s_{goal} = \{D_9, D_{10}\}$, and the set of all AFs $\mathcal{AF} = \{AF_0, AF_1, \ldots, AF_{10}, \ldots\}$. The AFs which are not cAFs of any superstate are not included in the ADD graph and thereby not shown. The final superstate $S_4 = \{D_0, D_1, \ldots, D_{10}\}$ satisfies $S_4 \models s_{goal}$.

8.5.2 Workflow Extraction

The pseudocode of workflow extraction is illustrated by Algorithm 8.2. Lines 3–10 calculates $ncDC(S)$, $ncAF(S)$, $altDC(S)$, and $altAF(S)$ from S_n to S_1 by analyzing AF data dependences. The principle is that if a cDC $D \in cDC(S_i)$

Algorithm 8.1: ADD graph creation

    Input   : initial state s_{init};   goal state s_{goal};   set of AFs $\mathcal{AF}$
    Output   : An ADD graph if a solution exists, or null otherwise

1 $S_0 \leftarrow s_{init}$ *// initialize superstate S_0*
2 $i \leftarrow 0$;   *// index of current superstate*
3 **while** $S_i \not\models s_{goal}$ **do**
        // calculate $cAF(S_i)$, see Equation 8.3 for the relation $\models$
4       $cAF(S_i) \leftarrow \{AF | AF \in (\mathcal{AF} - \bigcup_{j \in [0,i)} cAF(S_j)) \wedge (S_i \models$
       $AF.\mathcal{I}) \wedge (AF.\mathcal{O} - S_i) \neq \emptyset \}$
5   **if** $cAF(S_i) = \emptyset$ **then**
6 | **return** null   *// no solution found*
7   **else**
8 | calculate S_{i+1} based on Equation 8.4   *// next superstate*
9 | $i \leftarrow i + 1$ *// index of next superstate*
10   **end**
11 **end**
12 **return** the ADD graph based on the created superstates, the calculated cAF(S) and the dependences.

---

is an ncDC, then the cAF $AF_k \in cAF(S_{i-1})$ producing D is an ncAF, and $D' \in cDC(S_{i-1})$ input to AF_k is also an ncDC, and so on. Through this regression, all $ncDC(S)$ and $ncAF(S)$ can be determined. $ncDC(S_0)$ is calculated based on $ncAF(S_0)$ at the outside of the loop (Line 10). For example, in Fig. 8.2, $D_{10} \delta s_{goal}$, therefore, $AF_{10} \delta s_{goal}$ and $D_{8.2} \delta s_{goal}$. Since $D_2 \delta s_{goal}$ and $D_3 \delta s_{goal}$ (note that there exists a path D_3-AF_{10}-D_{10}), $ncAF(S_0) = \{AF_0, AF_1\}$. AF_2 is redundant and will be eliminated. $altDC(S_i)$ is calculated based on $ncDC(S_i)$ (Line 6). $altAF(S_i)$ is calculated when $ncAF(S_{i-1})$ and $altDC(S_i)$ are determined (Line 7). This is done by enumerating all possible AF combinations in $ncAF(S_{i-1})$, such that each of the AF combinations is sufficient to produce one alternative DC combination in $altDC(S_i)$, and eliminating the redundant AF combinations (the corresponding pseudocode is illustrated in Algorithm 8.3). Once all $ncDC(S)$, $ncAF(S)$, $altDC(S)$, and $altAF(S)$ are determined, Algorithm 8.2 eliminates non-necessary cDCs and cAFs, and checks whether the size of each $altAF(S)$ is one. If so, the ADD graph is a simple ADD graph, i.e., it contains a single workflow. The workflow can then be optimized in the next phase (Line 13). Otherwise, depending on the selection of alternative AF combinations in each $altAF(S)$, multiple ADD graphs can be extracted (Line 15). The process is repeated recursively for each extracted ADD graph, until a simple graph remains (Line 17).

In the ADD graph shown in Fig. 8.2, $ncAF(S_1)$ and $ncAF(S_2)$ each has three alternative AF combinations (see the table at the bottom part of Fig. 8.2), nine ADD graphs are extracted in the first invocation of Algorithm 8.2. When $\{AF_3, AF_5\}$ and $\{AF_6, AF_9\}$ are selected, there exist again three alternative AF combinations in $ncAF(S_1)$, i.e., $\{AF_3\}$, $\{AF_5\}$ and $\{AF_3, AF_5\}$. This is similar for other cases as well. Because some of the extracted ADD graphs are identical, in total, nine workflows are extracted when Algorithm 8.2 returns. For all of these

---

Algorithm 8.2: Workflow extraction: extractWorkflows()

Input   : ADD graph γ;   goal state s_{goal}
Output   : set of extracted simple ADD graphs (i.e., workflows) Γ

1 $\Gamma \leftarrow \emptyset$ *// initialize Γ*
2 $\mathcal{DC} \leftarrow s_{goal}$ *// set of DCs to be produced by previous superstates*
3 **for** $S_i \leftarrow S_n$ **to** S_1 **do**   *// regression*
4 $\quad$ $ncDC(S_i) \leftarrow \mathcal{DC} \cap cDC(S_i)$
$\qquad$ *// all AFs $\in cAF(S_{i-1})$ where $AF.\mathcal{O}$ entails at least one $DC \in ncDC(S_i)$*
5 $\quad$ $ncAF(S_{i-1}) \leftarrow \{AF \mid AF \in cAF(S_{i-1}) \wedge \exists D \in ncDC(S_i) : AF.\mathcal{O} \vDash D \}$
6 $\quad$ $altDC(S_i) \leftarrow$ calculate $altDC(S_i)$ based on $ncDC(S_i)$ *// alternative DC*
$\qquad$ *Combinations*
7 $\quad$ $altAF(S_{i-1}) \leftarrow calcAltAF(ncAF(S_{i-1}), altDC(S_i))$ *// alternative AF*
$\qquad$ *Combinations*
8 $\quad$ $\mathcal{DC} \leftarrow (\mathcal{DC} \cup (\bigcup_{AF \in ncAF(S_{i-1})} AF.\mathcal{I})) - ncDC(S_i)$
9 **end**
10 $ncDC(S_0) \leftarrow \bigcup_{AF \in ncAF(S_0)} AF.\mathcal{I}$
11 eliminate non-necessary cAFs and cDCs from γ
12 **if** $\forall i \in [0, n) : |altAF(S_i)| = 1$ **then**
13 $\quad$ $\Gamma \leftarrow \Gamma \cup \gamma$ *// is simple ADD graph*
14 **else**
15 $\quad$ $E \leftarrow \prod_{i \in [0,n)} altAF(S_i)$ *// cartesian product for extraction*
16 $\quad$ **forall** $e \in E$ **do**   *// for each extracted graph*
17 $\quad$ $\quad$ $\Gamma \leftarrow \Gamma \cup$ extractWorkflows(e, s_{goal}) *// recursive invocation*
18 $\quad$ **end**
19 **end**
20 **return** Γ

Algorithm 8.3: Calculate alternative AF combinations: calcAltAF()

Input   : set of AFs $\mathcal{AF}$;   set of DC combinations $altDC$
Output   : set of alternative AF combinations each of which can produce one DC
$\qquad\qquad$ combination in $altDC$

1 $alt\mathcal{AF} \leftarrow \emptyset$
2 **forall** $altDC \in alt\mathcal{DC}$ **do**
3 $\quad$ **forall** $D_i \in altDC$ **do**
4 $\quad$ $\quad$ $AF(D_i) \leftarrow \{AF | AF \in \mathcal{AF} \wedge AF.\mathcal{O} \vDash D_i\}$ *// set of AF whose output entails D_i*
5 $\quad$ **end**
6 $\quad$ $altAF \leftarrow \prod_{D_i \in altDC} AF(D_i)$ *// cross product*
7 $\quad$ $alt\mathcal{AF} \leftarrow alt\mathcal{AF} \cup altAF$
8 **end**
9 **forall** $alt \in alt\mathcal{AF}$ **do**
10 $\quad$ eliminate redundant AFs from alt
11 **end**
12 **return** $alt\mathcal{AF}$

---

workflows, the AFs in the same $ncAF(S)$ can be executed in parallel (via the AWDL construct `parallel`), and all AFs in the $ncAF(S_i)$ are executed before the AFs in $ncAF(S_{i+1})$ (via the AWDL construct `sequence`). Figure 8.4a–d show four generated workflows, represented with the UML Activity Diagram [176].

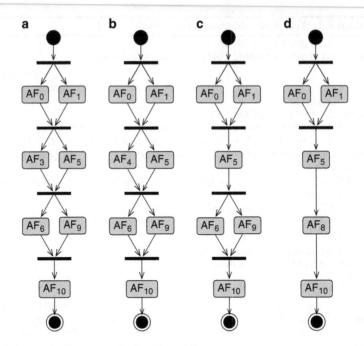

Fig. 8.4 Automatically composed scientific workflows

We can obtain another three workflows by substituting AF_6 with AF_7 in the first three workflows, and another two workflows by substituting AF_5 with AF_3, AF_4 respectively in the third workflow (Fig. 8.4c).

The extracted workflows can be assembled into an `alt` activity (see Sect. 3.2.2) as alternative branches to provide alternative execution paths in case of failure at runtime. For example, if AF_8 in Fig. 8.4d cannot be mapped to any AD or the execution of AF_8 fails, the workflow execution can continue with AF_6 and AF_9 (Fig. 8.4c) instead of returning an error to users. If AF_6 fails again, AF_7 can be used as a replacement. Users can also filter the extracted workflows by specifying the AFs they want (or do not want) to be included in the extracted workflows, e.g., based on the experiences they might have with previous workflow executions. The extracted workflows can be assembled into an `alt` activity, which provides a possibility for the workflow scheduler to schedule (without actual execution) all of these alternative workflows and select the best one (e.g., with minimum execution time or minimum cost) for the actual execution.

8.5.3   Workflow Optimization

The workflows extracted in the previous phase may still be optimized in terms of control flow. For example, in Fig. 8.2, AF_3 can be executed as long as AF_0 is finished, even if AF_1 is not finished at that time, because AF_3 does not

---

Algorithm 8.4: Workflow optimization

Input : simple ADD graph
Output : DAG of AFs

1   mark all AFs in $ncAF(S_0)$ as the root nodes of the DAG
2   **for** $ncAF(S_i) \leftarrow ncAF(S_1)$ **to** $ncAF(S_{n-1})$ **do**
3   **forall** $AF \in ncAF(S_i)$ **do**
4       $\mathcal{DC} \leftarrow AF.\mathcal{I}$ // unresolved inputs
5       $k \leftarrow i$ // index of current superstate
6       $\mathcal{AF}^p \leftarrow \emptyset$ // located predecessors
7   **repeat**
8         $\mathcal{DC}' \leftarrow \emptyset$ // temporarily unresolved inputs
9   **forall** $D \in \mathcal{DC}$ **do**
10   **if** $ncDC(S_k) \vDash D$ **then**
             // mark as predecessors, see Equation 8.2 for the relation $\vDash$
11              $\mathcal{AF}^p \leftarrow \mathcal{AF}^p \cup \{AF^p | AF^p \in ncAF(S_{k-1}) \wedge AF^p.\mathcal{O} \vDash D\}$
12   **else**
13   put D into $\mathcal{DC}'$ // mark as unresolved
14   **end**
15   **end**
16   **forall** $AF^p \in \mathcal{AF}^p$ **do**
17           $\mathcal{DC}' \leftarrow \mathcal{DC}' - AF^p.\mathcal{I}$ // ignore inputs of predecessors
18   **end**
19         $k \leftarrow k - 1$ // move to previous $ncDC(S)$
20         $\mathcal{DC} \leftarrow \mathcal{DC}'$ // update unresolved inputs
21   **until** $\mathcal{DC} = \emptyset$ // until all inputs are resolved
22   mark all AFs in $\mathcal{AF}^p$ as the predecessors of AF
23   **end**
24   **end**
25   **return** the DAG

---

depend on AF_1. Using only `parallel` and `sequence` constructs prevents such execution from happening, thereby may increase the workflow execution time due to unnecessary waiting.

In order to eliminate such delays in execution time, we introduce a workflow optimization phase, which, instead of using combinations of `sequence` and/or `parallel` constructs, composes AFs into DAGs, as illustrated by Algorithm 8.4. In this algorithm, two nested loops (Lines 2 and 3) are used to locate predecessors of each AF in each $ncAF(S_i)$. This is done by resolving (i.e., finding the producers of) input DCs of each AF. For each AF, Algorithm 8.4 initializes unresolved input DCs $\mathcal{DC}$ with $AF.\mathcal{I}$ (Line 4), then tries to resolve them by checking against previous $ncDC(S_k)$ (Lines 9–15). If an unresolved input DC is contained in $ncDC(S_k)$, we mark all the AFs in $ncAF(S_{k-1})$ which produce this DC as predecessors of the AF (Line 11). Otherwise, the input DC is marked as unresolved temporarily (Line 13). When all unresolved input DCs in $\mathcal{DC}$ are checked against $ncDC(S_k)$, $\mathcal{DC}$ is updated through $\mathcal{DC}'$ by eliminating input DCs of the located predecessors

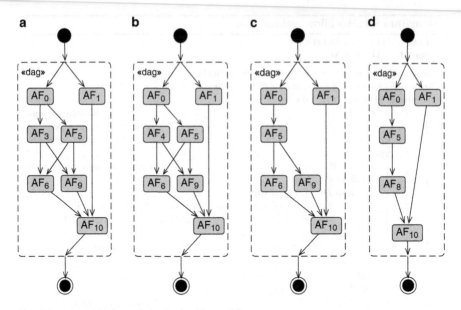

Fig. 8.5 Automatically optimized scientific workflows

(Lines 16 –18, 20). This is because these input DCs have been resolved in previous iterations and they are input to the predecessors of the AF. This process continues until all input DCs are resolved (Line 21).

Figure 8.5a–d show the optimized workflows of Fig. 8.4a–d, respectively. The optimization can be significant when the execution time of AF_1 is much longer than that of AF_0. Let us denote the execution time of AF_i by $t(AF_i)$. Figure 8.6 compares the execution of the workflow shown in Fig. 8.4d and that of its optimized version in Fig. 8.5d, where $t(AF_1) > t(AF_0) + t(AF_5) + t(AF_8)$. The processors P_1 and P_2 may be located in two different nodes. For the reasons of simplicity, the communication time between two processors and the overhead of the middleware are ignored. In Fig. 8.6, compared with the nonoptimized execution, AF_5 and AF_8 are executed in parallel with AF_1 in the optimized execution. This results in a total execution time of $t_4 - t_1 = t(AF_1) + t(AF_{10})$, which is less than the execution time of the nonoptimized workflow $t_5 - t_1 = t(AF_1) + t(AF_5) + t(AF_8) + t(AF_{10})$. The actual performance improvement achieved by employing workflow optimization on a real-world scientific workflow application is discussed in Sect. 8.7.

The scientific workflows composed by our control flow composition algorithm through the three phases achieve high quality because of (a) *portability*: the workflows are abstract and represented at the semantic level; (b) *fault tolerance*: the workflows may include alternative workflows thereby providing alternative execution paths in case some activities fail; and (c) *performance*: the workflows are optimized for execution time.

Fig. 8.6 Improvement of workflow optimization

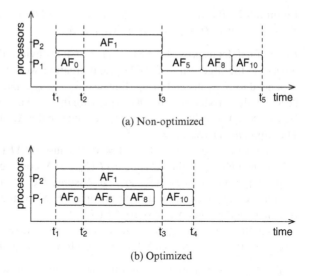

(a) Non-optimized

(b) Optimized

8.5.4 Algorithm Analysis

In this section, we present the four properties of our control flow composition algorithm, that is, *soundness*, *completeness*, *complexity*, and *quality*, through the following propositions.

Proposition 8.1 (Soundness). *Given an initial state s_{init} and a goal state s_{goal}, the workflows returned by the control flow composition algorithm, if any, are valid, that is, the inputs of each included AF are fulfilled either by s_{init} or by the outputs of other included AFs, and all required DCs specified in s_{goal} can be produced.*

Proof. In the phase of ADD graph creation, the ADD graph is built progressively based on data dependences. In other words, for each AF in $cAF(S_i)$, its inputs are fulfilled by the previous superstate S_i. In the phase of workflow extraction, $ncDC(S_i)$ and $ncAF(S_i)$ are calculated regressively from S_n to S_1. This ensures that whenever an AF in $cAF(S_i)$ is considered to be an ncAF, its input DCs are considered necessary. Its input DCs are fulfilled by the AFs in $ncAF(S_{i-1})$ where $i \in [0, n)$, or by s_{init}. Lemma 8.2 ensures that $\forall i \in [0, n), ncAF(S_i) \neq \emptyset$. Therefore, $altAF(S_i) \neq \emptyset$. According to the calculation of $altAF(S_i)$ given in Algorithm 8.3, any AF combination of $altAF(S_i)$ is sufficient to produce an alternative DC combination in $ncDC(S_{i+1})$. The phase of workflow optimization only removes unnecessary dependences among AFs. The fulfillment of the inputs of AFs is not affected. Therefore, the inputs of all AFs included in the generated workflows are fulfilled.

When a solution is found by the control flow composition algorithm, the final superstate S_n of the ADD graph satisfies $S_n \models s_{goal}$. Since all DCs in s_{goal} are ncDCs, they are kept in each extracted workflow. Therefore, all these DCs can be produced by each extracted workflow.

Lemma 8.2. *If a solution is found by the control flow composition algorithm, i.e.,* $S_n \vDash s_{goal}$, *then* $\forall i \in [0, n), ncAF(S_i) \neq \emptyset$

Proof. First, let us prove $ncAF(S_{n-1}) \neq \emptyset$. It is obvious that $S_{n-1} \nvDash s_{goal}$, because otherwise the algorithm of ADD graph creation would return when the graph is expanded to S_{n-1} instead of S_n. Because $S_n \vDash s_{goal}$ and $S_{n-1} \nvDash s_{goal}$, there must be an AF that produces some DCs which are in s_{goal} but not in S_{n-1}, that is, $AF.\mathcal{O} \cap (s_{goal} - S_{n-1}) \neq \emptyset$. This means, s_{goal} depends on the AF. That is, the AF is an ncAF. Therefore, $ncAF(S_{n-1}) \neq \emptyset$.

Then, let us prove $ncAF(S_{n-2}) \neq \emptyset$. Because $ncAF(S_{n-1}) \neq \emptyset$, let us assume $AF' \in ncAF(S_{n-1})$, then $AF' \in cAF(S_{n-1})$. According to the property (c) of the ADD graph, $AF'.\mathcal{I} \cap ncDC(S_{n-1}) \neq \emptyset$. Assume $DC' \in AF'.\mathcal{I} \cap ncDC(S_{n-1})$, DC' is an ncDC. Then, there must be an AF in $cAF(S_{n-2})$ that produces DC'. This AF is then an ncAF. Then we have $ncAF(S_{n-2}) \neq \emptyset$.

Continuing with this process, we can prove that the rest $ncAF(S)$ are not empty, i.e., $\forall i \in [0, n-2), ncAF(S_i) \neq \emptyset$. Therefore, $\forall i \in [0, n), ncAF(S_i) \neq \emptyset$.

Before the explanation of the following proposition, we present the definition of a *simple workflow*.

Definition 8.3. Given a set of DCs, and a DAG of AFs that can produce the set of DCs, the DAG of AFs is said to be a *simple workflow* if none of the AFs in the DAG is *redundant*. An AF is said to be *redundant* if removing the AF from the DAG does not affect the dependences of other AFs and the DAG can still produce the same set of DCs.

Proposition 8.4 (Completeness). *Given a set of AFs, an initial state* s_{init}, *and a goal state* s_{goal}, *if there exists a simple workflow* w *which accepts only the DCs given in* s_{init} *as input and can produce the DCs given in* s_{goal}, *then the workflow* w *can be found by the control flow composition algorithm.*

Proof. We split the AFs in the simple (i.e., DAG) workflow w into several groups. The first group gAF_0 includes all root AFs of the DAG. It is obvious that $\forall AF \in gAF_0, s_{init} \vDash AF.\mathcal{I}$ and applying such an AF to s_{init} can produce new DCs, i.e., $s_{init} \subsetneq (s_{init} + AF.\mathcal{O})$. This is because otherwise the AF would be redundant and w would not be a simple workflow. Then, we remove the AFs in gAF_0 from the DAG, and put all *new* root AFs of the resulting DAGs[1] into the second group gAF_1. It is obvious that $\forall AF \in gAF_1, s_{init} \cup \left(\bigcup_{AF' \in gAF_0} AF'.\mathcal{O} \right) \vDash AF.\mathcal{I}$. Because the new root AFs are not redundant, they can also produce new DCs. In the similar way, we can build other AF groups out of the rest AFs. By definition, each of these AF groups is actually part of $cAF(S)$ of each superstate in an ADD graph. That is,

---

[1]In the case where removing AFs from a DAG results in multiple small DAGs. *root AFs* means the root AFs of all those DAGs.

$\forall i \in [0, n) : gAF_i \subseteq cAF(S_i)$, where n is the number of AF groups. We put these AF groups into the ADD graph and connect them with data dependences according to their input and output. It is obvious that every AF in these AF groups will have a path to s_{goal} because they are not redundant. In other words, they are all ncAFs. Then, $\forall i \in [0, n) : gAF_i \in altAF(S_i)$. Then we can say that the workflow can be found by the control flow composition algorithm.

The execution time of our control flow composition algorithm is demanded mostly by the phase of ADD graph creation because this phase involves matching inputs of AFs with superstates through reasoning. This can also be proved by the experimental results given in Sect. 8.7. Therefore, the complexity analysis of the control flow composition algorithm focuses only on the phase of ADD graph creation. For the reasons of convenience, let us denote the set of all possible simple workflows by W and denote the number of AFs by x. As demonstrated by the following proposition, the worst case execution time taken by the control flow composition algorithm is a quadratic in x.

Proposition 8.5 (Complexity). *Given a set of x AFs, an initial state s_{init}, and a goal state s_{goal}, the time taken by the control flow composition algorithm to find W is quadratic in x if $W \neq \emptyset$.*

Proof. According to Sect. 8.5.1, the *basic operation* in the phase of ADD graph creation is to check whether an AF is a cAF for a given superstate. The number of the basic operation is determined by the number of AFs and the number of the superstates that are in an ADD graph. According to the property (a) of ADD graphs (see Sect. 8.4), the set of cAFs of each superstate are disjoint. Given x AFs, the maximum number of superstates in the ADD graph is $x + 1$, in which case, all sets of cAFs of each superstate have the minimum number of cAFs, i.e., 1. In other words, $\forall i \in [0, n) : |cAF(S_i)| = 1$. Here we assume that there are enough DCs defined in ASWO and associated with AFs such that the number of newly produced DCs in each superstate is greater than 0, i.e., $cDC(S_i) \neq \emptyset$. Note that if there are fewer DCs, the maximum number of superstates is less than $x + 1$; if there are more DCs, the maximum number of superstates is not affected. Therefore, given x AFs, the maximum number of superstates is $x + 1$. To expand the ADD graph to the superstate S_1, x basic operations are required because there are x AFs to be compared. Because $|cDC(S_i)| = 1$, expanding to S_2 requires $x - 1$ basic operations, expanding to S_3 requires $x - 2$ basic operations, and so on. The maximum total number of the basic operations is:

$$x + (x - 1) + (x - 2) + \ldots + 1 = \frac{x^2 + x}{2}$$

Therefore, the time complexity of the control flow composition algorithm is quadratic in the number of AFs.

Proposition 8.6 (Quality). *If a simple workflow is found by the control flow composition algorithm, the number of the superstates of the ADD graph is minimum, which also means that the length[2] of the found DAG workflow is minimum.*

Proof. Let us assume the control flow composition algorithm finds a solution when expanding the ADD graph to S_n. This means that $\forall i \in [0, n)$, $S_i \not\models s_{goal}$. Therefore, n is minimum.

8.5.5   Branches and Loops

With the help of AWDL constraints, the control flow composition algorithm can be extended to compose scientific workflows with loops and branches. The example constraints related to workflow composition are *to access the elements of a data collection in parallel, to produce a DC when another DC is produced*, etc.

Branches: Users can specify constrains for the goal state to obtain workflows with branches. For example, the goal state $s_{goal} = \{D_9, D_{10}(awdl:precondition= $ "$D_6=true$")$\}$ means that the composed scientific workflow must produce D_9 and D_{10}, and D_{10} must be produced when $D_6=true$ (assuming D_6 is a *boolean*). In this case, we first compose a workflow by invoking the control flow composition algorithm with $s_{goal1} = \{D_6, D_9\}$ as the goal state. The result is an ADD graph with $S_n \models s_{goal1}$. Then we compose another workflow with $s_{init} = S_n$ and $s_{goal2} = \{D_{10}\}$ as the goal state. Then we connect these two workflows through a *DecisionNode* which has an outgoing edge with the guard $[D_6=true]$ connecting to the second workflow, another outgoing edge connecting to an empty branch. Two branches are merged at the end of the second workflow.

Parallel Loops: In the initial state, users can also specify a data collection and how each data element is allowed to be accessed. For example, $s_{init} = \{D_1 \ (awdl:cardinality=multiple, awdl:access-order=parallel), D_2\}$ means that the user provided data is D_2 and a collection of D_1, and all D_1 can be accessed in parallel. In this case, we can compose a workflow by invoking the control flow composition algorithm with $s_{init} = \{D_1, D_2\}$ as the initial state. Then we can invoke the composed workflow in the loop body of a `for` construct with `parallel=`"*yes*" which iterates over the data collection of D_1. Automatic composition of workflows with counter loops is also possible with the help of the *range(start,stop,step)* construct. For example, users can specify an initial state $s_{init} = \{D_1(awdl:value-range=1:10:3, awdl:access-order=parallel), D_2\}$, where *1:10:3* indicates the loop counter, i.e., from 1 to 10 step by 3.

Sequential Loops: Users may specify a goal state $\{D_9, D_{10}(awdl:postcondition = $ "$D_{10} < 0.1)$"$\}$ which means when D_{10} is produced, its value must be less

---

[2]The length of a finite DAG is the number of edges of the longest directed path.

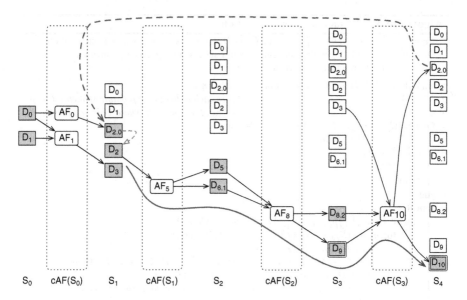

Fig. 8.7 An ADD graph for generation of sequential loops

Table 8.1 ncAF(S) and their input/output DCs

ncAF(S)	Input	Output
$ncAF(S_0)$	$\{D_0, D_1\}$	$\{D_2, D_3\}$
$ncAF(S_1)$	$\{D_1, D_2\}$	$\{D_5, D_6\}$
$ncAF(S_2)$	$\{D_5\}$	$\{D_8, D_9\}$
$ncAF(S_3)$	$\{D_3, D_8, D_9\}$	$\{D_2, D_{10}\}$

than 0.1 (e.g., a threshold value). A workflow with a sequential loop is required in this case. To compose a workflow with sequential loops, the control flow composition algorithm first composes a workflow with $s_{goal} = \{D_9, D_{10}\}$. Then it checks the possibility of sequential loops. Let us assume the workflow illustrated in Fig. 8.4d is considered for sequential loop generation. The corresponding simple ADD graph is shown in Fig. 8.7. Based on the ADD graph, we can obtain the input and output DCs of $ncAF(S)$ as Table 8.1. The control flow composition algorithm checks output DCs starting from $ncAF(S_3)$ (because it produces D_{10}) to see which DCs can be input to any previous $ncAF(S_i)(i < 3)$ and thereby produces new D_{10}. It is obvious that $D_{2.0}$ produced by AF_{10} can be input to AF_5 (indicated by the dash line), which consequently updates D_{10} (indicated by the solid line). Based on this, a workflow with a *do-while* loop can be generated, and AF_5, AF_8, and AF_{10} are sequentially executed in the loop body. In case of multiple possibilities of sequential loops found, user interactions are required. The pseudocode for the sequential loop generation is illustrated by Algorithm 8.5. Lines 3–9 find in which superstate the input Data Class D is first produced. Then, the algorithm tries to find

---

Algorithm 8.5: Sequential loop generation

Input	: simple ADD graph;	Data Class $D \in s_{goal}$ associated with a postcondition
Output	: A workflow with a sequential loop if successful, options of sequential loops for	
	users to select, or an error message	

1 build the $ncAF(S)$ input and output table, as Table 8.1
2 $\mathcal{T} \leftarrow \emptyset$ // *set of triples each indicating a possible sequential loop*
3 $k \leftarrow 0$ // *index of a superstate where D is first produced*
4 **for** $ncDC(S_i) \leftarrow ncDC(S_n)$ **to** $ncDC(S_0)$ **do**
5   $\quad$ **if** $D \in ncDC(S_i)$ **then**
6   $\quad\quad$ $k \leftarrow i$;
7   $\quad\quad$ break;
8   $\quad$ **end**
9 **end**
10 **repeat**
11 $\quad$ **forall** $D' \in \left(\bigcup_{AF \in ncAF(S_{k-1})} AF.\mathcal{O} - ncDC(S_k) \right)$ **do**
12 $\quad\quad$ **for** $ncAF(S_j) \leftarrow ncAF(S_{k-1})$ **to** $ncAF(S_0)$ **do**
   $\quad\quad\quad$ // *see Equation 8.1 for the relation* $\models$
13 $\quad\quad\quad$ **if** $\exists AF' \in ncAF(S_j) : AF' \, \delta \, D \wedge \exists D'' \in AF'.\mathcal{I} : D' \models D''$ **then**
   $\quad\quad\quad\quad$ // *D' in S_k can be input to AF' at $ncAF(S_j)$*
14 $\quad\quad\quad\quad$ put a triple $\langle D', k, j \rangle$ into $\mathcal{T}$ // *found a possible sequential loop*
15 $\quad\quad\quad$ **end**
16 $\quad\quad$ **end**
17 $\quad$ **end**
18 $\quad$ $k \leftarrow k - 1$
19 **until** $k = 0$
20 **if** $\mathcal{T} = \emptyset$ **then**
21 $\quad$ **return** sequential loop is impossible
22 **else if** $|\mathcal{T}| = 1$ **then**
23 $\quad$ **return** create a workflow with a *do-while* loop based on $\mathcal{T}$
24 **else if** $|\mathcal{T}| > 1$ **then**
25 $\quad$ **return** options of sequential loops to select
26 **end**

DCs $\in S_k$ which are not ncDCs and can be input to an ncAF of a previous superstate and thereby further update D (Lines 11–17). This process is done for all previous superstates except S_0 (Lines 10–19).

8.6   Data Flow Composition Algorithm

When control flow among AFs in scientific workflows is established (either manually or automatically based on our control flow composition algorithm presented in Sect. 8.5), data flow composition can be done automatically in two steps: (a) locating possible source data ports of each sink data port through backwards control flow traversing, and (b) matching source data ports against sink data ports based on data semantics.

Fig. 8.8 Data flow among
source and sink data ports

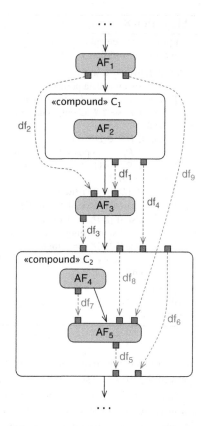

Figure 8.8 illustrates part of a scientific workflow, where compound activities C_1 and C_2 can be any compound activity such as if, for, while, dag, etc. The AF AF_2, AF_4, and AF_5 are children activities of C_1 and C_2, respectively. Some control flow edges in the compound activities are omitted for the reasons of simplicity. There are three cases to find source data ports for a given sink data port: (a) each input data port of an atomic or compound activity is a sink data port. The possible source data ports of such a sink data port are output data ports of all predecessors of this activity. For example, df_1 and df_2 illustrate possible data flow for input data ports of AF_3, and df_3 and df_4 show possible data flow for input data ports of C_1; (b) each output data port of a compound activity is also a sink data port. The source data ports of such an output data port can only be the output data ports of the children activities or some data ports (e.g., dataLoop ports) of this compound activity. For example, df_5 and df_6 show possible data flow for two output data ports of C_2; and (c) if an activity has a parent activity, the possible source data ports of each input data port of this activity includes not only the output data ports of its predecessors inside its parent activity, but also the input data ports of the parent activity and the output data ports of predecessors of the parent activity. For example, df_7, df_8, and df_9 show possible data flow for the input data ports of AF_5: from output data ports

---

Algorithm 8.6: Automatic data flow composition

Input	: a semantic scientific workflow w with control flow established.
Output	: workflow w with data flow established.

1 **forall** *Activity* $a \in w$ **do**
2 $\quad$ $\mathcal{DP} \leftarrow$ input data ports of a
3 $\quad$ **if** *a is a compound activity* **then**
4 $\quad\quad$ $|$ $\mathcal{DP} \leftarrow \mathcal{DP} \cup$ output data ports of a
5 $\quad$ **end**
6 $\quad$ **forall** $DP \in \mathcal{DP}$ **do**
7 $\quad\quad$ $\mathcal{DP}_s \leftarrow$ all possible source data ports of DP
8 $\quad\quad$ $\mathcal{DP}'_s \leftarrow \{DP' \mid DP' \in \mathcal{DP}_s \wedge$ the data class of DP' is a subclass of the data class of $DP\}$
9 $\quad\quad$ **if** $|\mathcal{DP}'_s| = 1$ **then** $\qquad\qquad$ *// exactly one matching source data port found*
10 $\quad\quad\quad$ $|$ set source of DP to DP' $\qquad\qquad$ *// compose data flow automatically*
11 $\quad\quad$ **else if** $|\mathcal{DP}'_s| > 1$ **then** $\qquad\quad$ *// multiple matching source data ports found*
12 $\quad\quad\quad$ $|$ list matching data sources for users to select
13 $\quad\quad$ **else if** $|\mathcal{DP}'_s| = 0$ **then** $\qquad\quad$ *// no matching source data port found*
14 $\quad\quad\quad$ $|$ notify users that no source data available
15 $\quad\quad$ **end**
16 $\quad$ **end**
17 **end**
18 **return** w

---

of its predecessor, from input data ports of its parent activity, and from output data ports of the predecessors of its parent activity.

The data flow composition algorithm is illustrated by Algorithm 8.6 which employs two nested loops (Line 1 and Line 6) to find matching source data ports for all sink data ports based on their data semantics. If the number of matching source data ports for a given sink data port is one (Line 9), the source of the sink data port can be set to the found source data port; thus data flow between the sink data port and the source data port is established automatically. Otherwise, if the number of the matching source data ports is zero, e.g., the input data port of workflows, users are required to provide the concrete data sources, e.g., *gsiftp://host/dir/file*. If the number of the matching source data ports is greater than one, users have to select one from the multiple matching data sources. Note that, since semantics are adopted in our approach, the likelihood that more than one data sources match a given sink data port is much less than the approach based on data type comparison. This will be demonstrated in Sect. 8.7.

8.7 Experimental Results

Our control flow composition algorithm is implemented in Java as part of the ASKALON scientific workflow composition tool where, to generate scientific workflows, users can specify input and output data semantics (i.e., data classes), and optionally the AFs which must be included or excluded. The reasoning part is implemented using the Jena APIs [85]. The data flow composition algorithm is implemented as a plugin of our workflow composition tool. The plugin composes data flow automatically while control flow is determined.

We evaluated our approach through a series of experiments: (a) the composition of a scientific workflow in a simulated domain, to test how our control flow composition algorithm behaves in the case where thousands of AFs are available; (b) the composition of a real-world meteorology scientific workflow application Meteo2 [151], to illustrate the execution time of the control flow composition algorithm for a real world case; (c) the comparison of the execution time of optimized and nonoptimized real-world scientific workflows; and (d) the composition of data flow of Meteo2, to see to what extend the data flow of Meteo2 can be composed automatically.

In the first experiment, we developed an ontology which contains thousands of AFs (namely, $AF_0, AF_1, \ldots$) and thousands of DCs (namely, $D_0, D_1, \ldots$). In order to measure the worst case execution time of the control flow composition algorithm, as described in Sect. 8.5.4, these AFs are defined in the following way: AF_i accepts D_i and a random number (between 0 and 10) of DCs from $\{D_0, \ldots, D_{i-1}\}$ as input, and produces D_{i+1} and a random number (between 0 and 10) of DCs in $\{D_0, \ldots, D_{i-1}\}$ as output. Thus, all AFs can be pipelined. The reason that we use a random number (between 0 and 10) of DCs as input and output of AFs is based on our experiences in multiple scientific domains such as material science, astrophysics, and meteorology where the number of the input and output ports of workflow activities varies from 0 to around 10. This observation actually makes the composition of scientific workflows more difficult if a classical state space searching-based Artificial Intelligence planning algorithm is used, due to the huge number of states. In this experiment, AFs are defined as below:

$$AF_0 : (D_0) \rightarrow (D_1)$$
$$AF_1 : (D_0, D_1) \rightarrow (D_2)$$
$$AF_2 : (D_2) \rightarrow (D_1, D_3)$$
$$AF_3 : (D_0, D_1, D_3) \rightarrow (D_4)$$
$$\ldots$$

Then we ran the control flow composition algorithm on a normal desktop computer (2 GB memory and one 2.4 GHz Intel Core 2 Duo CPU) to compose scientific workflows using these AFs. The Java runtime environment used was JRE 1.5.0_16. Obviously, we obtain a workflow consisting of a sequence of AFs. Although the structure of the composed workflow is simple, the number of the basic operations invoked in the control flow composition algorithm is maximized. By specifying a suitable initial state, e.g., $s_{init} = \{D_0\}$, and a goal state, e.g., $s_{goal} = \{D_{1000}\}$, we can obtain the worst case execution time of the control flow composition algorithm.

Figure 8.9 illustrates the experimental results of the execution time of the control flow composition algorithm with two curves: the total execution time, the execution

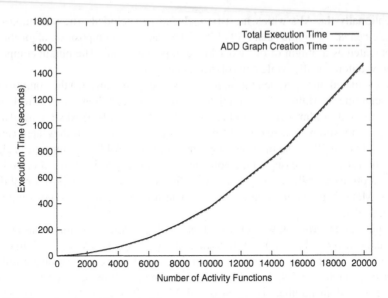

Fig. 8.9 Execution time of the control flow composition algorithm in the worst case

time of the ADD graph creation phase. The x-axis is the number of AFs. We can observe that the execution time of ADD graph creation is very close to the total execution time, i.e., most of the execution time of the control flow composition algorithm is spent in the phase of ADD graph creation. The trend analysis shows that the worst case total execution time of the control flow composition algorithm to compose a scientific workflow is a quadratic in the number of AFs. If 1,000 AFs are defined in ontologies in a certain domain, the control flow composition algorithm has a worst case execution time of 7.04 s; for 2,000 AFs, the worst case is only 20.70 s. We also measured the *heap* memory usage in the Java virtual machine (JVM) when composing these scientific workflows with the control flow composition algorithm. The results are illustrated in Fig. 8.10, where the values are calculated based on the measurements of *java.lang.management.MemoryMXBean*, the management interface for the memory system of JVM provided since Java 1.5. Because of the automatic garbage collection mechanism of the JVM, we consider the *heap* memory usage illustrated here as an estimation of the amount of the memory that are allocated for the objects of our workflow composition program, including the objects for storing the ontologies and the objects required by the control flow composition algorithm itself. According to what we observed, roughly 10% of the *heap* memory is used by the latter. We can conclude that our control flow composition algorithm uses a reasonable amount of memory. Note that the actual memory usage of our workflow composition program as provided by the operating system is usually higher than those measured here.

In the second experiment, we composed the real-world scientific workflow application Meteo2 [151] using the control flow composition algorithm on the

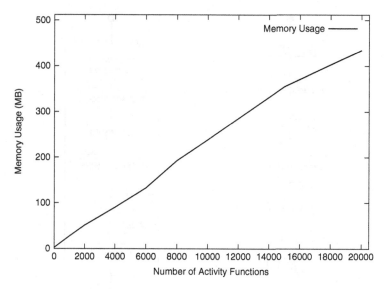

Fig. 8.10 Memory usage of the control flow composition algorithm in the worst case

same desktop computer. The ontology, provided by the Institute of Meteorology and Geophysics, University of Innsbruck, consists of 19 AFs. As input to the algorithm, users provide a list of input DCs and a list of output DCs as well as their corresponding constraints, e.g.,

Input: SimulationCaseData
   {awdl:cadinality= "multiple", awdl:access-order= "parallel"}
  SimulationDuration
  InitialSimulationDuration
  AnalyzedSurface
  MinValueOfHorizontalDiffusion
   {awdl:value-range= "0:80:10", awdl:access-order= "parallel"}
  TimeStepIndex
Output: RAMSModeledAtmosphereAndSurfaceAll
  DumpAll

Our control flow composition algorithm then builds an ADD graph, extracts workflows from the graph, and optimized the extracted workflows. Figure 8.11a illustrates the extracted workflow which consists of a combination of `sequence` and `parallel` constructs. Because the activity *REVUCompare* and *RAVER* can be executed before *RAMSAll* finishes, the workflow is optimized with a `dag` construct (Fig. 8.11b). The composed workflow so far corresponds one *simulation case*. Because a collection of *SimulationCaseData* and a collection of *MinValueOfHorizontalDiffusion* are provided and each elements of the collections can be accessed in

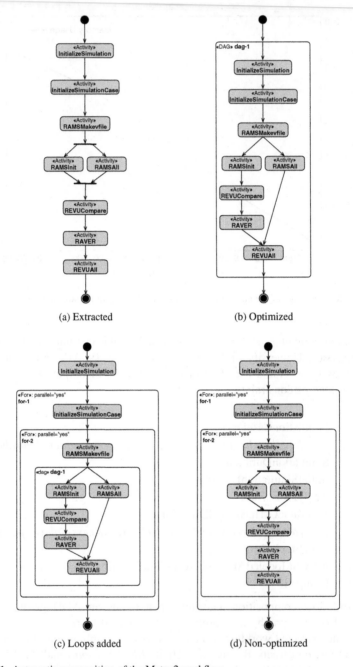

(a) Extracted   (b) Optimized

(c) Loops added   (d) Non-optimized

Fig. 8.11 Automatic composition of the Meteo2 workflow

Table 8.2 The nodes used for the execution of both Meteo2 workflows

Node	CPU	CPU Number	GHz	LRM	Location
karwendel	Dual Core AMD Opteron	8	2.4	SGE	Innsbruck
altix1	Itanium 2	8	1.4	PBS	Innsbruck
schafberg	Itanium 2	8	1.4	PBS	Salzburg
altix1jku	Itanium 2	8	1.4	PBS	Linz
c703-pc1801	Pentium 4	8	2.8	Torque	Innsbruck
c703-pc2601	Pentium 4	8	2.8	Torque	Innsbruck

parallel, the dag construct is put inside of two nested parallel for constructs. Since the activity *InitializeSimulation* consumes neither *SimulationCaseData* or *MinValueOfHorizontalDiffusion*, we put it outside of the two parallel for constructs to avoid unnecessary computations. Similarly, the activity *InitializeSimulation* is put outside of *for-2*. This leads to the final workflow as shown in Fig. 8.11c. If no workflow optimization is adopted, the final workflow would be the one shown in Fig. 8.11d. The total execution time for the composition of the workflow is 0.64 s for the optimized version and 0.54 for the nonoptimized version. We conclude that the control flow composition algorithm is fast enough for these two workflows.

In the third experiment, we executed the optimized and the non-optimized Meteo2 workflows on a distributed system installed on various sites in Austria [12] through ASKALON [51]. A subset of the computational resources which have been used for this experiment is summarized in Table 8.2. First, we executed one simulation case using one CPU (denoted by "1CPU,1CASE," and similar for the others). Obviously the execution time of both workflows are similar in this case because no parallelism can be employed. Since the maximum number of parallel jobs in one simulation case is two, we then increased the number of simulation cases and the number of CPUs such that the number of CPUs is twice the number of simulation cases. Note that if the number of CPUs is more than twice the number of simulation cases, the additional CPUs cannot be used. If the number of CPUs is less than twice the number of simulation cases, the execution time of both Meteo2 workflows are similar because the execution of all simulation cases are interleaved and the differences in control flow dependences in single simulation cases become insignificant. Figure 8.12 compares the corresponding average execution time of both Meteo2 workflows in our experiments. We can see that the execution time of the optimized Meteo2 workflow is less than that of the nonoptimized one. Specifically, when we execute four simulation cases on eight CPUs on *karwendel*, execution time is reduced by 25% (270.64s vs. 203.37s). The reduction in execution time in other cases varies from 9% to 20%. The corresponding speedup is improved by up to 2.24, as illustrated in Fig. 8.13.

In the fourth experiment, we applied our data flow composition algorithm to the meteorology scientific workflow Meteo2. Figure 8.14 compares the number of the available *data sources* for each data port of AFs in the workflow in three cases: the total number of *data sources*, denoted by *No heuristics*, the number of *data*

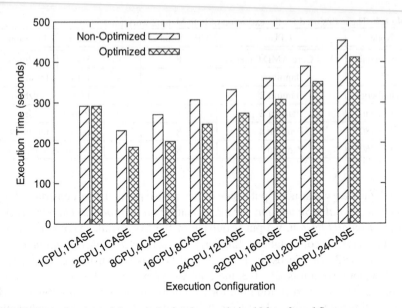

Fig. 8.12 Execution time of the optimized and nonoptimized Meteo2 workflows

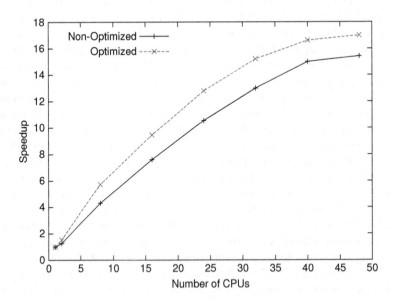

Fig. 8.13 Speedup of the optimized and nonoptimized Meteo2 workflows

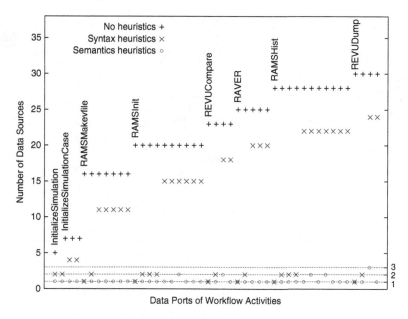

Fig. 8.14 Comparison of the numbers of available data sources for data ports in Meteo2

sources filtered based on data types of data ports, denoted by *Syntax heuristics*, and the number of *data sources* filtered based on semantics of data ports, denoted by *Semantics heuristics*. The horizontal axis indicates the data ports specified in the workflow, in the order in which they are available during the workflow execution. We marked the name of each AF above the plot point of the first data port of this AF in the figure. Obviously, if the number of available *data sources* for a data port is 1, the data flow of this data port can be established automatically because there is only one option. In the case of *No heuristics*, there is no change in the number of *data sources* for all input data ports of an AF because no syntactic or semantic information of data ports is considered. In the case of *Syntax heuristics*, most of the numbers of data sources are larger because many data ports in the workflow have type *awdl:file*. In contrast, the case *Semantics heuristics* shows that the numbers of *data sources* of 42 out of 45 (93%) data ports are 1, i.e., the corresponding data flow can be established automatically. The reason that some numbers in case of *Semantics heuristics* are still greater than 1 (which are 2 or 3) is as follows. Both AF *InitializeSimulationCase* and AF *RAMSMakevfile* produce data *Soil*, thus two *data sources* are available for the data ports with data semantics *Soil* of the successor AFs (e.g., *RAMSInit*); AF *RAMSInit* produces two *RAMSModeledAtmosphere* and AF *RAMSAll* produces one *RAMSModeledAtmosphere*, which means three *data sources* are available for the data port with data semantics *RAMSModeledAtmosphere* of AF *REVUAll*.

For those data ports which have more than one possible *data source*, Fig. 8.15 illustrates how the user interaction can be done to establish the corresponding data

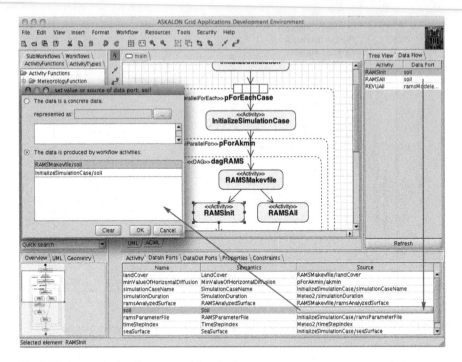

Fig. 8.15 Automatic data flow composition plugin

flow. When users click one of the three data ports in the GUI of the automatic scientific workflow plugin, the corresponding activity in the *drawing space* and the data port in the *attribute panel* are selected. Upon clicking the source field, multiple matching data sources for a particular data port are shown for the user to select.

8.8 Summary

In this chapter, we formalized the scientific workflow composition problem based on the STRIPS language and presented our algorithm for automatic composition of high quality (portable, fault tolerant, and optimized) scientific workflows. The control flow composition algorithm composes semantically described workflow activities, i.e., Activity Functions (AFs), into scientific workflows by employing progression to create an AF Data Dependence (ADD) graph and regression to extract workflows, including alternative ones if available. The control flow composition algorithm also optimizes extracted workflows in order to deal with the heterogeneous nature of distributed systems and workflow activities. The time complexity of the control flow composition algorithm is a quadratic in the number of AFs. With the help of AWDL constraints, we also extended the control flow composition algorithm for composition of scientific workflows with branches, as well as parallel and sequential loops. The composition of scientific workflows with the control flow composition algorithm in domains with up to 20,000 AFs further demonstrated the analyzed time complexity. The composition of a real-world meteorology workflow Meteo2 takes around half a second. By applying our workflow optimization techniques, the execution time of the Meteo2 workflow is reduced by up to 25% and the speedup is increased by up to 2.24. About 93% of data flow links in the scientific workflow Meteo2 can be composed automatically by our data flow composition algorithm.

We believe that our graph-based approach of automatic scientific workflow composition is the most feasible one among all methods introduced so far. Assuming that ontologies for application domains are given, it demonstrates good potential to be used as part of production workflow environments, in contrast to most related work, which has been largely evaluated against experimental implementations. Our approach has been integrated into ASKALON and is used by numerous application groups for their daily work and research with scientific workflows.

Part V
Related Work

Chapter 9
Related Work

9.1 Overview of Main Workflow Systems and Languages

In this section, we present an overview of the main workflow languages and systems with which our approach is compared. The list of these workflow languages and systems, by no means complete, includes BPEL [6, 39, 129], XPDL [179, 180], Kepler [2, 105], Pegasus [42], Taverna [133], Triana [36, 171, 174], Karajan [195], UNICORE [192], ICENI [110], GWENDIA [120], GWorkflowDL [1], P-GRADE [136], and IWIR [141].

BPEL is an XML-based OASIS [134] standard language for the specification of Web Service orchestration. BPEL was originally released as a combination of IBM's Web Services Flow Language (WSFL) [84] and Microsoft's XLANG [119] specification. In April 2007, OASIS released WS-BPEL 2.0 [129] with a significant enhancement. BPEL is an *execution* language. A BPEL process specifies the exact order in which participating services should be invoked, for example, sequentially, in parallel, depending on certain conditions, or iteratively. One can also declare variables, copy and assign values to them. By combining all these constructs, programmers can define complex scientific workflows. A BPEL workflow can also be presented as a new service, which is why BPEL is often described as a language for recursive composition. BPEL focuses only on Web Services, while scientific workflows may consists of not only Web Services, but also executables, shell scripts, and Java classes, etc.

XPDL is an XML-based, WfMC [178] standard language for the description of process definitions. XPDL aims to be an intermediate language used to interchange business process definitions between different workflow products such as modeling tools. In contrast to the *execution* language BPEL, the goal of XPDL is to store and exchange process diagrams. It does not guarantee precise execution semantics. Generally, it is not possible to take a workflow representation from the design tool of one vendor, and process it with the workflow engine of another vendor, because of vendor-specific information. XPDL is a process design format that literally represents the *drawing* of process definitions. Therefore, XPDL contains

J. Qin and T. Fahringer, *Scientific Workflows*, DOI 10.1007/978-3-642-30715-7_9,
© Springer-Verlag Berlin Heidelberg 2012

elements to hold not only executable aspects which would be used to execute processes, but also graphical information, such as the x and y positions of nodes. XPDL is effectively the file format or serialization of Business Process Management Notation (BPMN) [130], as well as any non-BPMN design method or process model which uses the XPDL meta-model in their underlying definition. XPDL specifies business processes mainly through the following XML elements: *Package*, *Application*, *WorkflowProcess*, *Activity*, *Transition*, *Participant*, *DataField*, and *DataType*. *Package* is the container holding a set of business processes which may share the same tools and participants. *Application* is a list of all applications, services, or tools required and invoked by the processes defined within the process definition or surrounding package. *WorkflowProcess* is used to define workflow processes or parts of workflow processes. A *WorkflowProcess* is composed of *Activity*, *Transition*, and process relevant data entities. *Activity* in XPDL is used to define each elementary activity that makes up a process. It is a boarder concept including not only computational tasks, but also transitions.

Kepler, mainly developed by the University of California, is built on the Ptolemy II system [40] which aims to model complex, heterogeneous, and concurrent systems and engineering applications. Kepler is a data flow-oriented Grid workflow development environment based on an actor-oriented modeling paradigm. Its workflow language, the Modeling Markup Language (MoML) [100], allows the specification of a workflow that includes *actors* and a *director*. *Actors* correspond to reusable workflow components. Actors have input and output ports which provide the communication interface to other actors. The *director* gives the execution semantics of dependencies among actors. The strengths of Kepler include its library of actors, which are local applications and Grid actors for access authentication, file transfer, job execution, job monitoring, and service discovery, and its suite of directors that provide flexible control strategies for the composition of actors.

Pegasus is developed by the University of South California. At the time of writing, Pegasus and DAGMan [37] have been integrated into a single system called Pegasus Workflow Management System (Pegasus-WMS) [139], which provides users with an end-to-end workflow solution. Pegasus takes an abstract workflow description in a form of a Directed Acyclic Graph in XML format (DAX) and generates a concrete executable workflow description by mapping computations onto Grid resources. The executable workflow can then be submitted to DAGMan for execution on the Grid. The generation of DAX can be done using Chimera Virtual Data System (VDS) [60], or using semantic technologies such as Wings [66]. Chimera VDS is a system to capture and reuse information on how data are derived by computations [7]. It consists of a Virtual Data Catalog (VDC), for representing data derivation procedures and derived data, and a Virtual Data Language (VDL) [207] interpreter that translates user requests into data definition and query operations on the data catalog. VDL formalizes descriptions of how a program can be invoked, and records its potential and/or actual invocations. The abstract description of how a program can be invoked (e.g., which parameters it needs, which files it reads as input, what environment is required, etc.) is called a *transformation*. Each invocation of a transformation with a specific set of input values and/or files is called a *derivation* [7]. Given a logical file name, VDS can generate a Directed Acyclic Graph (DAG) workflow which can be submitted to the Grid via DAGMan to create the requested file. Wings [66] is a workflow creation system that uses semantic representation and planning techniques to support the creation of workflow templates and instances.

Taverna, developed by the myGrid [123] team, is a data centric workbench for the composition and enactment of bioinformatic workflow applications. Taverna workflow is a linked graph of *processors* which represent Web Services or other executable components, each of which transforms a set of data inputs into a set of data outputs. Taverna workflows are represented in a high-level, XML-based, conceptual language called Scufl (Simple Conceptual Unified Flow Language) [133] in which each processing step of the workflow represents one atomic task. A Scufl workflow consists of three main entities: (1) *processors*, which is a transformation that accepts a set of input data and produces a set of output data. Processors are implemented as either local Java classes or Web Services [191], (2) *data links*, which mediate the flow of data between a data source and a data sink, and (3) *coordination constraints*, each of which links two processors and controls their execution. Unlike Kepler and Triana, Taverna does not provide an interactive visual workflow editor, instead, a static workflow viewer is available.

Triana, developed by Cardiff University, is a graphical Problem Solving Environment (PSE) providing a user portal for the composition of scientific applications. Users compose applications by dragging and dropping programming components, called *units* or *tools*. In the Triana workflow system, there is a middleware independent abstraction layer which consists of GridLab Grid Application Toolkit (GAT) [173], focusing on Grid-oriented tasks such as job submissions and file transfers, and the Grid Application Prototype (GAP) [36], focusing on service-oriented tasks such as Web service or JXTA service invocation. By using the GAT/GAP layer, Triana allows users to build workflows that mix existing technologies such as Globus job submission and Web Service invocation, and to incorporate new technologies as they become available by developing the corresponding adapters.

Karajan is a Grid parallel task management language and an execution engine, developed within the Java CoG Kit [195]. The Karajan language is a common purpose XML-based language which aims to provide an easy-to-use tool to define and manage complex jobs on computational Grids, while keeping scalability and offering some advanced features, such as failure handling, checkpointing, dynamic execution, and distributed execution. Karajan supports a range of Grid back-end services, through the Java CoG Kit Core abstraction layer, making it easy to work with heterogeneous Grid environments.

UNICORE is a Grid middleware system which aims to provide seamless, secure, and intuitive access to distributed resources for the German high performance computing centers and their users [49]. UNICORE also provides a programming environment to design and execute Grid workflows.

ICENI (Imperial College e-Science Network Infrastructure) is a collection of Grid middleware used for providing and coordinating Grid services for e-Science applications. Workflows in ICENI [111] are expressed in a simplified YAWL [193].

GWENDIA is a data-driven Grid workflow language. It leverages array programming principles to ease data-intensive workflow applications. Its *iteration strategies* allow programmers to express a wide set of data parallel executions in a compact framework.

Grid Workflow Description Language (GWorkflowDL) is developed in the European project *Knowledge-based Workflow System for Grid Applications (K-Wf Grid)* [88]. It is an XML-based language for representing scientific workflows based on High-Level Petri Nets (HLPNs), a bipartite graph in which nodes called *places* are linked to nodes called *transitions* by directed edges. GWorkflowDL consists of two parts: the generic part defines workflow structures, reflecting the data and control flow dependences in scientific workflows, and the execution part defines how the workflow should be executed in a specific Grid computing environment.

P-GRADE Portal conciliates both task and service-based workflows by providing a unique GUI for describing scientific workflow in a high-level framework [67]. P-GRADE is interfaced with both DAGMan for dealing with workflows of tasks and MOTEUR (hoMe-made OpTimisEd scUfl enactoR) [67] for handling workflows of services.

IWIR is a workflow language developed in the EU FP7 SHIWA project [163]. It is designed as an intermediate workflow language among scientific workflow systems, in order to enable interoperability of workflow systems across different languages and different Distributed Computing Infrastructures (DCIs).

In addition, xWFL is a simple and flexible XML-based workflow language used by the Workflow Enactment Engine (WFEE) [203]. The workflow structure consists of three parts, namely parameter definition, task definitions, and data link definitions. The Grid Service Flow Language (GSFL) [95] supports the specification of workflow descriptions for Grid services in the OGSA framework [59].

Many of these workflow systems and languages contain elements very similar to AWDL, albeit with different terminology. For example, AWDL *activities* are conceptually the same as Kepler *actors*, Pegasus *derivation*, Taverna *processors*, and Triana *units/tools*. In the following sections, we present a systematic comparison between the most relevant workflow systems/languages and our approach.

9.2   Programming

Recalling the motivations presented in Sect. 1.1, one can draw the following conclusions: A scientific workflow language that is abstract and independent of specific implementation technologies is essential for programming on the dynamic and heterogeneous distributed computing environment; a sophisticated type system (e.g., data types, activity types) in scientific workflow languages can help users find the potential workflow components and prevent composition time errors from happening in scientific workflow applications; complex control flow (e.g., conditional branches, sequential, parallel loops, etc.) and data flow (e.g., data collections) support is often required by scientific applications; workflow modularization and reuse can simplify the design of large and complex scientific workflow applications; with standards-based graphical tools, users can compose scientific workflows without knowing the exact syntax of scientific workflow languages; and semantic support in scientific workflow languages is desired in order to enable scientists to compose their scientific workflows with their own domain knowledge. Based on this consideration, in the following subsections, we will compare the related workflow systems and languages with our approach from the following aspects: *abstraction, type system, control flow, data flow, modularization and reuse, graphical tools*, and *semantic support*.

9.2.1 Abstraction

BPEL supports the specification of not only executable processes but also abstract processes. BPEL abstract processes describe process behavior partially without covering every detail of execution [18]. One of the purposes of BPEL abstract process is to use an abstract process as a starting point for developing an executable process [18]. However, this is often not done automatically. In contrast, the purpose of abstract scientific workflow in AWDL is to simplify scientific workflow specifications and abstract scientific workflows can be mapped to concrete (or executable) scientific workflows dynamically and automatically.

Services or tools required and invoked by XPDL processes can either refer to concrete computational entities or be declared without specific implementation, e.g., just by being named. The purpose of having named services or tools is to handle multi-platform environments, where a different program (or function) has to be invoked for each platform. From this point of view, XPDL abstracts from the concrete implementation or environment (thus these aspects are not of interest at process definition time). However, it is not clear how input and output of the named services or tools are specified. In addition, since XPDL only deals with the store of process definitions, XPDL does not provide how the named services or tools can be mapped to concrete computational entities.

Actors in Kepler can either be local processes or invoke remote services such as Web Services or a GridFTP transfer. These actors are implemented on per technology basis [171]. The example actors are *GridFTP* actor, *SSHFileCopier* actor, *WebService* actor, *Soaplab* actors, *GlobusJob* actor [90], etc. This approach does not shield the domain scientists from the low-level implementation technologies and make the Kepler workflows concrete. To free programmers from making technology decisions early on in the design process, Altintas et al. [3] presents a Grid workflow framework for Kepler by making abstract (i.e., implementation independent) actors for common workflow components such as data movement. However, in our opinion, the low-level tasks such as data movement should not be part of scientific workflow models but part of workflow engines which can execute those tasks dynamically based on where source actors and target actors are scheduled and executed. The work [28] presented a novel hybrid type system in Kepler for modeling scientific data that separates structural data types and semantic data types. This is very similar to the separation of data semantics and data representations in our approach.

The Chimera Virtual Data System (VDS) [60] aims to abstract workflows from the details of implementation through the separation of logical and physical data representation. Given a logical file name, VDS can generate a DAG workflow which is abstract in the sense that no information about physical resources where workflow tasks will be executed is encoded in the workflow. This idea of abstraction is similar to the idea of Activity Type adopted in AWDL.

Unlike VDS, the workflows created in Taverna are concrete due to the fact that Taverna relies on users to make the choice of resources or services, although in some cases users can also provide a set of services for a particular workflow component to support fault tolerance. According to [106], the future versions of Taverna will include late service binding capabilities. However, it is not clear whether the late binding will be done automatically.

Triana Grid workflows are abstract from underlying Grid middleware technologies through the use of the high-level programming interface GAT/GAP. The GAT/GAP layer is designed to hide implementation technologies but not hardware resources. In fact, Triana users are often required at composition time to provide the hardware resources where the workflow tasks are executed, except that in some cases, e.g., GRMS job submissions, the hardware resource information can be omitted and the selection of resources is left to the Grid resource manager [171].

GWorkflowDL [82] focuses on workflows of Web Services only. It supports Grid workflow descriptions at four different levels of abstraction, namely, *abstract operation*, *Web Service classes*, *Web Service candidates*, and *Web Service operations*. The level of *abstract operation* represents user requests. This level contains a single abstract operation which has not yet been mapped to potential workflows. The level of *Web Service classes* represents workflow functionalities. This level consists of operations of Web Service classes. The workflows at this level are abstract workflows which are independent from concrete resources. In the level of *Web Service candidates*, each Web Service class is mapped to a set of Web Service candidates that are currently available within the Grid environment. The level of *Web Service operations* represent concrete workflows. In this level, the workflow scheduler selects Web Service instances from Web Service candidates according to user-defined policies such as "fastest" or "cheapest."

IWIR [141] abstracts from specific implementations or installations of computational entities by using a concept called *Task Type*. A *Task Type* is composed of a type name and a set of input and output ports with corresponding data types. A *Task Type* is used as an abstract placeholder to represent a set of *Task Deployments* implementing the given *Task Type*. The Activity Type in AWDL has influenced the specification of IWIR's *Task Type*.

Other workflow languages like Karajan [195] and ICENI [110] include low-level tasks such as data transfers, the sending or receiving of data, etc.

In summary, most existing work either asks users to make technology decisions early on at workflow composition time or includes low-level tasks such as data transfers or sending/receiving data, etc. In contrast, AWDL is an advanced and user-oriented scientific workflow language that shields (a) specific implementation technologies; (b) low-level tasks; and (c) underlying data type systems (by using semantic technologies) from programmers. AWDL workflows are described at three levels (semantic, syntactic, and concrete) of abstraction. AWDL programmers compose scientific workflows at the semantic level. A semantic scientific workflow can be mapped to the corresponding syntactic representation, and then to the concrete one dynamically and automatically.

9.2.2 Type System

BPEL assumes that data are represented in XML. Data in BPEL are written to and read from typed variables. BPEL variables can be either WSDL message types, XML schema simple or complex types, or XML schema elements [18]. BPEL does not support *file* as a data type which is commonly used in scientific workflows. To the best of our knowledge, BPEL has no notion of similar concepts (e.g., web service type or service operation type) as the activity type used in the scientific workflow domain where for a given activity type, a specific implementation of the activity type can be selected dynamically at runtime based on its availability and certain (e.g., scheduling) decisions.

Like BPEL, XPDL also assumes that data are represented in XML. XPDL uses its own type system which include basic data types such as *string*, *float*, and *integer*, as well as complex data types defined by users by using XML schema syntax [180]. XPDL has concepts like *Application Type*, *Activity Type*, and *Implementation Type*. *Application Type* contains several pieces of information required by common applications such as calling an EJB component or invoking a Web Service. The *Application Types* supported in XPDL include EJB, POJO, XSLT, Script, WebService, BusinessRules, and Form. *Activity Type* can be *Route*, *Gateway*, *Event*, and *Implementation*. In case of *Implementation*, the *Implementation Type* can be *None*, *Application/Task*, *SubFlow/Subprocess*. A *Task* is an atomic activity that is included within a process. The type of a *Task* can be one of seven BPMN tasks (*TaskService*, *TaskReceive*, *TaskManual*, *TaskReference*, *TaskScript*, *TaskSend*, and *TaskUser*) or an application (*TaskApplication*). Although these types in XPDL are used to store information of workflow tasks, the functional information of workflow tasks, as that is referred by the activity type in the scientific workflow domain, is not encoded in these types. In addition, like BPEL, XPDL also does not support *file* type.

Kepler provides a static typing system to model data structural types in Kepler workflows [90] which includes common data types *Boolean*, *Int*, *Double*, *String*, etc., as well as other data types such as *Complex*, *General*, *Matrix*, and *Object*. The work [28] presented a novel hybrid type system in Kepler for modeling scientific data that separates structural data types and semantic data types, and allows them to be explicitly linked using hybridization constraints. This approach supports automatic structural data transformation which allows researchers to easily construct scientific workflows without having to focus on detailed, structural differences. While this idea is similar to the separation of data semantics and data representations, and automatic data conversions in our approach, we focus on general data instead of XML data only, and we further make use of the separation for building Activity Types (ATs) and Activity Functions (AFs), and then automate scientific workflow composition.

Data used in VDS workflows are file names and textual arguments, similar to command line parameters of executables [60]. In order to type dataset that spans files and directories, XML Dataset Typing and Mapping (XDTM) [121] in VDS defines the *logical structure* of a dataset via a subset of XML Schema. The corresponding *physical representation* is defined by *mapping descriptors*, which define how each element in the logical schema of the dataset is stored in and fetched from physical structures such as directories, files, and database tables [206, 207]. Multiple mappings may be defined for a single logical type. For example, an array of numbers might be physically represented, in different contexts, as a set of relations, a text file, a spreadsheet, or an XML document. XDTM is complementary to our approach and it can be used to deal with workflow data that have internal structures like XML data.

Unlike the aforementioned workflow systems, Taverna and Triana do not mandate typing. Input and output ports of Taverna *processors* may consume or produce single *string* values, lists, lists of lists, and so on [124]. In addition, to facilitate service discovery in Taverna, input and output ports can be associated with the semantic types that capture real world concepts. Example of the semantic types in the bioinformatics domain are *biological sequence* and *alignment report* [22]. Input and output data type of Triana *units* or *tools* can be any standard Java type (e.g., java.lang.String), Triana type (e.g., triana.types.SampleSet), or any other type that is on the Triana classpath [190].

Both GWENDIA [120] and IWIR [141] support basic types like *integer*, *string*, *double*, *file*, as well as nested data collections. Basic data types like *string* and *number* are also supported in Karajan. Karajan also provides support for common data types such as lists and maps that are specifically targeted to support parameter studies [195].

In contrast, AWDL has a sophisticated type system which consists of Data Representations (which include *storage type*, *content type*, *archive type*, and *cardinality*), data semantics or Data Classes (which are real-world concepts, i.e., meaning of data), Activity Types (each of which is a syntactic description of a group of *Activity Deployments* that all have the same functionality, the same input and output data structure), and Activity Functions (each of which is a semantic description of a group of *Activity Types* that all have the same functionality, and the same input and output data semantics).

9.2.3 Control Flow

While basic control flow constructs such as sequence and parallel are supported by almost all workflow languages or systems, this section focuses on the support of conditional branches, parallel iterations, and alternative constructs which are often required by scientific workflow applications.

A *flow* construct in BPEL is used to express parallel execution, like parallel section used in high-level programming languages. The *flow* construct can also behave as a DAG construct when dependences (optionally with transition conditions) are added among the activities enclosed in the *flow* construct. BPEL supports conditional constructs through its *if-else* activity, which allows to select exactly one branch of the activity from a given set of choices. The condition is formulated by using XPath [187]. BPEL also supports iteration constructs including *while, repeatUntil,* and *forEach. while* and *repeatUntil* are known from high-level programming languages. The *forEach* construct in BPEL is actually similar to the *for* construct used in high-level programming languages because of the use of the *counter* variable which is controlled by a start value and a final value, and can be used for indexed access to a specific element in a set of elements. By default, *forEach* executes its iterations sequentially. Parallel *forEach* can be achieved by specifying the attribute *parallel="yes"*. The *forEach* construct in BPEL supports the cases where not all iterations are required to complete, for example, when parallel requests are sent out and a sufficiently large subset of the recipients have responded. This is, however, rarely the case required by scientific workflows. As a combination of WSFL and XLANG, BPEL contains both graph-based and block-based [138] programming which makes BPEL more complex and harder to use for domain scientists.

XPDL uses *Gateway* to determine branching, forking, merging, and joining of flows. Parallel and conditional execution are supported by different Gateways, e.g., Exclusive/Inclusive Gateways, Parallel Gateways, etc. Iterations supported in XPDL include standard loops and Multi-Instance loops. A standard Loop activity has a boolean expression that is evaluated for each cycle of the loop, reflecting the programming constructs *while* and *until*. Multi-Instance loops reflect the programming construct *foreach* in which iterations can be executed either sequentially or in parallel.

Kepler supports iterative and branching constructs via special actors and directors [90]. For example, *if-then-else* and *do-while* can be implemented by using the *BooleanSwitch* actor and the *Dynamic Dataflow (DDF)* director. The *for-loop* construct is supported via the *Ramp* actor which controls iterations via its parameters: *firingCountLimit, init* and *step*, and the iterations parameter in the Synchronous Dataflow (SDF) director. Kepler uses a "map" operator to apply a function that operates on singletons to collections, thus implementing a *for-each* loop. Feedback loops (i.e., *while* loop) in Kepler are supported via special actors. For example, the actor *SampleDelay* under an SDF director provides initial outputs to be fed back to a loop such that the first iteration of the loop can start.

VDL [207] allows users to define procedures that accept, return, and operate on datasets with type, representation, and location defined by XDTM. A VDL procedure can be either an atomic procedure or a compound procedure. A compound procedure composes calls to atomic procedures, other compound procedures, and/or control statements. The control statements of a compound procedure supported in VDL include *if*, *switch*, *foreach*, and *while*, which have syntax and semantics similar to comparable constructs in high-level programming languages. The iteration of a *foreach* construct can be scheduled to run in parallel. In order to submit a workflow containing conditional (e.g., *if*, *switch*) and/or iterative (e.g., *foreach*, *while*) constructs to DAGMan for execution, a *dynamic node expansion* mechanism [207] is adopted: sub-DAGs are created and executed dynamically at runtime, and the main job waits for sub-DAGs to finish before proceeding.

There is no direct support of conditional branches and iterations in Taverna. Instead, Taverna supports implicit iterations with the help of its workflow enactment engine: when a processor that outputs a list of *string* is connected to a processor that takes a single *string* as input, the enactment engine will invoke the second processor multiple times (once for each element in the input list) and aggregate the results into a new list; when two or more lists are provided as inputs to a processor which takes single elements as inputs, the enactment engine will invoke the processor with either the cross product (i.e., Cartesian product) or the dot product of these lists [170]. Local services (tasks that are provided and executed by the Taverna workflow system itself) are used in Taverna to construct conditional branches, such as the *if-then-else* construct [198].

A major difference between the Triana workflow language and many other languages is that it has no explicit support for control constructs [36]. Loops and execution branching in Triana are handled by specific components. The argument is that this approach is simpler and more extendable and sustainable because it allows for a finer grained degree of control over these constructs than that can be achieved with a simple XML representation.

Similar to Taverna, GWENDIA also supports implicit iterations. It provides four *iteration strategies* to define how input data items received on several input ports of an activity are combined together for processing, namely dot product, cross product, flat cross product, and match product [120]. In GWENDIA, special activities are defined to express conditional branches and loops. Conditions in these activities are expressed using Java language. An interesting feature of these activities is that they are array-compliant, i.e., they can accept data arrays as input and produce data arrays as output.

The Karajan language can express complicated workflows including conditional control flow and loops. Inheriting from High-Level Petri Nets (HLPNs), GWorkflowDL also supports conditional control flow and loops [82] and has potentials to support many other workflow patterns [175]. Originally, workflows in UNICORE are represented as Directed Acyclic Graphs (DAGs) [15]. With the adoption of the Network Job Supervisor (NJS) component, UNICORE also supports conditional branches (e.g., *IfThenElse*) and loops (e.g., *DoN* and *DoRepeat*) [49]. While *DoN* depends on an execution counter (like a *for* loop), the execution of *IfThenElse* and *DoRepeat* is based on one of three types of runtime conditions: (a) *ReturnCodeTest*: check whether a task execution succeeded or failed; (b) *FileTest*: check whether a file exists, is readable, writable, etc.; and (c) *TimeTest*: check whether a given time and date have passed. However, the conditions in these constructs are not evaluated against the value of the data produced by scientific workflows. The P-GRADE portal provides a graphical interface through which users can easily construct workflows based on the DAG concept. The P-GRADE portal also supports parametric studies through *parameter spaces*. The parametric study applications can be sent to MOTEUR [67] for execution where implicit parallel iterations are applied. From this point of view, one could consider that implicit parallel iterations is supported by P-GRADE, although indirectly. There is no conditional branches and loops supported in P-GRADE. IWIR [141] supports basic control flow constructs including *blockScope*, *if*, *while*, *for*, *forEach*, and parallel constructs like *parallelFor* and *parallelForEach*. While others are similar to what we have in AWDL, *blockScope* groups a set of tasks to avoid naming conflicting and to build DAG-like constructs. Alternative executions are not supported in IWIR. Both xWFL and GSFL miss branches and loop constructs. Scientific workflows in the GriPhyN [13] project are limited to acyclic graphs.

In summary, control flow is not only an important aspect of scientific workflow languages, but also required for a scientific workflow language to be able to express various control flow constructs such as conditional branches and loops. In practice, data flow based scientific workflow languages and systems often provide control flow support through special mechanisms. For example, Kepler uses special actors and directors [90] to support iterative and branching constructs, and the "map" operator to provide implicit *for-each* loop support. The Grid workflow language Scufl in Taverna [133] adopts *coordination constraints* to express the case where two processors have to be executed in a certain order and yet there is no direct data dependency between them. For example, coordination constraints can be used to allow one processor to go from *scheduled* to *running* if another processor has status *completed* [133]. Similarly, GWENDIA also contains *control links* to interconnect two activities among which no data dependency explicitly defined but an order of execution should be preserved [120]. Iteration strategies is used in GWENDIA to provide implicit parallel iteration support. Triana makes use of special messages between units to support control flow [172].

Therefore, AWDL adopted the approach combing both control and data flow for easy expressing control and data flow requirements of scientific workflows. AWDL directly supports a rich set of control flow constructs including `dag`, `sequence`, `parallel`, `if`, `for`, `while`, and `alt`. In addition, to the best of our knowledge, the `alt` activity is not supported at the workflow language level by any of the aforementioned related work.

9.2.4   *Data Flow*

Data flow modeling in BPEL and XPDL is done in a similar way. Data in BPEL are written to and read from typed variables [18] which are shared among activities. Each activity can be specified as either a producer or a consumer for values associated with a variable [170]. Similar to BPEL, data in XPDL are modeled by DataFields [180] which can be produced or consumed by activities.

In Kepler, each actor contains one or more data ports. *Channels* are used to pass data from one port to another. In order to be able to transfer files to remote locations, data actors like *GridFTP* actor are added as nodes into Kepler workflows. This approach makes data flow representation of Kepler workflows less accurate because GridFTP operation clearly represents a data flow from one location to another, but with a specific GridFTP component this data flow is not visible to users [171]. In addition, *Relation* in Kepler allows a workflow to "branch" data flow. Branched data can be sent to multiple places in the workflow. For example, a user might wish to direct the output of an actor to another actor for further processing, and also to a display actor to display the data [90].

Unlike Kepler workflows, the abstract workflows generated by VDS in Pegasus-WMS are Directed Acyclic Graph (DAG) workflows where each task is represented by a node and each data flow dependence is represented by an edge instead of a data transfer task. Using edges instead of data transfer tasks to model data flow dependences is also adopted in AWDL workflows.

In Taverna, processors have input and output ports with an associated data type, and data travels from the output ports of a processor to the input ports of one or more subsequent processors [170]. Interaction among processors is defined by *data links* in data flow graphs. Data links mediate the flow of data between a data source and a data sink. The data source can be a processor output or a workflow input. The data sink can be a processor input port or a workflow output. Each data sink will receive the same value if there are multiple links from a data source [133]. This is similar to the data flow modeling used in AWDL workflows.

Unlike Kepler workflows which may contain file transfer tasks (actors), Triana workflows include file components in addition to job components. A file component represents a file accessible using the GAT File Capability Provider Interface (CPI) [171]. A file component is not generally associated with any data processing or handling operation, but simply represents a data location which can act as a data source and/or a data store. Data flow in Triana workflow is represented by a connection between two file components (i.e., file transfer, or file copy if both are local files), a connection from a file component to a job component (i.e., pre-stage the file into the job execution directory), or a connection from a job component to a file component (i.e., post-stage the file from the job execution directory).

In GWENDIA, data links interconnect output ports of an activity with input ports of another activity. Data links define a data dependency between two activities. Different outputs may be connected to different activities, causing the produced data to be replicated to all subsequent activities. Like GWENDIA, IWIR also supports data flow links from one data port to another. In addition, IWIR has union data ports which are used to collect and access data produced in different iterations or sequential or parallel loop constructs. Grid Job Definition Language (GJobDL) [83] uses a modified HLPN where *transitions* contain input and output ports which represent parameters and results, and edges connect *places* to ports instead of *transitions*. Compared with GJobDL, GWorkflowDL uses unmodified HLPN and models parameters and results with *places* [1].

Compared with business workflow languages like BPEL and XPDL where workflow tasks communicate via variables, scientific workflow languages or systems usually use data ports for the communication between workflow tasks. This is the case in AWDL as well. However, unlike Kepler and Triana, and similar to VDS and Taverna, AWDL represents data flow with data flow links among activities (strictly speaking, their data ports). No data transfer tasks or file components are represented separately as nodes in workflows. We believe this approach makes the workflow development simpler: users can consider a distributed system as a supercomputer where they can conduct their computations without dealing with when and where to do data transfers. In addition, in our opinion, data transfer should be handled by the workflow engines instead of the workflow developers because it is often unknown at composition time on which resource the data producer/consumer task will be executed due to the dynamic nature of distributed systems. Data transfers may be unnecessary if both the data producer task and the data consumer task are executed on the same resource, and the data consumer task only reads the data without modifying its content.

Petri Nets have traditionally been used for representing the control flow of workflows [76, 81, 193]. However, classic Petri Net has no explicit mechanism to model the data produced or consumed by the activities [48] without being extended to specialized high-level nets, for example, Colored Petri Nets (CPN) [86]. CPNs use nodes called *places* to model data types and values, and nodes called *transitions* to model activities. However, in our opinion, using Petri Nets to model scientific workflows is less intuitive because scientific workflows are often defined as directed graphs where nodes do not represent data but activities.

9.2.5 Modularization and Reuse

Subprocesses are used in practice to modularize large business process and to foster reuse of processes. This is often required in scientific workflows [72] as well. BPEL currently does not support the explicit definition of subprocess that can be invoked from within the same business process or from another business process [91]. The only approximate way in BPEL is to define a complete business process as an independent service and invoking it via an *invoke* activity. The main difference is that subprocesses are typically tightly coupled in terms of their life cycle to the invoking process. This is not the case when invoking via an *invoke* activity. XPDL support subprocesses via its *ActivitySet* and *SubFlow*. In Kepler, sub-workflows are supported via composite actors which are collections or sets of actors bundled together to perform complex operations. An entire workflow can be also represented as a composite actor and included as a component within an encapsulating workflow [90]. The sub-workflows in Pegasus actually refer to portions of workflows or workflow partitions which are used during the workflow mapping process in order to support the so-called *deferred mapping* [41]. Taverna supports sub-workflows (or *nested workflows* in Taverna terms) which are workflows that are reused inside another workflow [103, 191]. Sub-workflows is also supported in IWIR. In Triana, tasks can be grouped together. Grouped tasks can appear as any other Triana task and can be used in the same way [190]. No real sub-workflow is supported in Triana.

Altintas et al. [3] developed a framework that supports the design and reuse of workflows in the Kepler scientific workflow system. Their work focused on abstracting common used workflow components (e.g., for data movement, database querying, etc.) into a set of generic, reusable tasks. However, invocation or reuse of a sub-workflow or an entire workflow is not discussed in their work. Laszewski et al. [197] presented an architecture of a repository service for scientific workflow components. The GEMLCA [43] legacy code service solution also provides a repository service for scientific workflow components. These repositories are developed to facilitate the component reuse in scientific workflows. Cao et al. [29] presented a scientific workflow component model and discussed methodologies for reusing scientific workflow components. While workflow component reuse discussed in these papers is similar to our idea of Activity Types (ATs), no sub-workflow and workflow reuse are presented. Goderis et al. [71, 72] identified seven bottlenecks to scalable workflow reuse and repurposing in e-Science. Their work mainly discussed how reasoning over ontologies, written in the Web Ontology Language (OWL) and the Description Logic (DL), could help discovering and ranking workflow fragments for reuse and repurposing. The work [153] in the myExperiment project [122] identified multiple level of workflow reuse: workflows can be reused with different parameter and data, or shared with other scientists who conducting similar work; workflows, workflow components, and patterns can also be reused. However, no sub-workflow reuse is discussed.

In contrast, the AWDL modularization mechanism supports reusing not only workflow components but also sub-workflows and entire workflows. A sophisticated algorithm for detection of incorrect sub-workflow reuse at composition time is also presented. Furthermore, with the activity repository service GLARE and workflow libraries, we enable sharing and reusability at different levels and in a simple and consistent way.

9.2.6   *Modeling Support*

There are two ways to model scientific workflows: (a) text-based, e.g., GridAnt [96], GSFL [95] and Gridbus Workflow [203] use XML; and (b) graph-based, e.g., Condor DAGMan [37] and YAWL [193] use self-defined notations.

As far as graph-based modeling is concerned, GridFlow [30] uses Petri Nets [140] to model scientific workflows. Fraunhofer Resource Grid (FhRG) [81], which uses a hierarchical graph definition to model scientific workflows, is also built on Petri Nets. However, Petri Nets may be unable to model workflow activities accurately without extending its semantics [50]. This drawback has been addressed in UML Activity Diagrams. The work presented in [47] and [19] uses UML Activity Diagrams to model scientific workflows. However, the UML they used is UML1.x, in which Activity Diagrams had several serious limitations in the types of flows that could be represented. Many of these limitations were due to the fact that activities were overlaid on top of the basic state machine formalism and consequently constrained to the semantics of state machines [160]. Rather than following the standard syntax and semantics of Petri Nets and UML, some scientific workflow editor tools create their own graphical representation of workflow components [204]. For example, Triana [174], Kepler [105], and Taverna [133] use self-defined notations and allow users to predefine software components and reuse them. A lack of standards hinders the collaboration among different projects. Much work is thus replicated such as different user interfaces developed by different projects for the same functionality.

In a word, most of existing work suffers from one or several of the following drawbacks: the lack of the graphical workflow editor, the use of self-defined notations, the use of old UML 1.x Activity Diagram, or no adequate tool support. In contrast, we use the latest standard UML 2 Activity Diagram to model scientific workflow applications. Our approach can model graphically any scientific workflow application that can be expressed textually using AWDL [53].

9.2.7 Semantic Support

Kepler adopts semantic annotations to dataset schemas and services (and the corresponding input and output types) to facilitate workflow composition [24]. Leveraging the semantic annotations, Kepler provides (a) a semantic query system which assists users in locating components relevant to their analysis and modeling tasks, (b) a framework [27] for structural data transformation that allows researchers to easily construct scientific workflows without having to focus on structural differences, and (c) a hybrid type system [28] that separates structural data types and semantic data types and facilitates workflow verification and analysis (e.g., to check whether two connected data sources are semantically compatible). Compared with our approach, Kepler still presents syntax information (e.g., data types) to users when composing workflows, and the semantic annotations are used to verify whether two connected sources are "semantically compatible" instead of establishing data flow automatically as we do. Zhang [205] described an ontology-driven scientific workflow composition approach in Kepler for hyperspectral image processing applications. The author developed a workflow component ontology and a data type ontology and plugged them into Kepler. But the mapping from semantic data types to structural data types is considered to be inefficient and unnecessary in his work. Wings [66] for Pegasus uses semantic representations to describe compactly complex scientific workflow applications in a data independent manner (workflow templates), then automatically generates workflow of computations for given data sets (workflow instances). The work [22] presented the metadata management in Taverna workflow system, where the parameters of a workflow processing unit can be annotated with semantic types. However, how the semantic types can be used is not explored (to be done in their future work). Feta [104, 170] is a semantic discovery facility provided in Taverna. It includes a semantic service registry that maintains annotated description of services, and can be searched using terms from a publicly available ontology. Feta's data model of services distinguishes between the core unit of functionality, i.e., the *operation*, and the unit of publication, i.e., the *service*. The capabilities of *operations*, within Feta, are characterized by inputs, outputs, and several domain-specific attributes. Feta models the input and output data of service operations with *parameter* entities which is described by the properties *semantic type*, *format*, *collectionType*, *collectionFormat*, etc. The property *semantic type* is similar as the data semantics used in our approach (represented through the property *semantics* of data ports). The property *format* is similar to the property *hasContentType* of *DataRepresentation*. The properties *collectionType* and *collectionFormat* specify whether a service returns a set of results or a single item, which is similar to the *hasCardinality* property of *DataRepresentation*. Although these properties are similar as the properties of *DataRepresentation* in our approach (our approach has two additional properties: *hasStorageType* and *hasArchiveType*), we separate data *semantic type* (or data semantics) from the rest (which we call *DataRepresentation*) such that domain users can compose scientific workflows by only focusing on *semantic types* without dealing with the specific data representations. Furthermore, the semantic information in our approach is used not only for Activity Functions (AFs) discovery but also for automatic control flow and data flow composition. To our best knowledge, there is no support for semantics in BPEL, XPDL, and Triana.

In ICENI [110], Mayer et al. [109] presented a component description language which features a separation of concerns between component meaning, behavior, and implementation. While the idea sounds similar to ours, there are big differences between their approach and our approach. In their approach, the meaning level, i.e., the highest level of abstraction, concerns data flow, including data types. The behavior level concerns control flow. No semantic descriptions of data are used in their approach. In contrast, the three levels in our approach are the semantic level, the syntactic level and the concrete level. Further, ontologies are introduced in our approach to enable semantic scientific workflow composition. The Workflow Composition Tool (WCT) [77] in the K-Wf Grid project adopted an automatic workflow composition based on semantic descriptions of services' operations. The algorithm of Input-to-Output comparison is based on the concept *Data Template* which describes *content*, *format*, and *storage* constraints of data. While data representation in our approach is inspired by the concept *Data Template*, unlike WCT, our approach separates data representation from data semantics in the workflow language and users focus on data semantics to compose scientific workflows. The Model-Based Workflow (MBW) approach [155] generates abstract workflow representations based on the Workflow-Driven Ontologies (WDO) [156], which are developed by domain scientists and contain knowledge about *method* consumes *data* and produces *data* and *product*. While the generated abstract workflow representations in MBW are similar to our semantic scientific workflow representations, there is no data representation concept in MBW and it did not present an approach to map an abstract workflow representation to the corresponding executable one. As a part of the METEOR-S [117] project, Cardoso and Sheth [31] presented a formal description of *Web Service Template (ST)* and *Web Service Object (SO)*, and a detailed algorithm to compute the degree of similarity of ST and SO taking into account semantic, syntactic, and concrete information. Their work is complementary to our approach and their algorithm can be used to locate Activity Functions (AFs) by using free text or based on input and output data, and to map AFs to Activity Types (ATs). The Ontology-driven workflow management system [102] introduces ontologies into biosequence processing system to assist workflow composition and optimization. Chen et al. [33,34] presented a knowledge-based framework for semantic service composition. Nadarajan et al. [125] proposed a semantic-based hybrid workflow composition method within a three-layered framework. Majithia et al. [108] presented a framework of automated composition of semantic services with a dynamic and adaptive mechanism for service discovery and composition. However, none of them support separation of data semantics and data representation.

There is also some other work done by the Semantic Web Service community to describe services semantically and to compose services as workflows. OWL-S [184] is a set of ontology definitions designed to capture the behavior of services. The service presents the *service profile*, a description of what the service does. The service is described by the *service model*, which tell how the service works. Finally, the service supports the *service grounding* which specifies the invocation method for the service. The functionality provided by the service is specified through *hasInput, hasOutput, hasPrecondition*, and *hasResult* of the service profile. OWL-WS [21] extends OWL-S to support workflow descriptions. OWL-WS uses the OWL-S concept of Composite Process for modeling workflows that are not only intra service, i.e., a sequence of calls to different operations of a single service, but also inter services processes. WSDL-S [186] associates semantic annotations with elements of WSDL documents. However, none of them have the data representation concept and separate concerns between data semantics and data representation as we do.

9.3 Optimization

In this section, we outline the related work concerning data flow optimization at the workflow language level, with a special focus on data collection processing.

Kepler uses a *"map"* operator to apply a function, which operates on singletons, to collections. It is limited to processing one collection at a time. McPhillips et al. [113, 114] presented an idea to process nested, especially heterogeneous data collections scientific workflows. It uses *read scope* to specify portions of collections and *iteration scope* to control iterations of actions. Its collection operations are limited to invoking actions once for each item, or once for the entire collection. VDS supports iterations over datasets; however, it is limited to operating datasets (or slices of datasets) one element by one element, through the *foreach* statement in VDL. Taverna has no explicit iterative constructs. Its workflow language Scufl provides support for processing data collections through an implicit iteration mechanism, which is limited to the cross and dot products of lists (collections) being processed. Triana has no explicit support for control flow constructs. Loops and execution branching are handled by specific components. To the best of our knowledge, there is no data collection or similar concepts supported in Triana. GWENDIA supports data collection (or array, as called in GWENDIA) processing through its four *iteration strategies*: namely dot product, cross product, flat cross product, and match product [120]. The dot product and the cross product are similar to what Taverna does. The flat cross product is similar to the cross product, except for the indexing scheme of the produced data items: it is computed as a unique index value by flattening the nested-array structure of the cross product. The match product matches data items carrying one or more identical user-defined tags, independently of their indexing scheme. GWENDIA's conditional and loop activities also support array processing. As an intermediate workflow language which can be translated to or from many other scientific workflow languages including GWENDIA, IWIR also supports dot product, cross product, and flat cross product over data collections, as well as cross product over a combination set [142]. The Karajan [195] workflow language has parallel iterations. However, there is no flexible data collection-oriented data flow supported in Karajan.

Parallel computing patterns presented in [138] identified a data parallelism pattern and its variants *static/dynamic/adaptive* data parallelism for scientific workflows. These patterns have a close relationship to the classical *multi-instance* workflow pattern [154] and its variants. The work [154] identified 40 *workflow data patterns* which describe the manner in which data elements are defined and utilized in workflow systems. Among the workflow data patterns, Pattern 12 (Data Interaction—to Multiple Instance Task) defines the way to pass data elements from a preceding task instance to subsequent task instances of a multiple instance task, which may involve passing the data elements to all instances of the multiple instance task or distributing them on a selective basis. As an illustration for the *selective basis*, passing one data element to each task instance is provided in [154] as an example. Our work clarifies and extends the *selective basis* by explicitly defining some data collection distribution constructs. Pattern 13 (Data Interaction—from Multiple Instance Task) defines the way to pass data elements from a multiple instance task to a subsequent task. This is similar to the way we aggregate data elements as data collections. Based on the paper [154], among all the workflow systems examined, the only workflow system supporting both patterns is the commercial workflow management system FLOWer 3.0 [199]. YAWL [193] supports these two data patterns by defining four types of XQuery [188]: *accessor query*, *splitter query*, *instance query*, and *aggregate query* [135]. None of these patterns reflects the collection distribution constructs *BLOCK*, *BLOCK(b)*, *BLOCK(b,l)* and *REPLICA(r)*.

In contrast, AWDL supports mapping a portion of a *data collection* to activities or loop iterations. Furthermore, one iterative construct in AWDL (e.g., the for construct) can also process multiple data collections with each data collection being processed in an independent way in terms of how many data elements are processed in one loop iteration. All of these features can be specified at the workflow language level by users to control how datasets are processed by activities or iterative constructs.

9.4 Synthesis

Lautenbacher et al. [97] presented a survey of available workflow composition approaches in areas like scientific workflows, Semantic Web Services, and Business Process Management. The authors mainly focus on the question what features are supported by the existing approaches, e.g., whether semantic technologies are included, whether the approach works at an abstraction level, whether preconditions and effects are included, or whether advanced control flow constructs are supported. Little information about algorithms of automatic workflow composition is given.

Gil [65] described some ideas to use semantic technologies (e.g., application specific ontologies) and Artificial Intelligence planning algorithms to support assisted workflow composition. The author pointed out that (a) automatic completion of workflows is desirable in the stage of creating an executable workflow (where full information is specified) from a workflow instance (where tasks are not assigned to resources) by assigning tasks to resources; (b) automation can also be used to complete under-specified workflow templates by mapping an abstract task to a specific component or adding data conversion steps; and (c) full automation of the workflow composition process may be desirable for some kinds of workflows and application domains. However, no specific algorithms are presented. Wings [66] is a workflow creation system that combines semantic representations with planning techniques. It uses semantic representations to describe complex scientific applications in a data independent manner, then automatically generates workflows of computations for given data sets, and finally maps them to available computing resources via Pegasus [41]. While Wings can generate workflows of computations for given data collections, it can only generate workflow instances based on workflow templates (data-independent representations of workflows). The creation of workflow templates is still done manually. Furthermore, the creation of workflows is limited to DAGs. Gubała et al. [78], in the context of K-Wf Grid project, presented the Workflow Composition Tool (WCT) for automatic scientific workflow composition. The main idea of their work is to solve unsatisfied data dependences iteratively by contacting service registries until some dependences cannot be satisfied. The algorithm is limited to Petri Nets because the algorithm has to deal with the Petri Nets coherence by adding some dummy places and transitions. Furthermore, the algorithm cannot handle alternative control flow when a service operation requires multiple inputs which can be produced by many different combinations of multiple services, like the case presented in Fig. 8.3. A planning approach presented in [4] automatically constructs data processing workflows where the inputs and outputs of services are relational descriptions. Their planner uses relational subsumption to connect the output of a service with the input of another. Their approach focuses on the cases where inputs and outputs of services are relational descriptions.

In the area of Semantic Web Services, some Artificial Intelligence planning-based approaches for automatic web service composition have been proposed. Wu et al. [202] adapted the graphplan algorithm [26] with semantics for automatic composition of Semantic Web Services. Their work focused on addressing both process heterogeneity and data heterogeneity of Web service composition problems. Meyer et al. [118], in the context of the Adaptive Services Grid (ASG) project [11], uses an extension of the Enforced Hill-Climbing planning algorithm [80] for automatic service composition. Although the idea of graph-based planning is similar to our approach, there are a few differences: (a) our approach supports fault tolerance by generating alternative workflows, and (b) we consider workflow optimization. In addition, our algorithm focuses on scientific workflow composition and models workflow activities with input and output data classes and the consumption of data classes does not affect their availability. Therefore, mutual exclusion links, as used in the graphplan algorithm, are not needed in our approach. Ambite et al. [5] model the Web service composition problem as a Triple logic program and use Triple logic engine to generate workflows. Duan et al. [46] sketched an algorithm to synthesis BPEL4WS abstract processes. They assume that tasks are associated with ranks (positive integers), which, however, is not feasible for Web services which are developed by different organizations.

In addition, Lelarge et al. [101] presented an Artificial Intelligence planning based approach for automatic composition of secure workflows in the domain of stream processing systems. They compose a set of software components into an application. They model the state of the planning problem by a state vector indicating the set of currently available types. However, no Semantic Web technologies such as Ontology are involved.

In summary, existing work commonly suffers by one or several of the following drawbacks: only generating workflow instances from workflow templates, limited to special cases (e.g., specific workflow notation systems, relational service input and output data, tasks with ranks), no consideration of fault tolerance and workflow optimization, and no involvement of semantic technologies. In contrast, we provide a general and efficient approach for automatic composition of high quality (portable, fault tolerant and optimized) scientific workflows, including not only control flow composition but also data flow composition.

Part VI
Conclusions

Chapter 10
Conclusions

In this book, we have identified and addressed several research challenges in scientific workflow programming, optimization, and synthesis. This chapter concludes this book by highlighting the major contributions and outlining potential future research directions.

10.1 Contributions

The major contributions of this book fall into three areas: scientific workflow programming, scientific workflow optimization, and scientific workflow synthesis. Specifically, we have presented the XML-based Abstract Workflow Description Language (AWDL), a UML-based approach for scientific workflow modeling, collection-oriented data flow optimization, semantic scientific workflows, and automatic scientific workflow composition.

10.1.1 Scientific Workflow Language

We presented an Abstract Workflow Description Language (AWDL) for describing scientific workflow applications at a high level of abstraction (Chaps. 3 and 4). AWDL is an XML-based language and it has been designed such that the user can concentrate on specifying scientific workflow applications without dealing with either the complexity of distributed systems or any specific implementation technology. AWDL has the following features:

- AWDL is independent of implementation technologies such as Web services, Unix executables, and Java classes. An Activity Type (AT) is an abstraction of a group of Activity Deployments (ADs) which have the same functionality and input and output data structures.

J. Qin and T. Fahringer, *Scientific Workflows*, DOI 10.1007/978-3-642-30715-7__10,   191
© Springer-Verlag Berlin Heidelberg 2012

- AWDL workflows adapt to the dynamic nature of distributed systems because Activity Types (ATs) are abstract and can be mapped dynamically to available Activity Deployments (ADs) at runtime.
- AWDL provides a rich set of control flow constructs to simplify the specification of scientific workflow applications which includes `dag`, `sequence`, `parallel`, `if`, `for`, `while`, and `alt`.
- AWDL introduces the concept of data collection, which models both static and dynamic datasets at a high level of abstraction.
- There is no need to specify lower level tasks, e.g., starting or stopping activities, transferring data, queue activities, in AWDL.
- AWDL supports properties and constraints which provide additional information for workflow runtime systems to optimize and steer the execution of workflow applications.
- AWDL is a modularized language which supports sub-workflows and workflow libraries. AWDL provides a simple and consistent way to invoke Activity Types (ATs), sub-workflows, and workflows (Chap. 4).

10.1.2   Scientific Workflow Modeling

We presented an approach to model scientific workflows based on the standard UML Activity Diagram and implemented a graphical user interface based on it (Chap. 5).

- We presented a formal definition of scientific workflows (Definition 2.5) and compared it with that of UML Activity Diagrams.
- We extended the modeling elements of UML Activity Diagram by defining stereotypes which are used to model AWDL activities and control flow constructs.
- We implemented a graphical scientific workflow modeling tool based on the UML Activity Diagram with a model traverser, a model checker, and support for automatically locating data sources. The tool can also be extended by plugins.
- We implemented ASKALON Workflow Hosting Environment (AWHE) as a workflow library to facilitate workflow sharing and reuse.

10.1.3   Data Flow Optimization

In order to meet the complex data flow requirements of scientific workflows, we presented flexible collection-oriented data flow support in AWDL by introducing two AWDL built-in constraints *awdl:element-index* and *awdl:distribution* (Chap. 6). These constraints are used to specify collection distribution constructs which are used to map data collections to activities and to distribute data collections onto loop iterations. Five distribution constructs, inspired by High Performance Fortran

(HPF), are comma-separated colon expression, *BLOCK, BLOCK(b), BLOCK(b,l)*, and *REPLICA(r)*. The advantages of this approach are as follows:

- The approach enables the specification of more flexible and accurate dataset-oriented data flow in various scientific workflow domains such as mapping portions of data collections to activities, distribution of data collections onto loop iterations, processing multiple data collections with one parallel iterative construct independently in terms of how many data elements of each collection are processed in one loop iteration.
- It reduces data duplication, optimizes data transfers between workflow activities, and thus improves workflow performance. The experimental results with two real-world scientific workflow applications show the significant improvement in workflow performance.
- It also simplifies the efforts to port scientific applications onto distributed systems by reducing user efforts for code wrapping.

10.1.4 Semantic Scientific Workflows

In order to further simplify scientific workflow composition, we proposed a novel semantic approach by adopting ontology technologies in scientific workflow composition to separate concerns between data semantics and data representation and between Activity Functions (AFs) and Activity Types (ATs). The separation allows users to compose workflows at the level of data semantics and activity function and leave the task of dealing with data representations and activity types to the scientific workflow composition tool (Chap. 7). The main contributions of our approach are as follows:

- We introduce the concept of data representation in scientific workflows, and some comprehensive properties associated with the concept.
- We separate concerns between data semantics and data representation and between Activity Function and Activity Type, which makes AWDL more abstract and makes the scientific workflow composition tool easier to use for domain scientists.
- With the help of the generic AWDL ontology and the extended domain ontologies, scientific workflows in three different levels (i.e., semantic, syntactic, and concrete) of abstraction can be described with one single scientific workflow language.
- Data conversion among different data representations is automated.
- We applied our approach to a real-world meteorology scientific workflow application.

10.1.5 Automatic Scientific Workflow Composition

Based on our semantic approach for describing scientific workflows, we presented an approach for automatic scientific workflow composition (Chap. 8) which consists of two sub-algorithms dealing with control and data flow composition, respectively. The control flow composition algorithm is an Artificial Intelligence planning based algorithm using an Activity Function Data Dependence (ADD) graph. The data flow composition is done through backward control flow traversing and reasoning technologies. The main contributions of the approach are as follows:

- The control flow composition algorithm is general: not limited to any workflow modeling notation systems, and efficient: the complexity of our algorithm is a quadratic in the number of AFs.
- The composed scientific workflows are high quality (portable, fault tolerant, and optimized).
- (Semi-)automatic composition of scientific workflows with branches and loops.
- (Semi-)automatic data flow composition.

10.2 Future Research

Some research challenges in scientific workflow programming, optimization, and synthesis have been addressed in this book. The following potential directions are currently being considered for future research:

- With collection distribution constructs, more advanced data flow like *data stream* can be supported: as soon as the required data elements (instead of the entire data collection) are produced and ready to be processed, the corresponding subsequent activity (the consumer) can start. We will implement collection-based data stream support in ASKALON. Future extensions to allow more elaborate data collection distribution mechanisms such as *CYCLIC* and *CYCLIC(b)* distributions as well as distributions of nested collections will also be investigated.
- We will study the possibility of using machine learning technologies for further automation of data flow composition of scientific workflows in the cases where multiple matching data sources are found for a sink data port.
- Workflow sharing and reuse across workflow runtime systems and workflow languages will be studied. This will address the problem of workflow interoperability.
- We will study the provenance support in AWDL such that AWDL can capture scientific analysis processes at all levels of abstraction, from the semantic level, the syntactic level, the concrete level to the runtime level.
- The initial state, the specification of the initially available data classes, is considered fully known in our algorithm for automatic control flow composition.

We will investigate possible extensions to our algorithm to deal with cases with partially known initial states for further simplification of the scientific workflow composition process.

- We also plan to use more sophisticated semantic technologies in scientific workflow programming in order to provide a more user-oriented approach for scientists.

Part VII
Appendices

Appendix A
Acronyms

AD	Activity Deployment
ADD	Activity Function Data Dependence
AF	Activity Function
AGWL	Abstract Grid Workflow Language
ASWO	Abstract Scientific Workflow Ontologies
AI	Activity Instance
AT	Activity Type
AWDL	Abstract Workflow Description Language
AWHE	ASKALON Workflow Hosting Environment
cAF	Contributing AF
cDC	Contributed DC
DAG	Directed Acyclic Graph
DC	Data Class
dcAT	Data Conversion AT
DR	Data Representation
GUI	Graphical User Interface
HPF	High Performance Fortran
ncAF	Necessary cAF
ncDC	Necessary cDC
OGSA	Open Grid Services Architecture
OWL	Web Ontology Language
SOAP	Simple Object Access Protocol
RDF	Resource Description Framework
RDFS	RDF Schema
UML	Unified Modeling Language
W3C	World Wide Web Consortium
WSDL	Web Services Description Language
XML	Extensible Markup Language

J. Qin and T. Fahringer, *Scientific Workflows*, DOI 10.1007/978-3-642-30715-7,
© Springer-Verlag Berlin Heidelberg 2012

Appendix B
Symbols

Symbol	Description
g	A node
$\mathcal{G}$	A distributed system, i.e., a set of nodes
r	A resource
$\mathcal{R}$	A set of resources
w	A workflow
W	A set of workflows
a	An activity
A	A set of activities
$\vec{d}$	A dependence
$\vec{d}^{CF}$	A control flow dependence
$\vec{d}^{DF}$	A data flow dependence
$\vec{D}$	A set of dependences
λ	An Activity Diagram
n	A node of an Activity Diagram
$\mathcal{N}$	A set of nodes of an Activity Diagram
e	A directed edge of an Activity Diagram
$\mathcal{E}$	A set of directed edges of an Activity Diagram
AF	An Activity Function
$\mathcal{AF}$	A set of Activity Functions
AT	An Activity Type
$\mathcal{AT}$	A set of Activity Types
AD	An Activity Deployment

(continued)

J. Qin and T. Fahringer, *Scientific Workflows*, DOI 10.1007/978-3-642-30715-7,
© Springer-Verlag Berlin Heidelberg 2012

Symbol	Description
AI	An Activity Instance
DP	A data class, or a data port
$\mathcal{DC}$	A set of data classes
$\mathcal{DR}$	A set of data representations
$\mathcal{DP}$	A set of data ports
$\mathcal{I}$	A set of input data classes
$\mathcal{O}$	A set of output data classes
$AF.\mathcal{I}$	A set of input data classes of Activity Function AF
$AF.\mathcal{O}$	A set of output data classes of Activity Function AF
$\mathcal{DC} \cong \mathcal{DC}'$	$\mathcal{DC}$ is semantically compatible with $\mathcal{DC}'$
$\mathcal{DC} \models \mathcal{DC}'$	$\mathcal{DC}$ entails $\mathcal{DC}'$
C	A data collection
$|C|$	Cardinality of the data collection C
ei	The constraint *element-index*
ce	A colon expression
sa	A start element index
so	A stop element index
sr	A stride
I	A list of loop iterations
$|I|$	Cardinality of the set of loop iterations I
J^C	An index domain of a data collection C
K^I	An index domain of an iteration array I
i	An element index
$[i_1 : i_2]$	A set of element indices, defined by $[i_1 : i_2] := \{i \mid i_1 \leq i \leq i_2\}$
$\theta(i)$	A function mapping indices of a data collection C to indices of a list of loop iterations I
b	Block size
l	Overlap size
s	A state in STRIPS problems
s_{init}	Initial state
s_{goal}	Goal state
S	A superstate of an ADD graph
S_k	The k-th superstate of an ADD Graph
$\mathcal{D}$	A set of superstates of an ADD graph
$\vec{\mathcal{D}}$	A set of dependences of an ADD graph connecting either from a DC to an AF, or from an AF to a DC

(continued)

Symbol	Description
$cAF(S)$	The set of contributing AFs of the superstate S
$ncAF(S)$	The set of necessary contributing AFs of the superstate S
$cDC(S)$	The set of contributed DCs of the superstate S
$ncDC(S)$	The set of necessary contributed DCs of the superstate S
$\mathcal{A}$	The set of contributing AFs of an ADD graph
γ	An ADD graph, i.e., triple $\langle \mathcal{A}, \mathcal{D}, \vec{\mathcal{D}} \rangle$

Symbol	Description

References

[1] Martin Alt, Sergei Gorlatch, Andreas Hoheisel, and Hans-Werner Pohl. A Grid Workflow Language Using High-Level Petri Nets. Technical Report CoreGRID TR-0032, Institute on Grid Information, Resource and Workflow Monitoring Services, March 2006.

[2] Ilkay Altintas, Chad Berkley, Efrat Jaeger, Matthew Jones, Bertram Ludäscher, and Steve Mock. Kepler: An Extensible System for Design and Execution of Scientific Workflows. In *16th Intl. Conf. on Scientific and Statistical Database Management (SSDBM'04)*, Santorini Island, Greece, June 21–23, 2004. IEEE Computer Society Press.

[3] Ilkay Altintas, Adam Birnbaum, Kim K. Baldridge, Wibke Sudholt, Mark Miller, Celine Amoreira, Yohann Potier, and Bertram Ludäscher. A Framework for the Design and Reuse of Grid Workflows. In *Proceedings of Scientific Applications of Grid Computing*, 2005.

[4] José Luis Ambite and Dipsy Kapoor. Automatically Composing Data Workflows with Relational Descriptions and Shim Services. In *Proceedings of 6th International Semantic Web Conference and 2nd Asian Semantic Web Conference (ISWC 2007 + ASWC 2007)*, Busan, Korea, November 2007. Springer Berlin / Heidelberg.

[5] José Luis Ambite and Matthew Weathers. Automatic Composition of Aggregation Workflows for Transportation Modeling. In *Proceedings of the National Conference on Digital Government Research (dg.o2005)*, pages 41–49. Digital Government Society of North America, 2005.

[6] Tony Andrews, Francisco Curbera, Hitesh Dholakia, Yaron Goland, Johannes Klein, Frank Leymann, Kevin Liu, Dieter Roller, Doug Smith, Satish Thatte, Ivana Trickovic, and Sanjiva Weerawarana. Business Process Execution Language for Web Services Version 1.1. http://download.boulder.ibm.com/ibmdl/pub/software/dw/specs/ws-bpel/ws-bpel.pdf, May 2003.

[7] James Annis, Yong Zhao, Jens Voeckler, Michael Wilde, Steve Kent, and Ian Foster. Applying Chimera Virtual Data Concepts to Cluster Finding in the Sloan Sky Survey. In *Supercomputing '02: Proceedings of the 2002 ACM/IEEE conference on Supercomputing*, pages 1–14, Los Alamitos, CA, USA, 2002. IEEE Computer Society Press.

[8] Grigoris Antoniou and Frank van Harmelen. Web Ontology Language: OWL. In S. Staab and R. Studer, editors, *Handbook on Ontologies in Information Systems*, pages 76–92. Springer-Verlag, 2003.

[9] C. Archer. *Process Coordination and Ubiquitous Computing*. CRC Press, Inc., Boca Raton, FL, USA, 2002.

[10] Rob Armstrong, Gary Kumfert, Lois Curfman McInnes, Steven Parker, Ben Allan, Matt Sottile, Thomas Epperly, and Tamara Dahlgren. The CCA Component Model For High-Performance Scientific Computing. *Concurrency and Computation: Practice & Experience*, 18(2):215–229, 2006.

[11] ASG Team. Adaptive Services Grid (ASG). http://asg-platform.org.

[12] Austrian Grid Team. The Austrian Grid Project. http://www.austriangrid.at, 2006.

[13] P. Avery and Ian Foster. GriPhyN Annual Report for 2003–2004. Technical Report 2004–70, August 2004.

[14] Laurent Baduel, Françoise Baude, Denis Caromel, Arnaud Contes, Fabrice Huet, Matthieu Morel, and Romain Quilici. *Grid Computing: Software Environments and Tools*, chapter Programming, Deploying, Composing, for the Grid. Springer-Verlag, January 2006.

[15] Emir M. Bahsi, Emrah Ceyhan, and Tevfik Kosar. Conditional Workflow Management: a Survey and Analysis. *Scientific Programming*, 15(4):283–297, 2007.

[16] Mark Baker and Bryan Carpenter. MPJ: A Proposed Java Message Passing API and Environment for High Performance Computing. In *IPDPS '00: Proceedings of the 15 IPDPS 2000 Workshops on Parallel and Distributed Processing*, pages 552–559, London, UK, 2000. Springer-Verlag.

[17] Roger Barga and Dennis Gannon. *Workflows for e-Science – Scientific Workflows for Grids*, chapter Scientific versus Business Workflow, pages 9–16. Springer Verlag, 2007.

[18] Charlton Barreto, Vaughn Bullard, Thomas Erl, John Evdemon, Diane Jordan, Khanderao Kand, Dieter König, Simon Moser, Ralph Stout, Ron Ten-Hove, Ivana Trickovic, and Danny van der Rijn Alex Yiu. Web Services Business Process Execution Language Version 2.0 Primer . http://docs.oasis-open.org/wsbpel/2.0/Primer/wsbpel-v2.0-Primer.pdf, May 2007.

[19] Ricardo M. Bastos, Duncan Dubugras, and A. Ruiz. Extending UML Activity Diagram for Workflow Modeling in Production Systems. In *Proceedings of 35th Annual Hawaii International Conference on System Sciences (HICSS'02)*, Big Island, Hawaii, January 07–10, 2002. IEEE Computer Society Press.

[20] Sean Bechhofer, Frank van Harmelen, Jim Hendler, Ian Horrocks, Deborah L. McGuinness, Peter F. Patel-Schneider, and Lynn Andrea Stein. OWL Web Ontology Language Reference. Technical report, The World Wide Web Consortium (W3C), 2004.

[21] Stefano Beco, Barbara Cantalupo, Ludovico Giammarino, Nikolaos Matskanis, and Mike Surridge. OWL-WS: A Workflow Ontology for Dynamic Grid Service Composition. In *1st IEEE International Conference on e-Science and Grid Computing*, pages 148–155. IEEE Computer Society, December 5–8, 2005.

[22] Khalid Belhajjame, Katy Wolstencroft, Oscar Corcho, Tom Oinn, Franck Tanoh, Alan William, and Carole Goble. Metadata Management in the Taverna Workflow System. In *Proceedings of the IEEE International Symposium on Cluster Computing and the Grid (CCGrid)*, pages 651–656, Los Alamitos, CA, USA, 2008. IEEE Computer Society.

[23] Chad Berkley, Shawn Bowers, Matthew Jones, Bertram Ludäscher, Mark Schildhauer, and Jing Tao. Incorporating Semantics in Scientific Workflow Authoring. In *SSDBM'2005: Proceedings of the 17th international conference on Scientific and statistical database management*, pages 75–78, Berkeley, CA, US, 2005. Lawrence Berkeley Laboratory.

[24] Chad Berkley, Shawn Bowers, Matthew Jones, Bertram Ludäscher, Mark Schildhauer, and Jing Tao. Incorporating Semantics in Scientific Workflow Authoring. In *SSDBM'2005: Proceedings of the 17th international conference on Scientific and statistical database management*, pages 75–78, Berkeley, CA, US, 2005. Lawrence Berkeley Laboratory.

[25] Peter Blaha, Karlheinz Schwarz, Georg Madsen, Dieter Kvasnicka, and Joachim Luitz. WIEN2k: An Augmented Plane Wave plus Local Orbitals Program for Calculating Crystal Properties, 2001.

[26] Avrim L. Blum and Merrick L. Furst. Fast Planning Through Planning Graph Analysis. *Artificial Intelligence*, 90:281–300, 1997.

[27] Shawn Bowers and Bertram Ludäscher. An Ontology-Driven Framework for Data Transformation in Scientific Workflows. In *Proceeding of International Workshop on Data Integration in the Life Sciences (DILS 2004)*, pages 1–16, 2004.

[28] Shawn Bowers and Bertram Ludäscher. Actor-Oriented Design of Scientific Workflows. In *24st Intl. Conference on Conceptual Modeling*. Springer, 2005.

[29] Jian Cao, Yujie Mou, Jie Wang, Shensheng Zhang, and Minglu Li. A Dynamic Grid Workflow Model Based On Workflow Component Reuse. In *Proceedings of Grid and Cooperative Computing - GCC 2005*, 2005.

[30] Junwei Cao, Stephen A. Jarvis, Subhash Saini, and Graham R. Nudd. GridFlow: Workflow Management for Grid Computing. In *3rd IEEE/ACM International Symposium on Cluster Computing and the Grid (CCGrid 2003)*, Tokyo, Japan, May 12–15, 2003. IEEE Computer Society Press.

[31] Jorge Cardoso and Amit Sheth. Semantic E-Workflow Composition. In *Journal Of Intelligent Information Systems*, volume 21, pages 191–225, Hingham, MA, USA, 2003. Kluwer Academic Publishers.

[32] Rohit Chandra, Leo Dagum, Dave Kohr, Dror Maydan, Jeff McDonald, and Ramesh Menon. *Parallel Programming in OpenMP*. Morgan Kaufmann, 2000.

[33] Liming Chen, Nigel Shadbolt, Carole Goble, Feng Tao, Simon Cox, Colin Puleston, and Paul Smart. Towards a Knowledge-based Approach to Semantic Service Composition. In *Proc. of the 2nd International Semantic Web Conference (ISWC2003)*, pages 319–334, Florida, USA, 2003.

[34] Liming Chen, Nigel Richard Shadbolt, Feng Tao, Carole Goble, Colin Puleston, and Simon James Cox. Semantics-Assisted Problem Solving on the Semantic Grid. *Computational Intelligence*, 21:157–176, 2005.

[35] Roberto Chinnici, Jean-Jacques Moreau, Arthur Ryman, and Sanjiva Weerawarana. Web Services Description Language (WSDL) Version 2.0. http://www.w3.org/TR/wsdl20/, 2007.

[36] David Churches, Gabor Gombas, Andrew Harrison, Jason Maassen, Craig Robinson, Matthew Shields, Ian Taylor, and Ian Wang. Programming Scientific and Distributed Workflow with Triana Services. *Concurrency and Computation: Practice & Experience*, 18(10):1021–1037, 2006.

[37] Condor Team. DAGMan: A Directed Acyclic Graph Manager. http://www.cs.wisc.edu/condor/dagman/, July 2005.

[38] W. R. Cotton, R. A. Pielke, R. L. Walko, G. E. Liston, C. J. Tremback, H. Jiang, R. L. McAnelly, J. Y. Harrington, M. E. Nicholls, G. G. Carrio, and J. P. McFadden. RAMS 2001: Current status and future directions. *Meteorology and Atmospheric Physics*, 82:5–29, 2003.

[39] Francisco Curbera, Yaron Goland, Johannes Klein, Frank Leymann, Dieter Roller, Satish Thatte, and Sanjiva Weerawarana. Business Process Execution Language for Web Services Version 1.0. http://download.boulder.ibm.com/ibmdl/pub/software/dw/specs/ws-bpel/ws-bpel1.pdf, July 2002.

[40] John Davis II, Christopher Hylands, Bart Kienhuis, Edward A. Lee, Jie Liu, Xiaojun Liu, Lukito Muliadi, Steve Neuendorffer, Jeff Tsay, Brian Vogel, and Yuhong Xiong. Ptolemy II : Heterogeneous Concurrent Modeling and Design in Java. Technical Report UCB/ERL M01/12, EECS Department, University of California, Berkeley, 2001.

[41] Ewa Deelman, Gaurang Mehta, Gurmeet Singh, Mei-Hui Su, and Karan Vahi. *Workflows for e-Science – Scientific Workflows for Grids*, chapter Pegasus: Mapping Large-Scale Workflows to Distributed Resources. Springer Verlag, 2007.

[42] Ewa Deelman, Gurmeet Singh, Mei-Hui Su, James Blythe, Yolanda Gil, Carl Kesselman, Gaurang Mehta, Karan Vahi, G. Bruce Berriman, John Good, Anastasia Laity, Joseph C. Jacob, and Daniel S. Katz. Pegasus: a Framework for Mapping Complex Scientific Workflows onto Distributed Systems. *Scientific Programming Journal*, 13(2), November 2005.

[43] Thierry Delaitre, Tamas Kiss, Ariel Goyeneche, Gabor Terstyanszky, Stephen Winter, and Peter Kacsuk. GEMLCA: Running Legacy Code Applications as Grid Services. *Journal of Grid Computing*, 3(1–2):75–90, June 2005.

[44] Rubing Duan, Radu Prodan, and Thomas Fahringer. DEE: A Distributed Fault Tolerant Workflow Enactment Engine for Grid Computing. In *Proceedings of the International Conference on High Performance Computing and Communications(HPCC 05)*, Lecture Notes in Computer Science, Sorrento, Italy, September 21–25, 2005. Springer Verlag.

[45] Rubing Duan, Radu Prodan, and Thomas Fahringer. Run-time Optimization for Grid Workflow Applications. In *Proceedings of 7th IEEE/ACM International Conference on Grid Computing (Grid'06)*, Barcelona, Spain, 2006. IEEE Computer Society Press.

[46] Ziyang Duan, Arthur Bernstein, Philip Lewis, and Shiyong Lu. Semantics Based Verification and Synthesis of BPEL4WS Abstract Processes. In *Proceedings of the IEEE International Conference on Web Services (ICWS '04)*, page 734, Washington, DC, USA, 2004. IEEE Computer Society.

[47] M. Dumas and A. H.M. ter Hofstede. UML Activity Diagrams as a Workflow Specification Language. In *Proceedings of the International Conference on the Unified Modeling Language (UML'2001)*, volume 2185, pages 76–90, Toronto, Ontario, Canada, October 1–5, 2001. Springer-Verlag.

[48] Erik Elmroth, Francisco Hernández, and Johan Tordsson. Three Fundamental Dimensions of Scientific Workflow Interoperability: Model of Computation, Language, and Execution Environment. *Future Generation Computer Systems*, 26(2):245–256, 2010.

[49] Dietmar Erwin. UNICORE Plus Final Report - Uniform Interface to Computing Resources. http://www.unicore.eu/documentation/files/erwin-2003-UPF.pdf, 2003.

[50] Rik Eshuis and Roel Wieringa. Comparing Petri Net and Activity Diagram Variants for Workflow Modelling - A Quest for Reactive Petri Nets. In *Advances in Petri Nets: Petri Net Technology for Communication Based Systems; Lecture Notes in Computer Science (LNCS)*, volume 2472, pages 321–351, Heidelberg, Germany, March 9, 2003.

[51] Thomas Fahringer, Radu Prodan, Rubing Duan, Jürgen Hofer, Farrukh Nadeem, Francesco Nerieri, Stefan Podlipnig, Jun Qin, Mumtaz Siddiqui, Hong-Linh Truong, Alex Villazon, and Marek Wieczorek. *Workflows for eScience, Scientific Workflows for Grids*, chapter ASKALON: A Development and Grid Computing Environment for Scientific Workflows. Springer Verlag, 2007.

[52] Thomas Fahringer, Radu Prodan, Rubing Duan, Francesco Nerieri, Stefan Podlipnig, Jun Qin, Mumtaz Siddiqui, Hong-Linh Truong, Alex Villazon, and Marek Wieczorek. ASKALON: A Grid Application Development and Computing Environment. In *Proceedings of 6th International Workshop on Grid Computing (Grid 2005)*, Seattle, USA, November 2005. IEEE Computer Society Press.

[53] Thomas Fahringer, Jun Qin, and Stefan Hainzer. Specification of Grid Workflow Applications with AGWL: An Abstract Grid Workflow Language. In *Proceedings of IEEE International Symposium on Cluster Computing and the Grid 2005 (CCGrid 2005)*, Cardiff, UK, May 9–12, 2005. IEEE Computer Society Press.

[54] Hamid Mohammadi Fard, Radu Prodan, Thomas Fahringer, and Juan Jose Durillo Barrionuevo. A Multi-Objective Approach for Workflow Scheduling in Heterogeneous Computing Environments. In *Proceeding of the 12th IEEE/ACM International Symposium on Cluster, Cloud and Grid Computing (CCGrid 2012)*, Ottawa, Canada, 2012.

[55] Richard E. Fikes and Nils J. Nilsson. STRIPS: A New Approach to the Application of Theorem Proving to Problem Solving. *Artificial Intelligence*, 2(3–4):189–208, 1971.

[56] Ian Forster and Carl Kesselman. *The Grid: Blueprint for a New Computing Infrastructure*. Morgan Kaufmann, November 1998.

[57] Ian Foster. Globus Toolkit Version 4: Software for Service-Oriented Systems. In *Proceedings of IFIP International Conference on Network and Parallel Computing*, 2006.

[58] Ian Foster and Carl Kesselman. The Globus Project: A Status Report. In *Proceedings of IPPS/SPDP'98 Heterogeneous Computing Workshop*, 1998.

[59] Ian Foster, Hiro Kishimoto, Andreas Savva, D. Berry, A. Djaoui, A. Grimshaw, B. Horn, F. Maciel, F. Siebenlist, R. Subramaniam, J. Treadwell, and J. Von Reich. The Open Grid Services Architecture, Version 1.0. In *Informational Document, Global Grid Forum (GGF)*, 2005.

[60] Ian Foster, Jens Vöckler, Michael Wilde, and Yong Zhao. Chimera: A Virtual Data System for Representing, Querying, and Automating Data Derivation. In *14th International Conference on Scientific and Statistical Database Management (SSDBM'02)*, Edinburgh, Scotland, July 2002.

[61] Ian Foster, Yong Zhao, Ioan Raicu, and Shiyong Lu. Cloud Computing and Grid Computing 360-Degree Compared. In *Proceedings of the IEEE Grid Computing Environments (GCE08)*, 2008.

[62] Eric Freeman, Ken Arnold, and Susanne Hupfer. *JavaSpaces Principles, Patterns, and Practice*. Addison-Wesley Longman Ltd., Essex, UK, UK, 1999.

[63] Dennis Gannon, Randall Bramley, Geoffrey Fox, Shava Smallen, Al Rossi, Rachana Ananthakrishnan, Felipe Bertrand, Ken Chiu, Matt Farrellee, Madhu Govindaraju, Sriram Krishnan, Lavanya Ramakrishnan, Yogesh Simmhan, Alek Slominski, Yu Ma, Caroline Olariu, and Nicolas Rey-Cenvaz. Programming the Grid: Distributed Software Components, P2P and Grid Web Services for Scientific Applications. *Cluster Computing*, 5(3):325–336, 2002.

[64] David Gelernter and Nicholas Carriero. Coordination languages and their significance. *Communication of the ACM*, 35(2):97–107, 1992.

[65] Yolanda Gil. *Workflows for e-Science – Scientific Workflows for Grids*, chapter Workflow Composition: Semantic Representations for Flexible Automation. Springer Verlag, 2007.

[66] Yolanda Gil, Varun Ratnakar, Ewa Deelman, Gaurang Mehta, and Jihie Kim. Wings for Pegasus: Creating Large-Scale Scientific Applications Using Semantic Representations of Computational Workflows. In *Proceedings of the Nineteenth Conference on Innovative Applications of Artificial Intelligence (IAAI-07)*, Vancouver, British Columbia, Canada, July 2007.

[67] Tristan Glatard, Gergely Sipos, Johan Montagnat, Zoltan Farkas, and Peter Kacsuk. *Workflows for e-Science – Scientific Workflows for Grids*, chapter Workflow Level Parametric Study Support by MOTEUR and the P-GRADE Portal, pages 279–299. Springer Verlag, Argonne National Laboratory, Argonne IL, 60430, USA, 2007.

[68] gLite Team. gLite. http://glite.web.cern.ch/glite.

[69] Globus Team. The Globus Alliance. http://www.globus.org.

[70] Globus Team. The Globus Resource Specification Language RSL v1.0. http://www.globus.org/toolkit/docs/2.4/gram/rsl_spec1.html.

[71] Antoon Goderis, Ulrike Sattler, and Carole Goble. Applying DLs for Workflow Reuse and Repurposing. In *International Description Logics Workshop*, Edinburgh, Scotland, 2005.

[72] Antoon Goderis, Ulrike Sattler, Phillip Lord, and Carole Goble. Seven bottlenecks to workflow reuse and repurposing. In *Fourth International Semantic Web Conference (ISWC 2005)*, volume 3792, pages 323–337, Galway, Ireland, 2005.

[73] Li Gong. JXTA: A Network Programming Environment. *IEEE Internet Computing*, 5(3):88–95, 2001.

[74] Madhusudhan Govindaraju, Sriram Krishnan, Kenneth Chiu, Er Slominski, Dennis Gannon, and All Bramley. XCAT 2.0: A Component-Based Programming Model for Grid Web Services. Technical Report TR562, Department of Computer Science, Indiana University, 2002.

[75] Thomas R. Gruber. A Translation Approach to Portable Ontology Specifications. *Knowl. Acquis.*, 5(2):199–220, 1993.

[76] Zhijie Guan, Francisco Hernandez, Purushotham Bangalore, Jeff Gray, Anthony Skjellum, Vijay Velusamy, and Yin Liu. Grid-Flow: a Grid-Enabled Scientific Workflow System with a Petri-Net-Based Interface. *Concurrency and Computation: Practice & Experience*, 18(10):1115–1140, 2006.

[77] Tomasz Gubała, Daniel Harezlak, Marian Bubak, and Maciej Malawski. Constructing Abstract Workflows of Applications with Workflow Composition Tool. In *Proceedings of Cracow Grid Workshop (CGW'06), K-WfGrid - The Knowledge-based Workflow System for Grid Applications*, 2006.

[78] Tomasz Gubała, Daniel Hereżlak, Marian Bubak, and Maciej Malawski. Semantic Composition of Scientific Workflows Based on the Petri Nets Formalism. In *Proc. of the 2nd IEEE International Conference on e-Science and Grid Computing*, Amsterdam, The Netherlands., December 4–6, 2006. (c) IEEE Computer Society Press.

[79] Yousra BenDaly Hlaoui and Leila Jemni BenAyed. Toward an UML-Based Composition of Grid Services Workflows. In *Proceedings of the 2nd international workshop on Agent-Oriented Software Engineering Challenges for Ubiquitous and Pervasive Computing (AUPC'08)*, pages 21–28, New York, NY, USA, 2008. ACM.

[80] Jörg Hoffmann and Bernhard Nebel. The FF Planning System: Fast Plan Generation Through Heuristic Search. *Journal of Artificial Intelligence Research*, 14:253–302, 2001.

[81] Andreas Hoheisel. User Tools and Languages for Graph-based Grid Workflows. In *Grid Workflow Workshop, GGF10*, Berlin, Germany, March 9, 2004.

[82] Andreas Hoheisel and Martin Alt. *Workflows for e-Science – Scientific Workflows for Grids*, chapter Petri Nets, pages 190–207. Springer Verlag, 2007.

[83] Andreas Hoheisel and Uwe Der. An XML-Based Framework for Loosely Coupled Applications on Grid Environments. *Lecture Notes in Computer Science*, 2657:245–254, January 2003.

[84] IBM. Web Service Flow Language (WSFL 1.0). http://www-306.ibm.com/software/solutions/webservices/pdf/WSFL.pdf, May 2001.

[85] Jena Team. Jena Semantic Web Framework API. http://jena.sourceforge.net/.

[86] Kurt Jensen. An Introduction to the Practical Use of Coloured Petri Nets. In *Lectures on Petri Nets II: Applications, Advances in Petri Nets*, pages 237–292, London, UK, 1998. Springer-Verlag.

[87] Alexandru Jugravu and Thomas Fahringer. JavaSymphony, a Programming Model for the Grid. In *First International Workshop on Programming Paradigms for Grids and Metacomputing Systems (PPGaMS 2004)*, Krakow, Poland, June 2004. Springer Verlag.

[88] K-Wf Grid Team. K-Wf Grid: The Knowledge-based Workflow System for Grid Applications. http://www.kwfgrid.eu.

[89] Nicholas T. Karonis, Brian Toonen, and Ian Foster. MPICH-G2: a Grid-enabled implementation of the Message Passing Interfaces. *J. Parallel Distrib. Comput.*, 63(5):551–563, 2003.

[90] Kepler Team. Kepler User Manual. https://code.kepler-project.org/code/kepler-docs/trunk/outreach/documentation/shipping/UserM-anual.pdf, May 2008.

[91] Matthias Kloppmann, Dieter Koenig, Frank Leymann, Gerhard Pfau, Alan Rickayzen, Claus von Riegen, Patrick Schmidt, and Ivana Trickovic. WS-BPEL 2.0 Extensions for Sub-Processes. http://www.ibm.com/developerworks/library/specification/ws-bpelsubproc/, September 2005.

[92] Charles H. Koelbel, David B. Loveman, and Robert S. Schreiber. *The High Performance Fortran Handbook*. Scientific and Engineering Computation. The MIT Press, November 1993.

[93] Tevfik Kosar and Mehmet Balman. A New Paradigm: Data-aware Scheduling in Grid Computing. *Future Gener. Comput. Syst.*, 25(4):406–413, 2009.

[94] Sriram Krishnan and Dennis Gannon. XCAT3: A Framework for CCA Components as OGSA Services. In *Proceedings of 9th International Workshop on High-Level Parallel Programming Models and Supportive Environments (HIPS)*, April 2004.

[95] Sriram Krishnan, Patrick Wagstrom, and Gregor von Laszewski. GSFL: A Workflow Framework for Grid Services. Technical Report ANL/MCS-P980–0802, Argonne National Laboratory, July 2002.

[96] Gregor Von Laszewski, Kaizar Amin, Mihael Hategan, Nestor J. Zaluzec, Shawn Hampton, and Albert Rossi. GridAnt: A Client-Controllable Grid Workflow System. In *37th Annual Hawaii International Conference on System Sciences (HICSS'04)*, Big Island, Hawaii, January 5–8, 2004. IEEE Computer Society Press.

[97] Florian Lautenbacher and Bernhard Bauer. A Survey on Workflow Annotation & Composition Approaches. In *Proceedings of the Workshop on Semantic Business Process and Product Lifecycle Management (SemBPM) in the context of the European Semantic Web Conference (ESWC)*, pages 12–23, Innsbruck, Austria, June 2007.

[98] Craig Lee, Satoshi Matsuoka, Domenico Talia, Alan Sussman, M Mueller, Gabrielle Allen, and Joel Saltz. A Grid Programming Primer. Submitted to Open Grid Forum, August 2001.

[99] Craig Lee and Domenico Talia. *Grid Computing: Making the Global Infrastructure a Reality*, chapter Grid Programming Models: Current Tools, Issues and Directions, pages 555–578. John Wiley & Sons, Ltd, 2003.

[100] Edward A. Lee and Steve Neuendorffer. MoML – A Modeling Markup Language in XML – Version 0.4. Technical Memorandum UCB/ERL M00/12, University of California, Berkeley, CA 94720, March 2000.

[101] Marc Lelarge, Zhen Liu, and Anton V. Riabov. Automatic Composition of Secure Workflows. Technical Report W0607–005, IBM Research Division, July 2006.

[102] Melissa Lemos, Marco Antonio Casanova, Luiz Fernando Bessa Seibel, José Antonio Fernandes de Macedo, and Antonio Basílio de Miranda. Ontology-Driven Workflow Management for Biosequence Processing Systems. In *Proceedings of 15th International Conference Database and Expert Systems Applications (DEXA 2004)*, volume 3180/2004, pages 781–790, Zaragoza, Spain, August 30-September 3, 2004. Springer.

[103] Peter Li, Tom Oinn, Stian Soiland, and Douglas B. Kell. Automated Manipulation of Systems Biology Models Using libSBML within Taverna Workflows. *Bioinformatics (Oxford, England)*, 24(2):287–289, January 2008.

[104] Phillip Lord, Pinar Alper, Chris Wroe, and Carole Goble. *The Semantic Web: Research and Applications*, chapter Feta: A Light-Weight Architecture for User Oriented Semantic Service Discovery, pages 17–31. Springer, 2005.

[105] Bertram Ludäscher, Ilkay Altintas, Chad Berkley, Dan Higgins, Efrat Jaeger, Matthew Jones, Edward A. Lee, Jing Tao, and Yang Zhao. Scientific Workflow Management and the Kepler System. *Concurrency and Computation: Practice and Experience*, 18(10):1039–1065, 2006.

[106] Bertram Ludäscher, Ilkay Altintas, Shawn Bowers, Julian Cummings, Terence Critchlow, Ewa Deelman, David De Roure, Juliana Freire, Carole Goble, Matthew Jones, Scott Klasky, Timothy McPhillips, Norbert Podhorszki, Claudio Silva, Ian Taylor, and Mladen Vouk. Scientific Process Automation and Workflow Management. In Arie Shoshani and Doron Rotem, editors, *Scientific Data Management: Challenges, Existing Technology, and Deployment*, Computational Science Series, chapter 13. Chapman & Hall, 2009.

[107] Akshay Luther, Rajkumar Buyya, Rajiv Ranjan, and Srikumar Venugopal. Alchemi: A.NET-Based Enterprise Grid Computing System. In *ICOMP'05: Proceedings of the 6th International Conference on Internet Computing*, Las Vegas, Nevada, USA, June 2005.

[108] Shalil Majithia, David W.Walker, and W.A.Gray. Automated Composition of Semantic Grid Services. In S.J.Cox, editor, *Proceedings of the UK e-Science All Hands Meeting 2004*, Nottingham, UK, August 31 - September 3, 2004.

[109] Anthony Mayer, Stephen McGough, Murtaza Gulamali, Laurie Young, Jim Stanton, Steven Newhouse, and John Darlington. Meaning and Behaviour in Grid Oriented Components. In *GRID '02: Proceedings of the Third International Workshop on Grid Computing*, pages 100–111, London, UK, 2002. Springer-Verlag.

[110] Anthony Mayer, Steve McGough, Nathalie Furmento, Jeremy Cohen, Murtaza Gulamali, Laurie Young, Ali Afzal, Steven Newhouse, and John Darlington. *Component Models and Systems for Grid Applications*, volume 1 of *CoreGRID series*, chapter ICENI: An Integrated Grid Middleware to Support e-Science, pages 109–124. Springer, June 2004.

[111] Anthony Mayer, Steve McGough, Nathalie Furmento, William Lee, Steven Newhouse, and John Darlington. ICENI Dataflow and Workflow: Composition and Scheduling in Space and Time. In *UK e-Science All Hands Meeting*, pages 627–634. IOP Publishing Ltd, 2003.

[112] Deborah L. McGuinness and Frank van Harmelen. OWL Web Ontology Language Overview. Technical report, The World Wide Web Consortium (W3C), 2004.

[113] Timothy Mcphillips, Shawn Bowers, and Bertram Ludäscher. Collection-Oriented Scientific Workflows for Integrating and Analyzing Biological Data. In *3rd international Conference on Data Integration for the Life Sciences (DILS)*, Hinxton, UK, November 2006. LNCS/LNBI.

[114] Timothy McPhillips, Shawn Bowers, Daniel Zinn, and Bertram Ludäscher. Scientific Workflow Design for Mere Mortals. *Future Generation Computer Systems*, 25(5):541–551, 2009.

[115] Message Passing Interface Forum. MPI: a Message Passing Interface Standard. http://www.mpi-forum.org, June 1995.

[116] Message Passing Interface Forum. MPI-2: Extensions to the Message Passing Interface. http://www.mpi-forum.org/, July 1997.

[117] METEOR-S Team. METEOR-S: Semantic Web Services and Processes. http://lsdis.cs.uga.edu/projects/meteor-s/.

[118] Harald Meyer and Mathias Weske. Automated Service Composition using Heuristic Search. In *Proceedings of the Fourth International Conference on Business Process Management (BPM 2006)*, Vienna, Austria, 2006.

[119] Microsoft. XLANG Web Services for Business Process Design. http://www.gotdotnet.com/team/xml_wsspecs/xlang-c/default.htm, 2001.

[120] Johan Montagnat, Benjamin Isnard, Tristan Glatard, Ketan Maheshwari, and Mireille Blay Fornarino. A Data-driven Workflow Language for Grids Based on Array Programming Principles. In *WORKS '09: Proceedings of the 4th Workshop on Workflows in Support of Large-Scale Science*, pages 1–10, New York, NY, USA, 2009. ACM.

[121] Luc Moreau, Yong Zhao, Ian Foster, Jens Voeckler, and Michael Wilde. XDTM: The XML Data Type and Mapping for Specifying Datasets. In *Lecture Notes in Computer Science: Advances in Grid Computing - EGC 2005: European Grid Conference*, volume 3470, pages 495–505, Amsterdam, The Netherlands, February 14–16, 2005. Springer.

[122] myExperiment Team. The myExperiment project. http://www.myexperiment.org/.

[123] myGrid Team. The myGrid project. http://www.mygrid.org.uk/.

[124] myGrid Team. Taverna User Manual. http://www.mygrid.org.uk/taverna2/helpset/helpset.pdf, February 2009.

[125] Gayathri Nadarajan, Yun-Heh Chen-Burger, and James Malone. Semantic-Based Workflow Composition for Video Processing in the Grid. In *Proceedings of the 2006 IEEE/WIC/ACM International Conference on Web Intelligence*, Hong Kong, China, December 12–18, 2006.

[126] Farrukh Nadeem and Thomas Fahringer. Predicting the Execution Time of Grid Workflow Applications through Local Learning. In *Proceedings of the Conference on High Performance Computing Networking, Storage and Analysis (SC09)*, Portland, Oregon, US, 2009.

[127] Farrukh Nadeem, Radu Prodan, and Thomas Fahringer. Characterizing, Modeling and Predicting Dynamic Resource Availability in a Large Scale Multi-Purpose Grid. In *Proc. of the Eighth IEEE International Symposium on Cluster Computing and the Grid (CCGrid 2008)*, Lyon, France, May 19–22, 2008. IEEE Computer Society.

[128] Francesco Nerieri, Radu Prodan, Thomas Fahringer, and Hong-Linh Truong. Overhead Analysis of Grid Workflow Applications. In *Proceedings of the IEEE/ACM International Workshop on Grid Computing (Grid2006)*, volume 0, pages 17–24, Los Alamitos, CA, USA, 2006. IEEE Computer Society.

[129] OASIS Web Services Business Process Execution Language (WSBPEL) TC. Web Services Business Process Execution Language Version 2.0 – OASIS Standard. http://docs.oasis-open.org/wsbpel/2.0/wsbpel-v2.0.html, April 2007.

[130] Object Management Group. Business Process Modeling Notation (BPMN). http://www.bpmn.org/.

[131] OGF Community. Open Grid Forum. http://www.ogf.org.

[132] OGF JSDL Workgroup. Job Submission Description Language (JSDL) Specification, Version 1.0. http://www.gridforum.org/documents/GFD.56.pdf.

[133] Tom Oinn, Matthew Addis, Justin Ferris, Darren Marvin, Martin Senger, Mark Greenwood, Tim Carver, Kevin Glover, Matthew R. Pocock, Anil Wipat, and Peter Li. Taverna: a Tool for the Composition and Enactment of Bioinformatics Workflows. *Bioinformatics Journal*, 20(17):3045–3054, June 2004.

[134] Organization for the Advancement of Structured Information Standards (OASIS). http://www.oasis-open.org/.

[135] Chun Ouyang. Data Manipulation in YAWL. http://sky.fit.qut.edu.au/~terhofst/YAWLdocs/YAWLDataManual-beta7.pdf, November 2005.

[136] P-GRADE Team. P-GRADE: Parallel Grid Run-time and Application Development Environment. http://www.p-grade.hu/.

[137] Bijan Parsia and Peter F. Patel-Schneider. OWL 2 Web Ontology Language: Primer. Technical report, The World Wide Web Consortium (W3C), 2008.

[138] Cesare Pautasso and Gustavo Alonso. Parallel Computing Patterns for Grid Workflows. In *Proceedings of the Workshop on Workflows in Support of Large-Scale Science*, Paris, France, June 19–23, 2006.

[139] Pegasus-WMS Team. Workflow Management System (Pegasus-WMS). http://pegasus.isi. edu/wms/.

[140] James Lyle Peterson. *Petri Net Theory and the Modeling of Systems*. Prentice Hall PTR, Upper Saddle River, NJ, USA, 1981.

[141] Kassian Plankensteiner, Johan Montagnat, and Radu Prodan. IWIR: A Language Enabling Portability Across Grid Workflow Systems. In *WORKS'11: Proceedings of the 6th Workshop on Workflows in Support of Large-Scale Science*, Seattle, USA, November 12–18, 2011.

[142] Kassian Plankensteiner, Radu Prodan, Thomas Fahringer, Johan Montagnat, Andrew Harrison, Tristan Glatard, Gabor Hermann, and Miklos Kozlovsky. IWIR Specification v1.1. http://www.shiwa-workflow.eu/documents/10753/55350/IWIR+v1.1+Specification, March 2011.

[143] S. Pllana, T. Fahringer, J. Testori, S. Benkner, and I. Brandic. Towards an UML Based Graphical Representation of Grid Workflow Applications. In *2nd European Across Grids Conference, Nicosia, Cyprus, January 2004*. Springer-Verlag, 2004.

[144] Radu Prodan and Thomas Fahringer. ZEN: A Directive-based Experiment Specification Language for Performance and Parameter Studies of Parallel and Distributed Scientific Applications. *International Journal of High Performance Computing and Networking*, 2003.

[145] Radu Prodan and Thomas Fahringer. Overhead Analysis of Scientific Workflows in Grid Environments. *IEEE Trans. Parallel Distrib. Syst.*, 19(3):378–393, 2008.

[146] Protege Team. Protege-OWL Editor. http://protege.stanford.edu/overview/protege-owl.html.

[147] Jun Qin and Thomas Fahringer. Advanced Data Flow Support for Scientific Grid Workflow Applications. In *Proceedings of the International Conference on High Performance Computing, Networking, Storage and Analysis (SC07)*, Reno, NV, USA, November 10–16, 2007. IEEE Computer Society Press.

[148] Jun Qin and Thomas Fahringer. A Novel Domain Oriented Approach for Scientific Grid Workflow Composition. In *Proceedings of the International Conference on High Performance Computing, Networking, Storage and Analysis (SC08)*, Austin, Texas, USA, November 15–21, 2008. IEEE Computer Society Press.

[149] Jun Qin, Thomas Fahringer, and Maximilian Berger. Towards Workflow Sharing and Reuse in the ASKALON Grid Environment. In *Proceedings of Cracow Grid Workshop (CGW'08)*, Cracow, Poland, October 2008.

[150] Jun Qin, Thomas Fahringer, and Sabri Pllana. UML Based Grid Workflow Modeling under ASKALON. In *Proceedings of 6th Austrian-Hungarian Workshop on Distributed and Parallel Systems*, Innsbruck, Austria, September 21–23, 2006. Springer-Verlag.

[151] Jun Qin, Thomas Fahringer, and Radu Prodan. A Novel Graph Based Approach for Automatic Composition of High Quality Grid Workflows. In *Proceedings of the 18th International Symposium on High Performance Distributed Computing (HPDC 2009)*, Garching, Germany, June 11–13, 2009. ACM Press.

[152] David De Roure, Mark A. Baker, and Nicholas R. Jennings. *Grid Computing: Making the Global Infrastructure a Reality*, chapter The Evolution of the Grid, pages 65–100. John Wiley & Sons, 2003.

[153] David De Roure, Carole Goble, and Robert Stevens. Designing the myExperiment Virtual Research Environment for the Social Sharing of Workflows. In *E-SCIENCE '07: Proceedings of the Third IEEE International Conference on e-Science and Grid Computing*, pages 603–610, Washington, DC, USA, 2007. IEEE Computer Society.

[154] Nick Russell, Arthur H.M. ter Hofstede, David Edmond, and Wil M.P. van der Aalst. Workflow Data Patterns (Revised Version). Technical Report FIT-TR-2004–01, Queensland University of Technology, Brisbane, Australia, 2004.

[155] Leonardo Salayandía, Paulo Pinheiro da Silva, Ann Q. Gates, and Alvaro Rebellon. A Model-Based Workflow Approach for Scientific Applications. In *Proceedings of the 6th OOPSLA Workshop on Domain-Specific Modeling*, 2006.

[156] Leonardo Salayandía, Paulo Pinheiro da Silva, Ann Q. Gates, and Flor Salcedo. Workflow-Driven Ontologies: An Earth Sciences Case Study. In *Proceedings of Second IEEE International Conference on e-Science and Grid Computing (e-Science'06)*, volume 0, page 17, Los Alamitos, CA, USA, 2006. IEEE Computer Society.

[157] Mitsuhisa Sato, Taisuke Boku, and Daisuke Takahashi. OmniRPC: a Grid RPC system for Parallel Programming in Cluster and Grid Environment. In *CCGRID '03: Proceedings of the 3st International Symposium on Cluster Computing and the Grid*, page 206, Washington, DC, USA, 2003. IEEE Computer Society.

[158] S. Schindler, W. Kapferer, W. Domainko, M. Mair, E. van Kampen, T. Kronberger, S. Kimeswenger, M. Ruffert, O. Mangete, and D. Breitschwerdt. Metal Enrichment Processes in the Intra-Cluster Medium. *Astronomy and Astrophysics*, 435:L25–L28, May 2005.

[159] Felix Schüller, Jun Qin, Farrukh Nadeem, Radu Prodan, Thomas Fahringer, and Georg Mayr. Performance, Scalability and Quality of the Meteorological Grid Workflow MeteoAG. In *Proceedings of 2nd Austrian Grid Symposium*, Innsbruck, Austria, September 21–23, 2006. OCG Verlag.

[160] Bran Selic. What's New in UML 2.0. ftp://ftp.software.ibm.com/software/rational/web/whitepapers/intro2uml2.pdf, April 2005.

[161] Semantic Grid Community. Semantic Grid. http://www.semanticgrid.org.

[162] Keith Seymour, Hidemoto Nakada, Satoshi Matsuoka, Jack Dongarra, Craig Lee, and Henri Casanova. Overview of GridRPC: A Remote Procedure Call API for Grid Computing. In *GRID '02: Proceedings of the Third International Workshop on Grid Computing*, pages 274–278, London, UK, 2002. Springer-Verlag.

[163] SHIWA Team. SHIWA: SHaring Interoperable Workflows for Large-Scale Scientific Simulation on Available DCIs. http://www.shiwa-workflow.eu/, 2011.

[164] Mumtaz Siddiqui, Alex Villazón, and Thomas Fahringer. Grid capacity planning with negotiation-based advance reservation for optimized QoS. In *SC'06: Proceedings of the 2006 ACM/IEEE conference on Supercomputing*, page 103, New York, NY, USA, 2006. ACM.

[165] Mumtaz Siddiqui, Alex Villazon, Jurgen Hofer, and Thomas Fahringer. GLARE: A Grid Activity Registration, Deployment and Provisioning Framework. In *SC'05: Proceedings of the 2005 ACM/IEEE conference on Supercomputing*, Seattle, WA, USA, 2005. IEEE Computer Society.

[166] Laura Silva, Gian Luigi Granato, Alessandro Bressan, Cedric Lacey, Carlton M. Baugh, Shaun Cole, and Carlos S. Frenk. Modelling Dust in Galactic SEDs: Application to Semi-Analytical Galaxy Formation Models. *Astrophysics and Space Science*, 276(2–4):1073–1078, 2001.

[167] Harold Soh, Shazia Haque, Weili Liao, and Rajkumar Buyya. *Advanced Parallel and Distributed Computing*, chapter Grid Programming Models and Environments, pages 141–173. Nova Science Publishers, Inc., 2006.

[168] Harold Soh, Shazia Haque, Weili Liao, Krishna Nadiminti, and Rajkumar Buyya. GTPE: A Thread Programming Environment for the Grid. In *Proceedings of the 13th International Conference on Advanced Computing and Communications*, Coimbatore, Tamil Nadu, India, December 2005.

[169] Clemens Szyperski. *Component Software: Beyond Object-Oriented Programming*. Addison-Wesley Longman Publishing Co., Inc., Boston, MA, USA, 2002.

[170] Wei Tan, Paolo Missier, Ravi Madduri, and Ian Foster. Building Scientific Workflow with Taverna and BPEL: A Comparative Study in caGrid. pages 118–129, 2009.

[171] Ian Taylor, Matthew Shields, Ian Wang, and Andrew Harrison. Visual Grid Workflow in Triana. *Journal of Grid Computing*, 3(3–4):153–169, September 2005.

[172] Ian Taylor, Matthew Shields, Ian Wang, and Andrew Harrison. *Workflows for e-Science – Scientific Workflows for Grids*, chapter The Triana Workflow Environment: Architecture and Applications. Springer Verlag, 2007.

[173] Ian Taylor, Matthew Shields, Ian Wang, and Omer Rana. Triana Applications within Grid Computing and Peer to Peer Environments. *Journal of Grid Computing*, 1(2):199–217, 2003.

[174] Ian Taylor, Ian Wang, Matthew Shields, and Shalil Majithia. Distributed computing with Triana on the Grid. *Concurrency and Computation: Practice and Experience*, 2005.

[175] Arthur Ter Hofstede and Wil van der Aalst. Workflow Patterns: On the Expressive Power of (Petri-net-based) Workflow Languages. In *Proceeding of Fourth Workshop and Tutorial on Practical Use of Coloured Petri Nets and the CPN Tools*, August 2002.

[176] The Object Management Group (OMG). UML Activity Diagram. http://www.omg.org/spec/UML/2.2/.

[177] The Object Management Group (OMG). Unified Modeling Language (UML). http://www.omg.org/spec/UML/2.2/.

[178] The Workflow Management Coalition (WfMC). http://www.wfmc.org.

[179] The Workflow Management Coalition (WfMC). Process Definition Interface – XML Process Definition Language (XPDL) Version 2.0. http://www.wfmc.org/xpdl.htm, October 2005.

[180] The Workflow Management Coalition (WfMC). Process Definition Interface – XML Process Definition Language (XPDL) Version 2.1. http://www.wfmc.org/xpdl.html, March 2008.

[181] The World Wide Web Consortium. XML Schema Datatypes. http://www.w3.org/TR/xmlschema-2/.

[182] The World Wide Web Consortium. RDF Vocabulary Description Language 1.0: RDF Schema. http://www.w3.org/TR/rdf-schema/, 2004.

[183] The World Wide Web Consortium. Resource Description Framework (RDF). http://www.w3.org/TR/REC-rdf-syntax/, 2004.

[184] The World Wide Web Consortium (W3C). OWL-S: Semantic Markup for Web Services. http://www.w3.org/Submission/OWL-S/.

[185] The World Wide Web Consortium (W3C). Simple Object Access Protocol (SOAP) Version 1.2. http://www.w3.org/TR/2007/REC-soap12-part0-20070427/.

[186] The World Wide Web Consortium (W3C). Web Service Semantics - WSDL-S. http://www.w3.org/Submission/WSDL-S/.

[187] The World Wide Web Consortium (W3C). XPATH. http://www.w3.org/TR/xpath.html.

[188] The World Wide Web Consortium (W3C). XQuery. http://www.w3.org/TR/xquery/.

[189] The World Wide Web Consortium (W3C). Web Services Description Language (WSDL) Version 2.0. http://www.w3.org/TR/wsdl20/, 2007.

[190] Triana Team. Triana User Guide. https://forge.nesc.ac.uk/docman/view.php/\33/104/UserGuide.pdf, 2009.

[191] Daniele Turi, Paolo Missier, Carole Goble, David D. Roure, and Tom Oinn. Taverna Workflows: Syntax and Semantics. In *Proceedings of the IEEE International Conference on e-Science and Grid Computing*, pages 441–448, Bangalore, India, December 2007.

[192] UNICORE Team. Uniform Interface to Computing Resources (UNICORE). http://www.unicore.eu.

[193] Wil M.P. van der Aalst and Arthur H.M. ter Hofstede. YAWL: Yet Another Workflow Language. *Information Systems*, 30(4):245–275, June 2005.

[194] Snigdha Verma, Jarek Gawor, Gregor Von Laszewski, and Manish Parashar. A CORBA Commodity Grid Kit. *Concurrency and Computation: Practice and Experience*, 13:8–9, 2001.

[195] Gregor von Laszewski, Mihael Hategan, and Deepti Kodeboyina. *Workflows for e-Science – Scientific Workflows for Grids*, chapter Java CoG Kit Workflow, pages 340–356. Springer Verlag, Argonne National Laboratory, Argonne IL, 60430, USA, 2007.

[196] Gregor von Laszewski and Mike Hategan. Java CoG Kit Workflow Guide. http://wiki.cogkit.org/wiki/Java_CoG_Kit_Workflow_Guide, 2006.

[197] Gregor von Laszewski and Deepti Kodeboyina. A Repository Service for Grid Workflow Components. In *International Conference on Autonomic and Autonomous Systems*

International Conference on Networking and Services, Papeete, Tahiti, French Polynesia, October 23–28, 2005. IEEE.

[198] Ingo Wassink, Paul E. van der Vet, Katy Wolstencroft, Pieter B.T. Neerincx, Marco Roos, Han Rauwerda, and Timo M. Breit. Analysing Scientific Workflows: Why Workflows Not Only Connect Web Services. *IEEE Congress on Services*, 0:314–321, 2009.

[199] Wave-Front BV. FLOWer 3 Designers Guide. http://www.pallas-athena.com/, 2004.

[200] Marek Wieczorek, Stefan Podlipnig, Radu Prodan, and Thomas Fahringer. Bi-criteria Scheduling of Scientific Workflows for the Grid. In *Proc. of the Eighth IEEE International Symposium on Cluster Computing and the Grid (CCGrid 2008)*, Lyon, France, May 2008. IEEE Computer Society.

[201] Marek Wieczorek, Radu Prodan, and Thomas Fahringer. Scheduling of Scientific Workflows in the ASKALON Grid Environment. *ACM SIGMOD Record*, 35(3), 2005.

[202] Zixin Wu, Ajith Ranabahu, Karthik Gomadam, Amit P. Sheth, and John A. Miller. Automatic Composition of Semantic Web Services using Process and Data Mediation. Technical report, LSDIS lab, University of Georgia, February 2007.

[203] Jia Yu and Rajkumar Buyya. A Novel Architecture for Realizing Grid Workflow using Tuple Spaces. In *Proceedings of Fifth IEEE/ACM International Workshop on Grid Computing*, Pittsburgh, PA, November 2004.

[204] Jia Yu and Rajkumar Buyya. A Taxonomy of Workflow Management Systems for Grid Computing. Technical Report GRIDS-TR-2005-1, Grid Computing and Distributed Systems Laboratory, University of Melbourne, Australia, March 10, 2005.

[205] Jianting Zhang. Ontology-Driven Composition and Validation of Scientific Grid Workflows in Kepler: a Case Study of Hyperspectral Image Processing. In *Proceedings of 5th International Conference on Grid and Cooperative Computing Workshops*, 2006.

[206] Yong Zhao, Jed Dobson, Ian Foster, Luc Moreau, and Michael Wilde. A Notation and System for Expressing and Executing Cleanly Typed Workflows on Messy Scientific Data. *Sigmod Record*, 34(3), September 2005.

[207] Yong Zhao, Michael Wilde, and Ian Foster. *Workflows for eScience, Scientific Workflows for Grids*, chapter Virtual Data Language: A Typed Workflow Notation for Diversely Structured Scientific Data. Springer Verlag, 2007.

Index

Abstract Grid Workflow Language (AGWL), 9
Abstract operation, 174
Abstract process, 173, 188
Abstract Scientific Workflow Ontologies
    (ASWO), 10, 120, 121, 138
Abstract workflow, 31, 57
Abstract Workflow Description Language
    (AWDL), 8, 116, 127, 174
Activity, 23
  atomic activity, 32
  child activity, 35, 155
  compound activity, 32, 35, 124
  inner activity, 35, 36
  parent activity, 35, 155
  subsequent activity, 50
Activity Deployment (AD), 33, 77, 127, 176
Activity Function (AF), 10, 120, 176
Activity Instance (AI), 34, 106
Activity Type (AT), 10, 33, 55, 122, 174, 176
Activity type repository, 121
Adaptive Services Grid (ASG), 188
AF Data Dependence (ADD) graph, 11, 136,
    140, 144
  alternative DC/AF combination, 141
  contributed DC (cDC), 140
  contributing AF (cAF), 139
  dependence, 141
  necessary cAF (ncAF), 141
  necessary cDC (ncDC), 141
  simple ADD graph, 142, 144
  superstate, 139
Alternative branch, 44
Alternative execution, 44, 67
Application Programming Interface (API), 19
Artificial Intelligence, 137
Artificial Intelligence planner, 143
Artificial Intelligence planning, 188

Artificial Intelligence planning algorithm, 187
Artificial Intelligence planning problem, 138
ASKALON, 8, 25, 105, 121, 130, 131, 134,
    136, 156, 161
ASKALON Enactment Engine, 31
ASKALON scientific workflow composition
    tool
  attribute panel, 80, 164
  drawing space, 80, 129, 164
  GUI, 80, 130
  menu bar, 80
  misc panel, 80
  Model Checker, 80, 83
    dynamic model checker, 83
    static model checker, 83
  model panel, 80
  Model Traverser, 80, 83
  plugin, 83, 157
  resource panel, 80, 86
  standard toolbar, 80
  UML toolbar, 80
ASKALON user, 65
  application providers, 65
  workflow developers, 65
  workflow executors, 65
ASKALON Workflow Hosting Environment
    (AWHE), 12, 65, 86
Atomic condition, 40
Atomic procedure, 178
Automatic data conversion, 117
Automatic scientific workflow composition, 8
Automatic workflow composition, 45, 135

Backjumping, 126
Backtracking algorithm, 124
Backwards control flow traversing, 154

J. Qin and T. Fahringer, *Scientific Workflows*, DOI 10.1007/978-3-642-30715-7,
© Springer-Verlag Berlin Heidelberg 2012

217